elena vanishing

Also available:
Hope and Other Luxuries: A Mother's
Life with a Daughter's Anorexia,
by Clare B. Dunkle

elena vanishing

A MEMOIR

Elena and Clare B. Dunkle

CHRONICLE BOOKS

SAN FRANCISCO

Library of Congress Cataloging-in-Publication Data:

Dunkle, Clare B.
  Elena Vanishing / by Clare and Elena Dunkle.
      pages cm
  ISBN 978-1-4521-2151-2
  1. Dunkle, Elena—Health. 2. Anorexia nervosa—Patients—Biography.
I. Dunkle, Elena. II. Title.

  RC552.A5D87 2015
  616.85'2620092—dc23

                                    2014022164

Manufactured in China.

Design by Jen Tolo Pierce.
Typeset in Sabon and Helvetica Neue LT Pro.

Page 258, "We Should Talk about This Problem," from *I Heard God Laughing: Poems of Hope and Joy*, renderings of Hafiz by Daniel Ladinsky. Copyright 1996, 2006 by Daniel Ladinsky. Reprinted by permission of the author.

10 9 8 7 6 5 4 3 2 1

Chronicle Books LLC
680 Second Street
San Francisco, California 94107

Chronicle Books—we see things differently. Become part of our community at www.chroniclebooks.com/teen.

To the lights that lead me through the darkness:
My husband and soul mate, Matthew
My unwavering family
My little love, Lilly Arabella
My soul's echo, Rupert Brooke

And in remembrance of the souls
Who fought bravely alongside me against anorexia
But lost.

—Elena

> "Nor ever rest, nor ever lie,
> Till, beyond thinking, out of view,
> One mote of all the dust that's I
> Shall meet one atom that was you."
>
> —Rupert Brooke

A NOTE TO THE READER

This is a true story. But it is also a work of fiction.

Every incident, thought, and dream in this story happened as described, to the best of the authors' memories. Our goal has been to create an accurate portrait of anorexia nervosa in all its separate stages, just as Elena herself lived through them. But the portrait of a chronic illness comes through best in small moments: five minutes of action, one mental observation, or two lines of dialogue, sometimes separated by weeks. Skipping around like that is no way to tell an interesting story.

To solve this problem, the authors have grouped minor events around the major events. Each chapter creates one to three "typical" days out of a time period ranging from as short as half a week to as long as half a year. This means that in rare cases, we have moved a few minor events (episodes during Elena's time working in the ER, for example) months out of their real sequence. But such events did occur just as we have described them.

No events related to the progression of Elena's illness have been moved, and all significant events have stayed in their proper sequence.

The authors have reported important dialogue exactly as they remember it. But they have also abridged many conversations. Several therapy sessions have been condensed into one, for example, as well as several arguments. And the authors have created dialogue where they couldn't remember exactly what was said, although they took pains to make that dialogue match the topics and emotional tone of what they remember.

All journal and letter excerpts are real, with only clerical changes. All statements concerning when or how they were written are accurate.

While all the people in this book are real, all names outside the family have been altered. A few very minor plot or physical description details have been altered solely to protect the identities of others. And very minor physical details have been created, in a few cases, where such details have been forgotten (a person's clothing in a particular scene, for instance).

1

I wake up in a panic, and acid churns in my stomach. A nurse has walked into my hospital room. I was asleep. How long was I asleep? How long has it been since I last reached for the makeup bag under my pillow? Does the nurse see a girl with a bright future ahead of her? Or does he see a sweaty, tearstained mess?

As it turns out, I don't need to worry. All the nurse sees is my lunch tray. "You didn't eat any of this," he says. "You didn't even unwrap it."

I feel my face settle into a polite, neutral expression: forehead smooth and lips curved slightly upward. And I hear myself speak in the voice I save for strangers: slightly higher and more childlike than my normal voice, with a gentle lilt. People like that voice. They relax and smile when they hear it.

"I'm sorry," I say. "I fell asleep."

"So, if I leave it, will you eat it now?"

No. There's no way I can force that stuff down. This morning, I had three bites of pudding, and I'm still full. At the thought of more food, the familiar pains knife through me. But if I say that, I know what he'll think, so I purse my lips and arrange my face into a thoughtful expression.

"I don't know," I say. "I'm still sleepy. Maybe later, when I wake up again."

The nurse isn't happy with my answer. He growls and mutters as he takes my pulse and updates my chart.

I like this nurse. Yesterday he yelled at me, but I could tell he only did it because he was worried. Now he huffs, "Anorexia! You and my niece. Two beautiful girls, destroying your lives over a diet!"

I take careful note of the comment: *beautiful*. This nurse is the fifth person in the last four days to call me beautiful. But worry poisons my relief. What do I weigh now? I need to know the number that's made me beautiful.

"How's the heart?" asks the nurse. "Any pain in the chest?"

"No," I say, trying to keep annoyance out of my voice. That's because there's nothing wrong with my heart.

"Are you noticing any tightness? Any shortness of breath?"

"No." Of course not! One echo exam, and everybody freaks. Doctors read those tests wrong all the time.

"Do you need anything?"

"No thank you," I say with a shake of my head and a smile, as if he's a waiter taking my order. I feel the smile stay smooth and perfect on my face until he leaves the room.

As soon as the nurse is out of sight, I double up in agony, clenching my teeth to keep from groaning out loud. If I make a sound, I know he'll hear me and come rushing back to help. And I don't want anyone's help.

Anger and bewilderment are forms of admiration. It's pity I can't stand. Pity wraps you up inside your problem until the problem is all people see. *Did you hear what happened to her?* they whisper behind your back. *Can you just imagine? No wonder!* And when you do something amazing, nobody's jealous anymore. They hug you and cry and call you *brave*, when what they really mean by that is *damaged*.

So I lie still and take deep, quiet breaths. Pain doesn't bother me. I'm not afraid. I'm used to living with pain.

He saw you looking like a mess, warns the voice in my head. *You weren't careful enough. You let down your guard.*

That's my conscience. We all have one. Mine never lets me settle for second best. There's no place in life for losers.

So, even though the pain in my stomach still has me clenching my teeth in agony, I pull the little makeup bag out from under my pillow and touch up my face in the compact mirror.

Perfection. That's what I want people to see when they look at me. Nothing but perfection.

Anger is honest. Hatred is a backhanded compliment. Envy is the best gift of all. But let them turn you into a victim, and you're labeled for life.

Pity is the sea you drown in.

2

The psychiatrist sidles into my hospital room and looks grave when he sees my untouched tray. But then again, he always looks grave. He's a short man with sad brown eyes and a limp little brown mustache. He looks like he belongs in one of those old photographs, an explorer in a pith helmet with his arm draped around a half-naked tribesman.

I forget my pain and enjoy the feeling of how much I hate him.

I've only seen this moron for three short sessions, but he thinks he's figured out the solution to the Elena Dunkle mystery. He locked me in the hospital, and he told my parents I have anorexia nervosa. Now he wants to ship me back to the States.

I've lived in Germany for six years. It's a safe place for me, and I've earned that safety through hard work and plenty of angry tears when no one was around to see them. Germans think I'm one of them when they hear me speak. I know how to diss people in two languages. I love the Air Force base where my father works, too, with its neatness and discipline. It's a closed system, a small town, and I belong there.

I even love this hospital. It's like a second home to me. I volunteer here all the time. They're shorthanded right now down at the chaplain's wing because I'm stuck here in a hospital bed.

Being stuck here isn't why I hate the psychiatrist. I can respect drastic action. And I'm not an anorexic, but I know that anorexics are strong, smart people. I'm willing to take his diagnosis as a compliment.

No, the thing I hate about him is that he's still making pathetic attempts to be friends.

There are things I told this guy—little quirks about how I cope with food. If he shared them with the pediatrician and cardiologist, they might go along with his crazy diagnosis. But he's keeping those things from everybody—even from my parents. It's like those things I told him are our little secret. It's like he thinks we're two girlfriends away at summer camp together instead of what we really are, which is a maniac mad-scientist doctor and a prisoner he's locked away by force.

The psychiatrist wants me to be the one to tell my secrets. He actually believes he can persuade me to do this. But I haven't worked this hard this long at perfection just to throw it away.

It's an insult—that's exactly what it is. He's insulting my intelligence.

Now he sits down on the edge of my bed and gazes at me mournfully. "We're running out of time," he says.

I perk up. Maybe he's finally ready to do something on his own. Maybe he's finally going to quit treating me like his buddy.

In a way, it would be nice if he did. I've done nothing all week but wait. There are only so many interesting movies in the hospital library, and they won't let me leave this ward. The restricting is wearing me out, too. I've done my best to eat almost nothing, but it's exhausting to put up that kind of fight. I need a change. I hope he's finally ready to take action.

But no. He sighs and says, "Well, Elena, what are we going to tell them?"

We? Oh, for the love of God, will this loser just man up! When is he going to figure it out? I am *not* on his side.

"You know and I know how important this hospital stay is to you," he murmurs. "You can't fix this on your own. It's time to bring your parents in on this. Are you ready to tell them the truth?"

I stare straight ahead, and I keep my expression completely impassive. Maybe I can freeze him out. But the psychiatrist croons on in his confidential whisper as if we're Secret Santa pals.

Does he really think I'm nothing but some cute little girl who's going to burst into tears and sob on his shoulder?

"You don't want to disappoint your parents," he says. "I get that. Especially not after what they've been through with your sister."

White-hot daggers of rage flash through my brain and light up sparkling patterns behind my eyes. He shouldn't have done that. He shouldn't have brought up Valerie.

"I'm a perfectionist, too," he says. "I know how hard it is to give up on that perfect image. You think I don't know how you're feeling, facing an unhappy family? I'll tell you something. My wife and I divorced last year, and my daughter thinks it's my fault. She won't even talk to me."

"So that's what this whole thing is to you!" I snarl. "It's a Big-Daddy-to-the-Rescue crusade. You failed as a father with your own daughter, and now you've locked up another little girl so you can substitute-daddy me!"

The psychiatrist's mouth flops open, and he stares at me in shock. I have to stop myself from laughing. If he's got me figured out like he thinks he has, he should know that's what he gets for going up against me.

"Have you got a Messiah complex or something?" I say. "Is that what this is all about? You must think I'm going to *thank* you for doing this. You think you'll win my trust, and we'll fight this big bad problem together, and I'll wipe away a tear and tell you you've *saved* me."

I pause for breath. My chest hurts. But the psychiatrist just keeps staring. His face is turning the color of raw steak.

"Well, guess what?" I say. "I'm *not* grateful. You *haven't* saved me. Go daddy somebody else. *I'm* not going to be your replacement daughter!"

He jumps to his feet and rushes out of the room.

The psychiatrist mans up, all right. It's the end of Mr. Nice Guy. Within minutes of leaving me, he meets with my parents and the other two doctors in the conference room down the hall, and I go out to the corridor and listen as he makes an ass out of himself. He lays down the law, and he doesn't care what anybody else has to say about it. He's sending me to the States to a psychiatric institution.

The cardiologist argues with him. "I can't definitively state that her weak heart is eating disorder–related," she says. "You've hardly treated Elena. Where's the past history of eating disorder documented in her chart?"

"You haven't consulted with me at all," interjects the pediatrician. "What makes you so sure she's anorexic?"

Amazingly enough, the psychiatrist still keeps my secrets for me. Maybe he's forgotten about them. Or maybe he just doesn't care that he sounds like an ass.

In the hallway beside me, the ward nurses make *screw you* gestures at him behind the door, and my parents look stunned as the experts quarrel. But for the very first time, I feel a spark of sympathy for my psychiatrist.

So that limp little mustache had some fight behind it after all. I must have hurt his feelings pretty badly.

The cardiologist suggests a consultation at a children's hospital in the States. "They can run tests there that we aren't equipped for," she says. "They'll be able to find the root causes for this problem. She's lost six pounds in the week she's been here. I'd like to see them do a complete metabolic workup."

Six pounds. I've lost almost a pound a day! And I know my number now, the number that's made me beautiful. The relief I feel is so profound, my knees threaten to collapse. I totter back to my room, take off my glasses, and lie down.

Because it's like this: there's fat, and there's thin. Fat is bad, and thin is good. You take a girl sitting in the back of the classroom with her nose in a book. If she's fat, she's pitiful. If she's thin, she's sophisticated and mysterious. People say life's different, but people say there's a tooth fairy, too.

There's fat, and there's thin, and there's no in-between. You're one, or you're the other. But where does fat become thin? And where does thin become fat? In two pounds? Six pounds? Twelve pounds?

The girl in my mirror lies to everybody else. She'd lie to me if I let her. The camera lies, too. I can make my photos look like anything I want. Clothing sizes are clues (size 00 jeans, size XS). But clothes can stretch, and manufacturers change their sizes.

So I hunt obsessively through clues that tell me what people think of me, and I step on the scale twice a day. A number on the scale: that's the one and only thing I can trust. For a week, they've kept me away from the scale, but now I have my number again. I nestle into the pillow and close my eyes, at peace.

People burst into my room. I put on my glasses. It's the psychiatrist and my mother. Their meeting is over now, but he's still yelling—this time at me. It's just a bunch of shit, the stuff he's saying. I act like he's not there.

Yelling means he's lost the argument.

"You won't have that senior year with your friends," he says. "You'll spend six months in a hospital with a tube up your nose to feed you!"

Who is he kidding? Nobody gets locked up in institutions anymore. It's so mad-scientist, I can't help but smile.

"You think this is a joke? I'm serious, Elena! I'm very serious about this. You're getting sent out of here on the next transport plane, and you won't see Germany again."

I take off my glasses. The room blurs into vague, soft shapes, and the psychiatrist loses his angry expression. It doesn't matter what he says. I know my number again. And five people think I'm beautiful.

Eventually, the talk moves into the hall. Then it moves down the hall. I pull out my makeup bag and check my face again in the mirror:

Thin lips, plumped and filled in with gloss. Cheeks, brushed with blush in the hollows beneath the bones. Nose, squashy and powdered over to hide its pores. (God, I hate my nose!) First one brown eye and then the other to check the mascara on their lashes. (At least I have long eyelashes.)

What is a face? Nothing but the sum of its parts. If each part is right, the sum will be right, too.

Before I felt the worry over fat and thin, I felt the knot in my stomach. Stress used to gnaw and saw away inside me like a tiny black hole. I learned that in spite of the stress, I could do everything I needed to do: study, make top grades, shop for the right clothes, and put on that perfect smile. Some days, I felt just like Wonder Woman.

The only thing I couldn't do was eat.

At breakfast, I would fight to choke down half a bagel. When lunchtime came, I could still feel it sitting in my stomach, bloating me up. At supper, I was too tired and stressed to cope with the problem of food. I saved my energy to help me get through all the homework.

For months, I was afraid that my struggles over food were going to give me away. I wore baggy clothes and lived in fear of the day when pity would find me and smother me: *You're having trouble, Elena. I'm so sorry for you! I think you're being so brave.*

But my not eating turned out to be the best disguise of all.

As the girl in my mirror got thinner, I became more popular. And I didn't have to do a thing! Guys treated me differently. Girls came to me and begged, "Please, please tell me how you did it."

The girl in my mirror wasn't me anymore, so I started avoiding her eyes. They had nothing to say to me. I got used to putting on my makeup one feature at a time: lips, nose, one cheek, the other cheek, forehead, eye, eye. That was all I looked at. I didn't need to look at the whole thing.

Then one night, I woke up out of a nightmare and stumbled into the bathroom and looked in the mirror, and the girl I saw there was a total stranger. The fear of the nightmare was still heavy in my mind, and I felt sure that girl was about to disobey me.

If she smiled when I didn't smile, what would happen to me? Who would I be then?

I haven't looked at the mirror girl since.

But I don't need to. It doesn't matter what I see. It only matters what other people see: cool, calm, in-control perfection that can deal with yelling psychiatrists and still smile.

I put away the makeup bag and try to get comfortable. The mound of blankets does no good; I haven't been able to get warm in longer than I can remember. I close my eyes.

The nice nurse who got mad at me and called me beautiful carries in a supper tray, and the smells rising from it make me sick. I'd like to take a bite to please him, but I'm still too full to eat. This morning I broke down and ate a piece of toast, and it's turned into a hard knot inside my stomach, a rock that the acid churns around. Earlier today, that rock made me throw up three times, but I still can't get rid of it.

You knew it was a mistake to eat the toast, says the voice in my head. *Now that toast is rotting in there.*

And the thought of my full, hard, bloated stomach full of rotting food makes me shake, until I have to run to the bathroom and vomit again.

But the high of purging boosts me, and the dreamy haze of restriction wafts me along. I crawl back beneath the covers, feeling pure and holy.

No worries now. Nothing.

Nothing at all.

3

I wake up. It's twilight in the featureless room, that never-quite-dark-
enough half-light that means it's nighttime in a hospital. The quiet
is complete in the almost-empty ward. There isn't even the click of a
keyboard or the rustle of a page from the nurses' station.

The dim room swims. My hands are shaking, and I'm cold, but
I'm also drenched with sweat. My chest aches. My heart pounds: the
heart with thin walls. Except that's not real, is it?—there's nothing
wrong with my heart. Did I dream the cardiologist and her exam? Did
I dream the psychiatrist who lost the argument because he couldn't
stop yelling?

You'll spend six months in a hospital with a tube up your nose!
You'll never see Germany again!

That's crazy. It must have been a dream. It sounds like a bad
novel. It sounds like an old black-and-white movie. In my mind, the
psychiatrist morphs into a villain in a black cape and hat. They go
perfectly with his silly mustache.

But my heart won't stop hurting, and the room wavers before
my eyes. I'm not sure I'm strong enough to sit up. *Am* I having a heart
attack? I can't think straight. My arms and legs are so heavy, I can
barely move.

Out of the corner of my eye, I see feet by the door. A pair of Converse sneakers. Green scrubs—the hospital uniform of untucked cotton shirt and cotton pants. Red hair.

A nursing tech with red hair is standing in my room.

But when I turn my head to look, there's nothing there.

Over by the bathroom, I see a scrap of floral cloth. A flowered dress. Brown hair in a bun.

A woman is sitting in the rocking chair by my bed. She's huddled into herself, with her head on her chest, in sorrow or in pain.

I look straight at her. But she's gone.

Dead people, warns the voice in my head. *Maybe they died in this room.*

I try to summon up the energy to feel afraid, but my mind won't focus.

Dead people, says the voice in my head again. *Are they still here? Look again.*

But I don't look. I won't let them see that I've noticed them. If you ignore something, it goes away, no matter how bad it is.

I close my eyes and sink back into unconsciousness.

"Hey, Elena," calls a cheerful voice. "Are you ready to go?"

Is it the dead woman by my bed? Or did I dream her, just like I dreamed about getting sent back to the States by the villain in the black cape and hat?

I open my eyes and reach for my glasses. The room is full of light. The dead people are gone, and a nurse is pushing an empty gurney over to me.

She says, "Ready to catch that plane?"

Transport to the States. But wasn't it just a dream?

It's a stupid idea. It's crazy!

Mom comes in. She looks tired but still interested in everything. Mom writes books, so she says that everything she learns is useful because in order to write a book, you have to know a little bit about a lot of things.

Before Mom wrote her books, her stories were special, just for me and my sister. But now our special stories are out in bookstores for anybody to buy.

Mom's hair is very short and mostly gray. I've tried to get her to color it, but she says she likes gray hair. She's not wearing any makeup, as usual, even though makeup would hide the starts of creases in her forehead and the tiredness in her eyes. Mom would look better if she didn't let everybody see how she's feeling.

At that thought, I reach for my makeup bag and touch up my face. No worries. This is just a mistake. I don't need to do a thing. At some point, my pediatrician will walk in to stop this insanity, and there will be explanations and apologetic laughter. So I smile at the nurse, and I read her appreciation in her answering smile. *What a mature young woman!* she's thinking now. *Such a joy to work with.*

You've got her fooled! laughs the voice in my head.

The nurse pushes me down the halls and through the emergency room. It's nice to see the ER, which is one of the places I volunteer, but I hope I don't meet anybody I know. I adjust my expression in case that happens: slightly bored, mouth in a line, as if I'm putting up with a couple of preschoolers. People need to know that even though there's drama going on, I'm not part of that drama.

Now we're outside in front of the hospital. At least I'm getting a few rays of sunlight. My friend Barbara and I have been working on our tans this summer, but this week in bed has pretty much trashed mine.

Dad finds my gurney. He's in his button-down dress shirt, ready for his workday. He's an important manager who does engineering for the Air Force; a deputy squadron commander, in fact. Dad's tall and a little scary-looking, with thinning hair and a closely trimmed gray beard.

But this year has been too much for Dad. I pretend not to notice that he's crying. I want to tell him not to worry, but it's better if we don't talk about it.

Ignoring things is what makes them go away.

Other gurneys gather on the asphalt drive outside the ER. All around me are wounded soldiers swathed in bandages and casts. "You kind of wonder what it feels like to get shot," one Marine says thoughtfully to another. "Anyway, we've checked that box."

This is getting embarrassing. I should be doing something to help, not lying here like this. Just last week, I met some of these same soldiers and helped get them settled in.

Nurses in scrubs go through the crowd now and prep the patients for transport. They come by and move me onto a primitive-looking stretcher with long wooden rods down the sides. The stretcher has a big feather pillow in a plastic sack that's as heavy as lead. My nurse helps them pull up an ultra-itchy dark green wool blanket that looks like it's been through World War II.

Then they tighten a strap around my middle. Now I can't sit up.

I don't like the strap. I want to protest, but if I do, they'll think I'm scared. I can't let that happen, so I smile at them as graciously as if they've just brought me flowers, and they move on to someone who actually needs their help.

Dark blue buses back up into the drive, just like school buses except for the color and the fact that they don't have seats inside.

Swinging doors in the back open, and one by one, soldiers in camouflage fatigues carry us onto the buses and lock our stretchers into brackets on the walls.

I don't want to be carried on a stretcher. I'm not a patient. I'm not a victim! But they heave me into the bus, and I grip the long poles on either side as my stretcher rocks up and down. Then, with a *clump*, they lock me into place.

"What's wrong with the girl?" I hear the wounded soldiers asking. "What's the matter with her? Will she be okay?" My stretcher is so high that it's up by the school bus windows, where anybody can see me. I can look right down to the asphalt drive below.

Now we're bouncing along the highway. Pine trees flash past my feet, and I feel lightheaded and short of breath.

You've screwed up your heart, warns the voice in my head. *It's thin. That's what the cardiologist said.*

But the cardiologist is wrong. She can't be right about my heart. And this can't be happening. It isn't happening, is it? It's like I'm watching a movie that's all around me.

The bus makes its way through square beige buildings to the flight line, where the big planes sit. The flight line is a massive concrete field with mysterious stripes and symbols painted on it. It's so wide that I can't see its edges. There's concrete to the horizon.

I've lived here for six years, and I've never even thought of walking onto the flight line. A red stripe runs around its edge, and if you stick a toe over that line, the security guards up in the tower send a jeep patrol with machine guns racing over to find out what you're doing. Breaking red is serious business. No Air Force kid would even think about it. But here I am, breaking red, rolling down the dead center of all this concrete. It's crazy. It's like I've been sucked into the middle of a war film.

The C-17 airplane is big, fat, and ugly. It looks like a metal goose. Its back end is open, with a wide ramp reaching down to the ground. The bus stops, and our nurses unlatch the doors at the back and jump out. The fingernail-screech of airplane engines gets very loud.

Knots of Army and Air Force soldiers start carrying stretchers up the ramp: six to a stretcher, three to a side, like bearers for a coffin. I don't want them to carry me that way, flopped out flat like a dead body. I don't want to watch this movie anymore.

They'll drop you, warns the voice in my head. *They'll drop you, and your heart will burst. Feel it? Feel how it's pounding?*

I struggle to sit up, pulling at the strap around my middle. My nurse from the children's ward bends over me. "I can't breathe," I tell her in what I hope sounds like a calm, in-control voice. "I think there might be something wrong with my heart."

Impersonal faces and battle fatigues are next to me in the bus. With a *thunk*, they unhook my stretcher. Camouflaged torsos, tan and gray, walk me under the shadow of the C-17. The noise vibrates my teeth. I can feel them grinding together.

They're going to drop you! shrieks the voice in my head. *You're sliding backward off the stretcher!*

I can't see my nurse. My heart gives a stab of pain. The hot, humid wind of German high summer rushes across the concrete and blows directly into my face.

"I can't breathe," I gasp. "I can't breathe!"

That's all I remember.

4

I open my eyes because someone is screaming. When I open my eyes, the screaming stops. I close them, but the screaming starts up again, so I slip away to a place where it can't find me.

Now I'm choking. There's a burning pain in my nose. I open my eyes long enough to see my pediatrician's face.

"I'm sorry," he says. "We have to do this."

I can't ask him what he has to do because I'm gagging on something in my throat. But I don't wonder about this. I don't wonder about anything. I close my eyes and slip away again.

Beeps. Steady, rhythmic beeps. Little by little, they pull me into myself. Wires tangle under my fingers. Sticky-tape dots itch on my chest.

Smoke over fire, I think with my eyes closed. That's how nurses place the sticky-tape dots. *White is right.* That's how I've placed the three ECG leads on the chests of dozens of patients. But I have more leads stuck to me than that. Lines are snaking everywhere, across my chest and out the arm of my hospital gown.

Lines. Snakes. Medusa.

Another line crosses my cheek and dives down my nostril. Inside my throat, it chokes me and rubs the flesh raw. I try to open my eyes, but they're gummy, and the light from the television across the room stabs into them before I can shut it out.

"Elena, honey. What is it?"

That must be a nurse. She sounds nice. I'm going to be a nurse.

"Popsicle," I whisper.

"Her throat hurts," I hear Mom say. "From the feeding tube."

A tube up your nose to feed you.

Endless steady beeps of the monitor. I try to count them, but I keep getting lost. One, two. One, two. One, two, three, four.

Even numbers comfort me. They will help me in this new world I'm lost in—a soft continent, circumnavigated by lines and tubes.

Lines. Snakes. Medusa.

Mom is here. But Valerie is not.

Where is Valerie? My sister kept me safe from the monsters. She should be here to keep me safe in this new world.

One, two, three, four.

"Honey. Elena, honey."

A hard edge pushes against me, bringing me out of the soft darkness. I squint my eyes open. Powder blue. A plastic basin full of mashed-up popsicles. Grayish-purple slush.

I close my eyes and spoon in the icy slivers, and my burning throat gets a little relief.

Voices murmur and whisper around me. They rise and fall like the looping curves of the monitor by the bed. I've come unstuck from the day-to-day routine of life. Things I knew about myself once— these things no longer seem to be true.

You have anorexia! he told me sternly, like he blamed me for it. *You won't have a senior year with your friends!*

Or maybe it was a dream, like the dead people in my room. If I close my eyes, I don't see them. So I keep my eyes closed as the voices murmur and whisper. Valerie isn't here to tell me it's going to be okay.

One, two. One, two. One, two, three, four.

Now there's a rumbling in my ears, and my bed is shaking. My teeth are jolting together. I open my eyes and see nothing familiar in the fuzzy shape of my room. It's much too long, and the unexpected distance frightens me.

I grope around and find my glasses in my hand. I put them on.

A steel-gray barrel-vault ceiling comes into view. Yellow bundles of electrical cords and cherry-red ducts wind down it, and black stencil numbers run along its metal sides.

Where am I? What's happened to the world I belong to? I reach up and try to push this scary place away.

A man in Army fatigues catches my hand in his. I realize he's been here the whole time. His face looks young, but his hair is white, and his eyes look like they've seen everything. He's doing something with my arm. A thin line: there's an IV there.

"Elena," he says. "It's going to be okay."

"It is?" I ask him. This makes no sense. How can it be okay?

But then it is okay, because darkness comes back—the safe kind of darkness I'm getting used to. The man and the noise and the light all fold up and disappear together.

I feel a jolt. I open my eyes, and I'm outside in sunlight. Everything is in sharp focus this time. I reach up to find my glasses on my face.

I'm lying on a stretcher. Two men are rolling me over to an ambulance. They aren't in fatigues. They're in green scrubs. The man with white hair has disappeared.

"Um. This is for you," one of them says. Awkwardly, he hands me a small stuffed bear.

Why? the voice in my head frets. *Why? What's going on? Do you look okay? Is your makeup okay?*

Mom is there, too. She climbs into the front seat, just beyond my head, and I hear her talking in a bright, polite voice.

Mom has a voice just for strangers, too.

I glance around the ambulance. This is an American ambulance. I know the difference. At the ER, I've helped clean vomit out of the German ones.

So they did it—what they threatened to do. I'm not in Germany anymore.

You won't see Germany again.

I wait for that to hurt, but all that comes back is dull disinterest. My life feels like a book I read a long time ago.

The man who gave me the bear climbs into the ambulance beside me, and the back door slams shut. I close my eyes as we start to move.

You won't see Germany again. You'll have a tube up your nose to feed you.

I swallow. Sure enough, I have a tube.

The ambulance stops. Doors slam. I am being wheeled down a hall and into an elevator. Once upon a time, I would have hated to feel so helpless. Once upon a time, I lived in a different world.

I roll into a room with white ceiling tiles and a view of roof gravel out a window. Its privacy curtain is covered with pink cartoon fish. The ambulance driver slides me onto the hospital bed as if I'm a doll. Then he says good-bye. He leaves me an awful plastic-bag pillow full of feathers and an itchy green wool blanket that I have seen somewhere before.

A nurse comes in and sticky-tapes me into a new harness of wires. Then she starts the hypnotic beeping of a new machine. Steady beeps are even more soothing than even numbers. I close my eyes and let them carry me away.

Now a beautiful, beautiful Indian woman with large brown eyes like a fawn's is leaning over my bed. "I'm the doctor in charge tonight," she says. But she doesn't look like a doctor. She looks like a fairy tale. I close my eyes, then open them again. The fairy-tale doctor is gone.

Is this a movie? Is this real? Do I care what's real?

I close my eyes again.

Fuzzy gray drowsiness floats me along, like the soft waves of a sunless sea. They rock me in time to the steady beeps beside my bed. But eventually, the waves recede. I open my eyes to see where they have left me.

White ceiling tiles—big rectangles edged by metal bands. Maybe they have patterns of dots on them, but to me, they're just soft white. I touch my face. I'm not wearing my glasses.

"I need to go to the bathroom," I announce to the white ceiling.

"Do you promise not to pass out and hit the floor?"

I fumble for my glasses and find them next to my pillow. A blond-haired nurse comes into view. She doesn't look like a fairy tale. She looks real.

"I wouldn't pass out," I say.

"Yes, you have, every time we've let you sit up," she answers.

I've been sitting up? When?

"I'll let you try again," she says, "but you have to promise me to stay conscious. We don't want you cracking your skull."

Clutching her arm, I navigate the few feet to the bathroom. My legs feel so rubbery, it's like they haven't been used in weeks. We make it back to the bed, and she hooks me back up to the machine. The end of my nose tube connects to a feeding pump.

Have they been stuffing me full of calories while I've been asleep? Have I gotten fat? What's my number?

After the blond nurse leaves, I lie there, listening to the beeping machine. I wait for the gentle waves to come back, but they don't. My bed doesn't feel like a soft continent anymore. It feels more or less like a bed. Mom is sitting across the room by the window, tapping away on her laptop. She turns to look at me, but I close my eyes.

You're trapped, says the voice in my head. *He yelled at you, and he won.*

I roll away from that thought as far as the wires will let me.

No matter how hard you fight, they always win. They hold you down, and they hurt you, and they win.

I shiver like a beaten dog, and feelings that have been numb for days burst inside my brain all at once.

Then I'm not in the hospital anymore. I'm in a dollhouse. I float down the halls and through rooms, admiring the gorgeous furnishings. I have left my body behind, the awkward, ominous girl who haunts my mirror. All that is heavy about me is gone, and I fly over the beautiful rugs and past the gilded furniture in joy and in peace.

Outside, a deep voice is talking. And then a soft voice answers it, taking turns. I try to stay in the dollhouse, but it slides away from me.

I open my eyes. Mom is having a conversation with a big African American man in a splendid white lab coat. Two other doctors are with him, but they don't speak. They watch him in respectful silence, one on either side.

"It's *dissociation,*" he's telling Mom, rolling the word in his mouth like it has a taste he enjoys. "Dissociation doesn't have a basis in medical or physical causes. She's retreating from reality, to another place in the mind. A safe world the patient can control."

"I was in a dollhouse," I say.

Mom and the two other doctors look at me in surprise, but the man in the lab coat keeps right on talking.

"Yes, a dollhouse—that's what it's like," he continues smoothly. "That's a great metaphor for the dissociative state."

"That's not what it's *like*," I say. "That's what it *is*. That's where I *was*." But he doesn't listen to me. He's another man who doesn't need to listen because he already knows all about me, even though he doesn't know me at all.

That's how I know that I've got another psychiatrist.

The three men leave. Mom goes back to her typing. I close my eyes and try to slip away again, but this time, I can't leave my body behind. My hair feels like it's been coated with wax, and my mouth feels like I'm chewing cotton. I try to remember the dollhouse, but worries prick me instead. Senior year starts in another month. My coursework is all planned out. Did Mom pack the books I'm supposed to read for AP English?

You won't have a senior year, says the voice in my head.

Why shouldn't I have a senior year? Valerie did. Valerie walked around like a groupie at a death-metal concert, and she even got to go to college. After she ran away, it took nine big gray plastic bags to clean all the trash out of her room.

In my mind, those trash bags crackle open and release a swarm of ugly thoughts. With a jolt of pain, the black hole starts spinning and resumes nibbling away inside me. Can anybody tell the black hole is there? What do people see? What do I look like?

You look like a mental patient, says the voice in my head. *You look like some kind of a freak.*

I reach under my pillow, find the makeup bag, and check my face. The little tube sticking out of my nose is bright yellow. My hair doesn't just feel like it's dipped in wax, it pretty much looks like it's dipped in wax, too. My lips are scaly, and my pores are a disaster. The skin on my nose is dull and covered in black dots.

I look like hell. I need to fix this. Did Mom bring my facial masks?

There's a bustle at the doorway: techs in hospital scrubs bring in a small table and two folding chairs. It's part of the anorexia protocol, they say. I'm supposed to sit there to eat supper, and a tech is supposed to sit opposite to watch me.

The black hole spins faster, and a searing pain stabs through my gut. Food? Really? They think I can eat with this tube poking down into my stomach?

They've been pumping calories into you while you were asleep, says the voice in my head. *They've fattened you up. You're obese!*

The techs tell Mom she needs to leave while I eat. She folds up her laptop, picks up her purse, and heads off down the hall.

I sit on one side of the little table, and a tech sits on the other side. After days of lying in bed, it feels weird to be sitting. My body feels like a puppet, ready to flop over. I have to think about which strings to pull to keep it upright. The nurses let me wear scrubs at the last hospital. Now I'm not in scrubs anymore, but a hospital gown. I feel inadequately dressed.

Is the tech really going to sit there and watch me eat?

I never let strangers see me eat. It's one of my rules.

The tech is only a couple of years older than me and cute in a mousy kind of way. She's wearing pale shades of rose eye shadow, and a pink bead tie holds her ponytail.

I resist the urge to touch my stiff, dirty hair.

The other tech brings in my meal: a fat, squashy white-bread sandwich, pickle spears, and a bag of chips. More food than I've eaten in I don't know how long. More food than I could possibly eat! Soaked in sodium and preservatives—that stuff makes the body swell up like a sponge. It takes all my self-control to keep from bursting into tears.

You can't eat those chips, says the voice in my head. *Nineteen grams of fat at least—you better not eat those chips!*

"I'm kind of sick to my stomach," I tell the tech, settling an apologetic smile onto my face to convey the impression that I'd love to eat if only I felt better. "They've had me on such crazy medications the last few days. What if I can't eat this?"

"I don't know," she confesses, a little embarrassed by her role as enforcer. "I don't do anything about it anyway. I just report it to the doctor."

"The psychiatrist?" I ask, and I picture the African American man with his deep voice, freshly ironed lab coat, and habit of talking about me right in front of me as if I'm some kind of animal.

"I guess so," she says, and we avoid each other's eyes for a minute. I count my breaths to give myself courage, one-two, one-two, and pick up a pickle spear as a gesture of good will. Pickles are safe. They don't have many calories.

The sodium will bloat you up, says the voice in my head.

"I like your eye shadow," I say to the tech and then bite the pickle spear. It tastes nasty, so I put it back down.

"Thanks," she says, brightening.

"Do you like working here? Are you an RN?" I ask.

As I talk, I pick up the sandwich with one hand. With the other, I pick up the plastic wrap. I spread the plastic across my lap. Then I hitch my chair closer to the table so the wrap won't show.

"I love it here!" she says. "I started this spring. I'm an LVN right now, but I'm going to start an RN program in the fall."

"Have you always wanted to be a nurse?" I ask. "When did you know that's what you wanted to be?"

"Let's see . . . ," she says, shifting her gaze to stare thoughtfully into the distance. People generally stare into the distance when they're trying to remember.

That's when I slip the cheese from the sandwich and drop it into my lap.

By the time the meal is over, I feel like I've made a new friend. I've also managed to stuff half the food into the plastic wrap. I hold it in a fold of my gown while the tech clears away the table, and I stash it under my pillow until she leaves.

She's supposed to stay with me till Mom gets back, but she and the other tech take a minute to haul away the little table. That's a lucky break. There's no time to get to the bathroom, but I slip out of bed and hide the contents of the plastic wrap inside a low cabinet by the door. I've managed to keep hold of the chip bag, too. An empty bag might be useful. My stomach feels tight, and the pickle has bloated me up, but it's not as bad as it could have been.

Take *that*, you damn psychiatrists! Let's see you figure this one out.

This new psychiatrist is just as bad as the other one, says the voice in my head. *He's going to have you locked up with real anorexics.*

The thought staggers me. I'm nowhere near thin enough to handle that! Anorexics have serious willpower. They'll see me as a big fat failure. They'll think being in an institution is my idea, like I'm trying to join their club, and they'll hate me for it. I already wasn't thin enough to meet real anorexics before, and who knows how much I've ballooned thanks to this feeding pump?

My hand flutters nervously to my collarbone to feel how much flesh is there. I can poke my finger into the fat on either side of it. This isn't good! If there's even a chance I could end up with real anorexics, I've got to find a way to lose more weight.

Mom comes back from the cafeteria. Her face is older than I remember. She ought to wear makeup. Everyone can see how tired and pale she is.

"What did you do while you were thrown out of the room?" I ask, trying to cheer her up.

"I went and ate supper, too, at the hospital cafeteria," she says. "Chicken-fried steak and collard greens—you can tell we're in the South. And chocolate pudding for dessert."

"I wish I'd had pudding," I joke. "I guess there's no dessert on the anorexia protocol."

"That's too bad," Mom says, and she means it. Mom has a sweet tooth.

The blond nurse comes back to check on me. I like her because she's so direct. "No passing out, remember," she warns me, and she moves a chair into the shower stall so I can wash my hair. I take note of how she turns off the machine alarms and unhooks me from everything. "Now let me go get some plastic to cover up your IV."

"You don't need plastic," I tell her. "Hand me a glove and I'll show you." Borrowing her scissors, I cut the fingers off the latex glove and pull the wide band that's left up over my IV tube. "Now all it needs is a little tape around the edges, and you don't have to worry about water leaking through the wrap."

"That's a neat trick," she says. "I'm going to remember that."

"I learned it in Germany," I say. "I volunteer at the hospital there because I'm planning on being a nurse, too. Next year, I'll be working fifteen hours a week in the ER."

"That's great!" she says. "We need good nurses."

All my worries leave me under the hot, steamy spray of the shower. Nothing feels better than getting clean. I put on a new gown.

I even get to brush my teeth. And there are fresh sheets on my bed. It's like Christmas.

As soon as I settle into bed, Mom comes over. She has a big smile on her face.

"Look what I've got," she says in a conspiratorial whisper, and she pulls a container of chocolate pudding out of her purse.

Not pudding! shrieks the voice in my head. *A hundred and fifty calories—more with those Oreo bits! And you need to lose weight. You don't know your number. Who knows how much weight they've pumped into you already!*

But Mom looks happier than she's looked in a long time. There's no way I can ruin this for her.

"Great!" I say, and it takes every bit of control I have to match her smile.

Mom and I lie on my bed together and share the pudding bite for bite. *SpongeBob* is on. How could that crazy square not distract me? But the voice in my head is relentless.

Twenty-five grams of simple carbs, it hisses. *Twenty-five grams at least! Insulin is flooding your bloodstream right this minute, turning sugar molecules into fat!*

The monitor shows that my heart is speeding up. I feel sweat prickling my face. "I've got to go to the bathroom," I say, swinging my feet over the side of the bed.

"I think somebody's supposed to help you," Mom says.

"No, I'm not that dizzy anymore. You can help me." Quickly, I pop the leads out of the heart machine and grab my IV pole to steady myself.

"No, I think someone's supposed to monitor you," Mom says. "Part of the anorexia protocol."

But practice makes perfect, and I'm steadier on my feet than I was before the shower. Trundling the noisy IV pole, I'm across the room before she can hit the call button.

Inside the bathroom, I lock the door and turn on the faucet at the sink.

Get that crap out of there! says the voice in my head. *A hundred and fifty calories! How will you face real anorexics now?*

But I can't do it. I can't break faith with Mom after everything she went through with Valerie. I pound my fists on my rock-hard stomach and curse under my breath. But I can't do it. I can't flush Mom's pudding.

You're stupid, fumes the voice in my head. *You're a fat, stupid bitch! She wouldn't know anyway. It doesn't matter.*

But it does matter. It matters a lot. I won't do it.

Knocking sounds on the door. "Elena! Come out of there," calls the nurse. She sounds upset, but I haven't done anything wrong.

"Just washing my hands," I call back and open the door.

This isn't the blond nurse. It's a new nurse I haven't seen before. She's heavyset, and she's angry. "We have to monitor your output," she lectures as I trundle the IV pole back to bed.

Output? They're monitoring my *output*?

"You shouldn't have flushed," she says. "You should have rung for help."

"Sorry," I say. "I didn't know."

The nurse glares at me as she hooks my lines back up. Seriously, what is her problem? She gives a quick glance around to make sure Mom isn't nearby. Then she leans in close to my ear.

She whispers, "*We* don't think you deserve to be here!"

Shock tingles through me. I smooth my face into an expressionless mask, but the shock lingers even after she's gone. *We?* Who's *we?* Even the blond nurse? Even the tech with the rose-colored eye shadow? They're whispering about me behind my back! What are they saying?

They think you're fat, says the voice in my head. *They know you're not an anorexic. They all think you're a big fat fake.*

Anxiously, I wrap my fingers around my wrist. Is that true? Am I fat? What's my number?

You're swelling up, says the voice in my head. *The feeding pump is swelling you up. You're not anorexic! Who do you think you're fooling? You're obese! You're a stupid, fat bitch!*

The angry nurse comes back with a tech, and together they hook up the feeding pump. Out of the corner of my eye, I see them load it with strawberry Ensure, but I lie still and pretend they don't exist.

The tech stays behind on a chair by the door. "Anorexia protocol," she tells Mom. "I'll be here all night. They want your daughter to have twenty-four hour supervision."

She looks sweet and concerned while she tells this to Mom, but I bet she's been whispering about me, too.

Mom turns out the light and settles down on her foldout bed. The tech reads a nursing textbook by the light from the hall. I lie in my bed in torment as the feeding pump fattens me up. The pump grinds, grinds, grinds, like someone chewing. My stomach is going to burst!

They've got you right where they want you, flat on your back, sneers the voice in my head. *You deserve it, too, you fat, stupid bitch!*

Hour after hour, I lie awake, rigid, while calories force their way into my body. The grind of the pump is like a taunt, like a boast: *We've got you! You can't get away. We hate you! You can't fight us. We win!*

The ward grows still. The tech by the door stops turning pages. I peek at her. She's slumped over her book.

She doesn't think you deserve to be here, says the voice in my head.

Well, I don't think I should be here, either, and you can stick your damn strawberry Ensure up your ass!

Holding my breath, I hit the pause button on the feeding tube. The room drops into stark, sudden silence. I don't dare unhook my heart leads because that will ring an alarm, but the wires will stretch far enough to let me get to the sink and to the cabinets by the door.

I kneel down next to the cabinet and pull out the empty chip bag. I smooth its crinkles out one by one. Then I dump Ensure from the feeding pump into the chip bag and empty it out into the sink.

I'm tiptoeing right past the sleeping tech. She could get fired for sleeping on the job. But I'm willing to swear that she was wide awake all night and that she watched every single drop of Ensure go through the line.

A second trip, and then a third. My heart's pounding, and my breath hurts. I feel like a cat burglar, or a spy.

But by the third trip, the feeding pump is empty.

A syringe lies on the platform under my heart monitor. I saw the nurse use it earlier to clear the line on my nose tube. I disconnect the tube from the pump and, with infinite care, pull a vacuum on the tube with the syringe. The Ensure that has already been pumped into my stomach flows out through the nose tube again.

I hold the end of my nose tube so it can drain into the sink. Its contents join the pale puddle already there.

Hey, you big bad psychiatrists and bitchy nurses, I'm not your victim. I'm not some cute little girl who's going to get yelled at and cry. You want to lock me up? Go right ahead! But you better want what you want as much as I do.

Slowly, cautiously, I turn on the faucet. Its dripping stream sounds like a drumbeat on the metal sink. It's so loud, I almost jump out of my skin. But the tech right beside me doesn't stir. She's worn out from school and working extra shifts.

Careful! frets the voice in my head. *If she wakes up now—if she sees you—!*

So what? What can she possibly do? There's nothing anybody could do to me that's worse than what's been done already. And if she does something worse, I'll deal with that, too.

I wash the pale, viscous puddle down the drain and refill the feeding pump with water. Then I rinse out my chip bag and hide it away. Finally, I hook my nose tube back to the feeding pump.

My heart is pounding as I crawl back into bed. I lie there and listen to the feeding pump grind as it fills my stomach with water. I should be able to relax now, but worries nag at me and keep me on edge. I need to talk to Mom in the morning about correspondence school. I need to figure out some way to take online classes.

Because if they're really going to keep me here until I've gained weight, then I'm never getting out of this place.

5

It's finally happening. After almost two weeks of enforced bed rest at the children's hospital, they're sending me to an eating disorder treatment center.

Another hospital. A mental hospital! And nothing is wrong with me!

Two EMTs are hauling my stretcher down the halls. I'm strapped down around my middle again. I can't believe Mom is letting this happen. I can't believe they can do this to me.

You'll spend six months in a hospital, says the voice in my head. *You'll spend six months in a hospital with a tube up your nose.*

Without meaning to, I raise my hand to my face. That damn tube is still there, snaking down inside my throat. Its free end has been taped to my cheek, and the tape feels stiff and itchy. I have to force myself not to pull it loose.

I'm a prickly bundle of nerves, and my stomach feels like it's stuffed with razor blades, but I have myself under control. If I yell and scream, I might feel better, but I'll sound like I belong in a mental hospital. If I'm polite, I might shame my kidnappers a little, but the transport will be easier for them. So I've decided on silence. I stare up at the ceiling tiles and adjust the expression on my face: as stiff and blank as a stone statue.

With a jerk and a heave, the techs lift my stretcher into an ambulance. Mom climbs in the back with me, and we start off. The only view I have is out the tiny back window, where the street unrolls behind us. I hate riding backward. It's making me sick.

The young EMT is telling Mom his life story, but I know he's really telling it to me. Apparently, he's worked overtime for so long now that I'm the closest thing to a date he's had in weeks.

I pretend I've gone deaf and keep my eyes fixed on the cars nosing up to our back bumper. This guy isn't going to get the satisfaction of thinking I'm listening.

An eating disorder treatment center. Anorexics. Oh, God! What will they think of me? I did my best, but they weighed me right before the ambulance came. They wouldn't let me see my number, but I know it was more than it was when the transport plane brought me in.

What's my number? I don't know my number!

You're obese, says the voice in my head. *You're huge!*

The ambulance slows down, then stops. We're there. But we're not there. We're at Patient Intake. They won't even let us see the place, much less talk to anybody, till Mom's signed dozens of forms.

Minutes tick by while a big woman with big hair puts form after form on the desk in front of Mom. Mom skims each one before she signs it. It's like she's buying a new house. Or buying the whole center. Or selling me!

A tech comes with a wheelchair and rolls me outside. Mom walks beside us past big brick buildings and tall trees. Then the tech buzzes us through a door and takes the wheelchair away.

My first impression of Drew Center is doors: handsome, heavy, wood-paneled doors—New England doors, front doors—the kind you'd see in *The Amityville Horror*. But these doors aren't just on the outside. They're everywhere.

Mom and I walked through the first front door, the one that buzzed, and it left us in a small waiting room. Now another big front door opens on the other side of the room. It leads into a bare office. Mom isn't with me in the office. They made her stay behind.

A girl maybe four years older than me with straight brown hair and badly plucked eyebrows sits on the other side of a desk. "I'm going to be asking you some questions," she tells me. "Your answers are confidential."

Bullshit! warns the voice in my head.

Still, I surprise myself by being more candid than I thought I would be. I tell her stuff nobody else knows. Maybe it's because I'm finally at a real anorexia treatment center. That's kind of cool. I feel like I'm talking the bouncer into letting me into a club.

"Do you restrict?"

"Yes."

"What's the longest time you've gone without eating?"

"Twenty-one days."

My friends and I were doing a three-week juice fast, but I was the only one who made it. I think about the willpower I exhibited then and feel a glow of pride.

The girl pauses before she writes this down. "No food at all?"

"It was a juice fast."

"Ah."

She makes a note, and I feel the glow slip away.

All those bottles of juice! laments the voice in my head. *So many grams of simple sugars! You could have made it without them.*

"Have you ever experienced sexual assault?" the girl is asking in the meantime.

This jars me out of my thoughts.

"Why don't people say 'rape' anymore?" I snap. "What's wrong with calling it what it is?"

The girl looks serious. "Sexual assault covers more than rape," she says. "It covers any kind of unwanted sexual contact."

"Oh."

"Well?" she prods.

"What?" I say.

"Have you ever experienced sexual assault?"

Her pen hovers over the paper, waiting to check a box. There are several lines below that so she can write down the juicy details.

I'm a big fan of writing things down. I keep boxes full of letters and notes, and I even save old text messages on my phone. I like to go back and reread them. They make things real for me.

Since I was eleven years old, I've kept a journal. I've written down every single important thing that's happened.

Except one.

You were so stupid! mutters the voice in my head.

"Why would I tell you?" I say out loud.

The girl looks startled. "What do you mean?"

"Let's say I've been 'sexually assaulted.' Why would I want to tell you?"

"It's important to work with a therapist if you're a victim of sexual trauma," she says. "Remember, your answers here are confidential."

"Yeah," I say. "Just between you and me and about thirty other people who work here, so you can all whisper about me behind my back."

"We wouldn't do that!"

"Oh, yeah? Well, how about I say you're going to 'consult' about me instead? No thanks! And I'm not a *victim* of anything."

Her pen still hovers over the paper.

"So that's a no?" she says. "Is that your answer?"

Since I was eleven years old, I've kept a journal. But I didn't write about one thing. And then I burned the notebook I didn't write it in, just to make sure.

"My answer," I say, "is that it's none of your business."

We finish up the interview, and the girl leads me further into the center through more big wooden doors. Two nurses in white uniforms sort my luggage into "allowed" and "forbidden" piles while I change into a set of green scrubs with DREW CENTER printed across the back.

This is just like prison. I know. I've watched the shows.

Then the nurses march me down to the cafeteria for my very first eating-disorder-center meal.

Skinny girls, skinny women, and one skinny man sit along both sides of long, bare, cafeteria-style tables. The skinny people look like political prisoners being tortured for their beliefs. They're staring down at huge plates of food like they're looking into the muzzle of a gun. More staff in white uniforms walk up and down behind them.

I am issued a plate. My stomach is churning, but for once, I'm not thinking about the food. So these are real anorexics! I sneak quick looks to my left and right as we all toil through the ordeal of eating.

They think you're fat, whispers the voice in my head. *They think you don't deserve to be here.*

Is that true? No one has even looked at me. Do they think I'm fat? I don't have my makeup bag. I didn't get to check my makeup. What do they see?

The girl across the table starts shaking and crying. She's eaten all she can, and her lunch is gone, but she can't choke down dessert, which is a piece of chocolate cake garnished with Oreos. If she can't eat the last few bites of Oreo cake, they'll force her to drink as much Boost as the calories of her whole meal.

That's not fair. It's not medicine, it's punishment, but that's the way they wrote the rules here.

They've got you both where they want you, says the voice in my head. *You're helpless. You can't do a thing.*

I can barely breathe. Is that true? Am I helpless? My chest hurts, and my heart pounds faster. But maybe I can do something after all—something to stop these evil white uniforms from winning.

I catch the girl's eye and make a tiny gesture: *I'll take your cake.* She gives me a grateful look. But as soon as she starts to slide the cake over to me, a staff member swoops down on us, yelling.

"That's it! Boost for both of you, the entire lunch's worth of Boost. You know it's against the rules to share food!"

The girl sobs out loud and shoves her tray off the table.

Two staff members take my arms and pull me up from my seat. They march me into a nearby room and sit me down on an examining table.

"Where do you think you are?" scolds the first one. "Do we look stupid to you? What do you think we are, blind?"

Stupid bitch! adds the voice in my head.

"Is that what you got away with at your last center?" scolds the second. "Well, you're not going to get away with it here!"

Stupid bitch! Stupid bitch! Stupid, fat bitch!

It's too sudden. I didn't see it coming. I can barely breathe from shock. My heart gives a painful lurch—my damaged heart!

Then they're gone. Everything is gone.

I open my eyes. I'm in a small, dim room. White light shines in at the open doorway. I'm lying on a bed, but I can't remember where I am. Everything around me is blurry.

I reach beside the pillow for my glasses. No glasses. I sit up in a panic and fumble around for them.

My nose jerks like I'm a fish on a hook. I reach up to feel it and discover that my tube has been hooked up to a feeding pump again. I squint at the pump. A big bag dangles from it, the color of mud, but it's probably just chocolate Ensure.

Now my nose hurts deep inside, and the back of my throat

hurts. My forehead is aching, too. I touch it and discover a big tender lump between my eyes.

Careful of the tube, I continue searching the bed. My glasses! Where are my glasses?

A hazy, faceless blob floats into the twilit room and comes close enough that I can identify it as a nurse.

"Do you have my glasses?" I ask.

"So you've had enough of being a drama queen," she says. "Stunts like that aren't going to get you anywhere! You're off to a great start, trying to cheat the minute you arrive. Well, breaking rules isn't going to work out anymore, I can tell you that."

This makes me feel bad for a minute. She's right, I did break the rules. And I've always been the good girl, the one teachers love. How did that good girl end up in prison?

"Do you have my glasses?" I ask with a little more humility.

"So she's stopped her charade," says a man's voice, and another blob floats through the door. I parse this one out to be a doctor with a stethoscope around his neck. He comes close enough that I can read the name on his coat. It isn't Drew Center. I'm in a hospital emergency room. My heart lifts briefly. I work in an ER like this.

"You know what this has been?" says the doctor blob to the nurse blob. "This has been a complete waste of your time. I don't know how you put up with it."

Now I realize that those are people hurrying past the white light coming in at my doorway. My eyes are so bad, I see nothing but splashes of shimmer and shadow, like a view of pond water through a microscope. Paramecium-shaped forms propel themselves about in the hallway outside. They block and overlap one another.

"My head hurts. Where are my glasses?" I say helplessly. This is a caring profession! Aren't these people supposed to care?

"You pitched off the table onto your face," the nurse says sternly. "You might as well stop the nonsense. We've seen it all, trust me. We've seen it ALL."

"Next time, be more careful," admonishes the doctor. "Pitching fits!" he adds to the nurse. "I don't know how you put up with it."

"Oh, I don't," says the nurse. "I don't put up with it at ALL."

In a flash, I'm so boiling mad that it takes all my self-control not to scream. I didn't ask these two blobs to judge me. I didn't ask for anything! All I did was leave my hospital volunteer job, where I was actually *nice* to our patients, in order to attend a counseling session with the limp-mustached shrink three weeks ago.

Or has it been four weeks now?

The blobs continue bullying me until they run out of things to say. I sit stock-still, a blank expression smooth across my face, and stare at the pond water beyond them. What the *hell* has happened to my so-called life? This is starting to get surreal!

As soon as the blobs leave, I unhook my nose tube from the pump and go padding around the ER in my bare feet. The nose tube drips brown streaks down the front of my prison top, but I don't care what people think. They don't look like people to me anyway since I don't have my glasses on. I might as well be alone.

Eventually I find a tiny bathroom, complete with shiny handrails and an emergency pull cord that knocks me in the face as I bend over the toilet. I shove it aside and vomit every one of their hateful, bullying, mud-brown calories right out of my stomach. The nose tube comes flying out, too. I rinse my mouth and peer at the yellow tube in the bathroom mirror. It threads into my nose and out the corner of my mouth. It looks disgusting.

You look like a mental patient, says the voice in my head. *You look like the kind of person they lock up.*

So I yank out the nose tube and throw it into the toilet. Let it stop the thing up.

Let the toilet vomit it out, too!

I'm shaky and weak now. I wander back through the pond water, clutching doorframes, until one of the dim rooms beyond feels familiar. I crawl back into bed. Eventually, the nurse blob comes to retrieve me and drives me through windy darkness back to Drew Center.

She says nothing about my missing nose tube or my chocolate-streaked shirt. Doesn't she even notice?

Or—have I dramatically defied her in a way she expects?

You broke down and acted like a mental patient, growls the voice in my head. *You look like a loser! You deserve to be locked up.*

It's the middle of the night. For my first day out of bed, it's been pretty stressful. The nurse blob walks me down a wide empty hall to a room with two twin beds. I squint. Another girl is already sleeping in one of them. She doesn't stir while I change into pajamas.

My glasses are on the bedside table. I fall asleep with them in my hand.

Next morning, the girl who tried to give me her Oreo cake isn't at the table for breakfast. I feel frail and sick. My forehead throbs where the knot is. As I stare at the plate of food facing me, I can hear someone down the hall screaming hysterically and very loudly. The staff are giving each other looks they seem to think I can't see or understand—but I can and do.

"Shit!" the tiny woman to my right says. "Why does someone always wig out every damn meal? Like I can eat to this background music." She's cutting a blueberry pancake into little pieces and grouping them according to blueberry percentage in each piece.

"Karen, you aren't allowed to do that." A nurse leans over her with a new pancake. "Eat it normally, okay?"

"Screw you!" Karen screams. "You messed me up! Screw you!"

The nurse sighs. "You have twenty minutes left to eat, so get started."

Karen begins to cry quietly, spearing her new pancake with her fork until it's imprinted with tiny holes. She sags against me, and I squeeze her hand in sympathy.

Instantly, the nurse is back. "Elena, honey, move over here."

Eyes smarting, I pick up my tray and move to the next table. Can't I do anything right?

"What the *hell*?" Karen says. "She wasn't doing anything!"

She flips over her tray and runs down the hall. Staff run after her. I keep my eyes on my plate and try to ignore the sounds of the scuffle that ensues.

Listlessly, I begin to chew dry pieces of pancake. No butter. No syrup. It isn't like eating pancakes at all. At first I glance at the other thin, unhappy eaters, but they avoid my eyes. So I give up and stare at my plate.

Not even one full day, and already I hate this place.

When my plate is empty, I can leave the table. But I can't go to the bathroom. We're not allowed into the bathroom for an hour. The toilets there flush with a key that we don't have, and a staff member inspects what's in them before they get flushed.

I can't bear to even think about that.

I wander out into the main hallway. Big locked New England doors range down one side of it. Big windows line the other. Next to the nurses' station sits Susannah in a yellow plastic chair. She's really scrawny, and with her big brown eyes and long hair scrunched up on top of her head in a ragged ponytail, she looks very much like a little girl who is lost and can't find her way.

That's the punishment chair. You're put there for doing things wrong.

Susannah was sitting in the yellow chair yesterday when I came in. That's how I know her name. I smiled at her as we walked by with my suitcases, but the nurse noticed.

"Baby," she said, "don't even try with that one. Susannah won't change, so don't even try."

That made me look back at her as we walked away. And Susannah leaned forward in the yellow chair, hair spilling over her thin little face, and she smiled back at me.

Now I slide into the seat next to hers, and together we watch a squirrel dance up the side of a tree trunk outside. I'm so tired. The sunlight is almost hypnotic. It dazzles me.

"You're very young," Susannah says. "When I first saw you, I thought you were old. But you're very young."

Her voice sounds disappointed, as if she needs something desperately, but I'm not it.

She doesn't see perfection, whispers the voice in my head. *What about your makeup? Have you checked your makeup?*

But I'm not allowed to have my makeup bag here.

My face burns. "Actually, I'm seventeen," I say.

Susannah smiles, opens her journal to a blank page, and begins to write. We sit in silence. Bathroom break is announced. I need to go. But I need people not to look in my toilet when I go, so I stay where I am.

Now it's time for art therapy group. Groups are mandatory, so I get up. Susannah doesn't. She reaches out to touch my arm.

She whispers, "I am going to be here forever."

In art therapy, we're doing something with construction paper. I'm too tired to grasp what it is. Then a staff member calls me out of the art room and walks me through a door she unlocks. She says the psychiatrist will be meeting with Mom and me.

It feels strange to walk into a normal-looking office and be able to sit down on a couch next to Mom. After what I've been going through, I expect her to be on the other side of a glass wall, talking to me through an orange phone.

Mom looks upset.

"They called me last night," she says, "but they wouldn't tell me where you were. Good Lord! What made that goose egg on your forehead?"

She doesn't look any happier when I tell her.

The psychiatrist comes in—another psychiatrist. He's short and neatly dressed, and he has the sloping shoulders and comfortable belly of a penguin.

Mom starts talking right away.

"All the literature I've been able to find," she says, "explains that pseudoseizure patients don't really go unconscious, and they take care not to hurt themselves. But what about that bruise? And I've seen my daughter stuck with a needle while she was unconscious, and she didn't react. What's causing these blackouts, and what exactly are they? Are they related to the thyroid problems the hospital found? Elena's never blacked out a single time before this summer."

That's not true. I think I did black out once before. But I'm not going to remember that.

"I couldn't say," the psychiatrist answers. "It's too early to tell."

"Too early?" asks Mom. "What do you mean? Why too early? She's been in hospitals now for almost a month. They ran so many tests on her that her chart's an inch thick. What data do you need?"

"Well, I haven't had time to look at her chart yet."

I watch Mom struggle to hold on to her good manners. It's nice to be on the sidelines and see someone else get angry for a change.

"Elena's been here for twenty-four hours," she points out. "You knew she was coming for a week. You could have asked for her chart at any time. When is someone going to look at her chart?"

The psychiatrist smiles disarmingly. "These things take time," he says.

"I can appreciate that you have your routine," Mom says. "But we've already spent the time. My daughter has been in the hospital for a month, and in spite of all the care they could give her, she's done nothing but lose more weight. Protocols, feeding pumps, the whole nine yards—she's still below the weight she was the day she went in."

Relief floods through me. After weeks of not knowing, I almost have my number again. I don't know what it is, but I know what it isn't: as much as it was the day this all started.

Take *that*, you damn psychiatrists!

"Yes, well. Their protocols weren't like ours," this psychiatrist says with a touch of pride.

That washes the happy feelings out of me again.

He's right, says the voice in my head. *He'll get you fattened up.*

Mom glances at my bruised forehead. "Yes, I can see that your protocol is different," she snaps. "With all due respect, I'm reluctant to let doctors continue to experiment on my daughter. I want quantifiable evidence that this is the right treatment and that it's working. Your facility didn't even want to take her at first. Her weight was too high, you said. And she's got these other health problems going on—heart problems, thyroid problems. At least tell me this: does she even have anorexia?"

"Well, we really can't be sure yet," the psychiatrist says.

They keep talking, but that's all I hear. Oh, my God! I knew it. I *knew* it!

It's true! shrieks the voice in my head. *It's true! You're a fat, flabby mess. You don't deserve to be here!*

The room whirls. My stomach upends, and I feel myself choke on acid. They didn't want to take me. My weight was too high. Whatever my number is, it's too high!

You're a failure! wails the voice in my head. *You can't even do self-destruction right! You think they care about getting you healthy? You're not even sick enough for them to care!*

The psychiatrist and Mom are standing up now. The meeting is over. But I can't go back out there. I can't face the real anorexics, the ones who know what I am.

They're rolling their eyes behind your back! They can't believe you're in here. The staff get together and whisper about you: "Did you hear about her weight? Can you believe it?!"

"I just don't know what to do," Mom says after the psychiatrist leaves. "I keep waiting for a doctor to sit down and talk to us like he's got a grasp on the facts. This is all so touchy-feely, this whole 'maybe, maybe not' stuff. I swear, it wasn't this bad when I had cancer!"

"Please get me out of here," I beg her, close to tears. "I don't belong here, I know I don't!"

"I tell you what," Mom says, "I'll go back to the hotel and call Dr. Harris—you remember, the psychiatrist who saw Valerie in Texas. He's the only psychiatrist who's ever given me a straight answer, and I know he specializes in eating disorders."

Mom leaves, and a tech takes me back to the main hallway where the nurses' station is. Patients are everywhere. I retreat into a corner, sit on the floor, and pull up my knees to make myself as small as possible.

Please don't look at me. Please stop looking at me!

Group sessions are over for the morning. There's nothing for the patients to do right now, and they don't have a lot of options for places to go, so they're drifting around the wide hallway like restless souls in hell. I study them out of the corner of my eye, the anorexics—what I thought I might be, but I'm not.

They look like children, no matter what their age. They look like refugees.

Several of the girls are standing in a clump right in the middle of the hall. They look attenuated, taller than they should be, with their coarse hair pulled back in clips and their faces gaunt and solemn. They turn their heads to and fro as they talk, like meerkats on a mound.

The only man is thin and lively. He looks like Pinocchio. He's laughing and gesturing with his stick-thin arms, entertaining several of the others. Any second, I expect to see him leap into the air and crow, "I'm a real boy!"

One woman catches my eye, but I look away quickly and rest my sore forehead on my knees. Mom needs to call to tell them I'm leaving. I need to get out of here!

The room is starting to go gray around the edges. I can feel my breath, cold, rushing in and out of my chest. My heart hurts—my damaged heart. My heart is thin, even if I'm not.

"Hey," says a low voice in my ear.

It's Karen, the woman who threw her pancake. She's crouching beside me in the corner. "You're having a bad time, aren't you?" she says. "Yeah, you are. You're having a bad time."

My face feels cold. I touch it and realize I've been crying. Karen sneaks a look at the nurses' station. "Come with me," she says.

She leads me into the rec room, keeping a cautious eye on two patients who are sitting on the couch and watching TV. She stops behind them, by the far wall. A big metal shelving unit there holds everything from books and games to yoga mats. With the tips of her fingers, Karen waves me closer.

"This is one of my best spots," she whispers. "Not the bottom shelf, because they look there, but the second shelf, behind the stack of yoga mats. You can crawl in there and pull the mats back in front of you. No one's ever found me there."

It doesn't look like there would be room for a person behind the mats, but Karen is like a toothpick. I'm not surprised no one has thought to hunt for her there.

She waves again, and I follow her down the hall. Two small palms and a luxurious fiddle-leaf fig share the corner by the window.

"I curl up behind the pots," she murmurs. "It's crazy that it works. You're not hidden that much. You'd think they'd spot you, but their eyes slide right past."

Next, she leads me through a door at the end of the hall. I didn't know this room was unlocked, but Karen tells me this is the cooldown room. Prepared for what's coming, I scan for hiding places, but I don't see any. It's sparsely furnished, and you can take in the whole room from the doorway.

"Back here," breathes Karen, with a quick look toward the door. "There, behind the couch cushion. It's a futon, see? All one piece. You just push it forward and slide in between it and the frame, and no one will ever, ever find you."

I stare at Karen in awe. This woman is a genius!

"Because sometimes, you have to be where they can't see you," Karen says. Her face is urgent, like she's telling me how to defuse a bomb. "Sometimes, you have to get away."

I nod. "You do. You absolutely do."

"You can use my places," Karen whispers, with another cautious look toward the door. "I know I can trust you. You won't tell."

"I won't. I absolutely won't."

And Karen slips away.

Right after supper, a nurse calls me to the phone. It's Mom, and I can tell from her hello that she's feeling a hundred percent better.

"You can start packing," she says. "I talked to Dr. Harris, and he's offered to see you in his office day after tomorrow. He says he'll have an EEG and an MRI done to make sure there's nothing medical causing the blackouts, and he'll do a full psychiatric evaluation to see if you have an eating disorder. It's going to take two days to get there. We'll rent a car and drive. I'm getting ready to call rental places right now, so I won't make it to visiting hour."

I don't tell her that the staff have already put me on the blacklist for visiting hour. It would just make her mad.

I hang up the phone. So I'll be leaving. That's good, right? No need to worry anymore about what the patients think of me. No need to wonder whether we're alike or different.

"I need my suitcase," I tell the nicest nurse. She turns and stares at me in surprise. "I'm leaving. My mom's going to pick me up after visiting hour."

"Has she cleared that with Dr. Moore?"

"I guess so."

"I'll check with him. In the meantime, you just have a seat and watch the world go by. Nothing's going to happen until Dr. Moore says it can, and it won't take you more than a couple of minutes to pack."

Visiting hour begins. A staff member unlocks the waiting room door, and parents and siblings file in and empty their pockets in front of the nurses' station. The visitors are all wearing identical resolutely cheerful expressions.

Behind the main part of the group is a young man with a baby. I love babies. Back home in Germany, I do as much babysitting as I can.

You'll never see Germany again.

The young man finishes his pocket-and-bag check and walks toward us with a dazed half smile on his face—an expression that wants to turn into a real smile if he can only see the right thing to make that happen. But after a few seconds, the smile falters, and I realize that the right thing isn't going to happen today.

He notices me watching him and comes over.

"I'm Karen's husband," he says. "Have you seen her?"

Uh-oh!

I turn and scan the room. No Karen anywhere. I remember the urgent look on her face: "Sometimes, you have to get away."

The young man gives a shuddering sigh. He looks bewildered but not surprised. He asks, "Do you have any idea where she might be *this* time?"

I do. But I made a promise, so I shake my head.

He turns to scan the crowd again, hopelessly this time, and shifts the baby in his arms. It opens its eyes and starts to fuss.

"I have to talk to the nurses," he says. "Where can she *go*?" he adds under his breath.

Probably behind the yoga mats. But I don't say that. Instead, I say, "Can I hold your baby?"

He surrenders the child gratefully and heads to the nurses' station, where a bustle of activity immediately ensues. But I ignore it. I ignore everything in the world except the wonderful little creature in my arms.

Holding Karen's baby: this is the best thing that has happened in weeks. The baby is soft and beautiful and smells so pure that it aches my chest to hold it. I don't even wonder if it is a boy or a girl. It doesn't matter. It is already perfect.

I sit down in the yellow chair by the nurses' station and balance the baby on my knees. I sing to it, and it waves its little starfish hands in the air and opens its round dark-blue eyes very wide.

I marvel at its fresh start in the world. It has no regrets, no memories, no fear of the future. It is new. New, new, new. Amazing.

Visiting hour ends, and the crowd ebbs away. Looking crushed and miserable, the man comes back to retrieve Karen's baby. I wander into the rec room and sit down on the couch to watch a soap opera somebody else has turned on.

A few minutes later, Karen sinks onto the couch next to me, her face set in a look of grim determination.

I don't have the heart to ask what she's determined to do.

"Elena," calls the nice nurse. She doesn't say anything else, but I can already see it in her face. She holds out the phone, and then Mom's telling me something in a voice that's just a shade less than a shriek.

I drop the phone and burst into tears.

Patients surround me. "What is it?" they ask. "What's wrong?"

"They won't let me leave," I sob. "They're forcing me to stay here!"

"Bastards!" That's Karen's voice.

"This place is a damn prison!" That's Susannah's.

Hands reach out to me, propel me to a chair, pat my shoulders, and give me tissues. Patients are bending over me or kneeling down next to me. Their eyes are alight with encouragement.

"Don't let them get to you," they tell me. "Stay strong! We can't let them win!"

We. It's the only word I hear. Over and over, I hear it: *we.*

This place is a prison. But maybe—just maybe—I belong.

6

I am sitting in group therapy. The pretty young woman leading the group today is wearing a light blue peasant blouse and has a string of chunky wooden beads around her neck. She is talking with great animation, and her short black hair flips in shiny layers as she turns from us to the dry-erase board and back. I take in her bright, serious expression and her dynamic gestures, but I'm not listening anymore. What she just said has shocked me to the bone.

"Remember," she told us, "it's up to you to do the work to recover from your eating disorder. You are all you have to rely on. You can't look to your family for help. Your parents are the ones who made you sick."

I stare at her ballet shoulders, her embroidered blouse, and her eloquent hands.

Is that true? Did my parents make me sick?

In my mind, I see a fried egg on a plate. Its edges are crunchy and brown, and its white is pockmarked with oil-filled dimples. The yolk has burst and leaked a puddle of golden goo that is in the process of crusting onto the plate. Dad is sitting across from me, jaw tight and eyes blazing. I am to sit there until I eat that egg.

Avoiding Dad's glare, slightly bored and very angry, the younger me pops her knuckles and works through her repertoire of table-time activities. She tap-dances against the chair legs, daydreams a story about a mouse that knows karate, and hums through snatches of songs. She makes her fork and butter knife fall in love with each other and plan to run away to Dallas. She fans her fingers and peers around the kitchen through them, pretending she's hiding in a jungle.

Eating the egg doesn't even occur to her.

The older me watching this childhood drama can tell that my father is beside himself. Dad intends personally to make sure I eat the egg, so he can't leave the table, either. His precious free time is draining away. Soon it will be bedtime, and then the grind of another workday. Also, his repertoire is more limited than mine: he doesn't know tap-dancing or understand the fun of soap operas with cutlery.

He drums his fingers against the table.

We are at a standoff.

Inevitably, Dad's patience cracks, and he opens negotiations. "Eat five more bites." Then, as the younger me's eyes light up: "*Big* bites."

"Not the runny stuff."

"Okay, you can skip the yolk. But eat all the white. That wasn't five bites! Eat one more."

The younger me risks a childish wail. "It's too much! The last one was *h-u-g-e*!"

"Oh, fine!" Dad snaps as his chair scrapes back. "Take your plate to the sink."

I remember exactly how the younger me feels when this happens: she has wrestled with the giant and won. He stalks off to his lair—the office. She runs off to her waiting dogs and her stuffed cloth cow and her older sister, who gives a very grown-up sigh.

"Why, Elena?" the sister asks with exaggerated patience. "Why does every minute with you have to mean drama?"

Well, look at you now, Valerie. Look at your cigarette burns and your fingerless gloves and your loser junkie friends.

Who's the drama whore now?

"Thank you, Steph," the pretty woman is saying, while a girl I don't know stares unhappily at her toes. "And now Karen has something she would like to share."

This brings me out of my reverie. She does?

"I do?" asks Karen with a frown.

"You remember," prompts the pretty woman. "What we talked about this morning."

The frown on Karen's face deepens.

"Okay. So my father, if you can call him that, wasn't around when I was a kid. More of a sperm donor, I guess. Anyway, my mother . . ."

She trails off into silence.

After a few seconds, the pretty woman coaxes, "You can do it. Go on. We're listening."

"I know I can do it!" Karen snaps.

There is another quiet pause.

"Anyway, not much to say about my mother," she goes on. "I don't remember much about her. I came home from school, and the front door was locked. Nobody was home. My mother was gone. Moved out. Moved while I was at school. That sounds like a joke, doesn't it?"

She looks around at us with a grim smile, but we aren't smiling. So she shrugs and continues, "The neighbors called the police, the police put me in foster care, and here I am."

The pretty woman waits for a minute, but Karen is done. So the woman turns to the rest of us.

"You see here how Karen's parents set up her disorder," she says. "But she's the one doing the work to make herself well. That's the challenge to each and every one of you. They made you sick, but you can make yourself well."

I look at Karen's gaunt face as she stares down at the ground. It's wearing the same look of determination I saw the night before. If parents make us sick and screwed-up parents make us more sick, then what does that mean for Karen's baby?

And in a flash, I have it all. I know why Karen has to get away. Fury bubbles up inside me. They made this woman afraid to hold her own child!

You see how they try to make you weak, says the voice in my head. *They make you stop believing in yourself.*

A staff member comes to fetch me for my first individual therapy session. I walk behind her, still boiling with rage.

They'll get inside your head, says the voice in my head. *They want to break you down.*

Once again, a young woman faces me across the small office. What is it with all these young women? Are they anorexia wannabes? This one is Indian or Middle Eastern, and her face wears an expression as determined as Karen's was, as if her life depends on how well we get on together.

Scorn adds itself to the fury I feel. This young woman hasn't done this very many times.

The woman wants to talk about my disorder. I don't think I have one, so at first I don't talk. But when she starts asking questions about my parents, I find that I have things to say.

"My parents didn't mess me up!"

"What makes you say that?" she asks.

"The session today. You people think our parents screwed us up. Well, mine didn't!"

"*Are* you screwed up?" she asks.

But I don't bite on that one.

"The problems you're having now," she rephrases. "What do *you* think brought them about?"

"My sister, Valerie. Two years ago, she was fine. Then she started spending all her time in her room and listening to this really hard-core music, 'I am my nightmare,' leather-and-chains kind of stuff. Pretty soon, she was cutting and burning herself all over, on her arms and legs and hands. She didn't care that people could see it."

I fall silent, thinking about the time Valerie came to my high school with four-letter words written all over her ripped clothes. I was humiliated! I couldn't bring myself to admit she was my sister.

The young woman is trying to control her face to keep it from reacting to what I say, but she isn't too good at it yet. This purely drives me crazy, the gamesmanship of the psychiatric people, who refuse to ask a normal question or have a normal reaction.

Maybe that's why I taunted the first psychiatrist until he blew up. I wanted to know if he was a real human being.

"Did your sister get help?" the woman asks.

"Eight weeks in a *Lifestyles of the Rich and Famous* clinic in England," I say. "It was a Gothic mansion from the 1800s. She had tea on the lawn every afternoon."

"That must have made you angry," suggests the therapist—which, of course, makes me angry at *her*.

"Hey, Val went to a lot of trouble," I say. "Might as well get something out of it."

"So you started restricting after your sister began to self-harm."

"No, I was doing that in boarding school."

"Boarding school?" she prompts.

"In Germany," I say. "We were a hundred and twenty girls from Germany and Switzerland and the Netherlands, too—even one girl from Australia. The headmistress was this big tall nun who wore the whole black habit. She had thick glasses and a deep voice that could make you jump out of your skin when she came up behind you and suddenly said your name."

"A foreign girls-only boarding school," the young woman says, and even though she's trying to stay expressionless, I can see that she's got her answer: the answer to What Went Wrong. "It must have been very hard for you," she adds, "to go to school so far from home."

"It wasn't that far," I say.

"A foreign country," she continues meaningfully.

"I live in Germany!" I say. "We moved there when I was eleven. America's the foreign country!"

But the young woman isn't about to give up. She's like a dog chewing a bone.

"To have to leave your parents," she murmurs. "To have to spend months away from home . . ."

"We went home every three weeks!"

But her conviction acts like battery acid. It corrodes my confidence. Away from home at twelve—that does seem pretty cruel.

A memory flashes into my brain of my own voice, crying: "Please don't make me go back!"

And then my mother's calm voice: "Elena, this is a great opportunity for you."

Now I'm holding my own face expressionless—or trying to.

"So you started restricting there," the therapist says. "Did you know any other anorexics?"

"There was Anna Anton. She was anorexic."

"And how did you know Anna Anton?"

"She sat next to me at meals."

The thought of *that* little irony almost makes me giggle.

When I first got to the boarding school, I was one of the younger girls in the middle-school grades. We didn't play with dolls anymore, but we collected stationery with cute cartoons on them, and we brought our games and stuffed animals from home. I brought my old cloth black-and-white cow, even though her black patches had faded to purple. She stayed on my bed, and my classmates called her the Milka cow.

The boarding school went up to class thirteen, one class higher than in America, and because of how the German school system works, it wasn't unusual for those seniors to be nineteen or twenty. It was the custom for each of the young girls like me to pick an upper-class girl to idolize. We wrote them little notes, and some of them treated us like pets. It was supposed to be good for us since we were so far from home, like having an older sister.

I picked Anna Anton, who was in charge of my table in the cafeteria. She was quiet, she liked to read, and she was nice to me. That was enough to make her my idol. I studied her like my very own manual for how to be a real almost-grown-up woman. And what did I learn from Anna Anton?

Anna Anton sat right next to me at the table. And Anna Anton didn't eat.

Most meals, all she did was drink hot tea. Maybe once a day, she would eat a slice of bread, and she could make that bread last through the whole meal. No one corrected her because she was the oldest person at the table. Anyway, I think I'm the only one who noticed. You're pretty selfish when you're sitting down to eat in a school cafeteria. All you care about is what's on your own plate.

When Anna Anton had her wisdom teeth taken out, they couldn't wake her up after the surgery. They tried to bring her back around, but her exhausted body slept right through it. She stayed unconscious the whole day.

I heard about that and thought, *Wow, that's so wonderful! I'd love to sleep for a whole day.*

Anna Anton fainted in church a lot. She'd black out right there in the pew. Then there would be a big commotion, with two older girls putting her arms around their necks and dragging her out to the fresh air.

I used to think, *Wow, that's so cool! I'd love to faint in church.*

So I worshipped Anna Anton, and I studied her day by day, trying to be just like her. And when I finally had her system down— the hot tea, the one piece of bread—she had the nerve to call up my parents.

"Your daughter is dying," she told them. "Your daughter won't eat!"

And I had to lie my way through a whole frantic parent-housemother meeting to convince them Anna Anton was wrong.

"Did you admire this person?" the therapist asks me now.

"No. Anna Anton was a lying, backstabbing bitch."

"I see. You knew an anorexic at boarding school, but you didn't like her."

"Not that one. But Anita was amazing."

The young woman's expressionless expression slips again. "You went to school with *another* anorexic?"

"It was a gymnasium," I explain. "The highest level of German high school. We were under a lot of stress."

"And was this girl Anita under stress?"

"Yes. Because she always got A-pluses. No matter what she did."

I realize as I say this that it won't make sense. The therapist would have to understand the whole system of favoritism that went on at my school. Anita made the best grades because Anita had always made the best grades. She was the school's favorite student. It was that simple.

There's no question that Anita deserved those A-pluses most of the time. She had an amazing mind. Once, she decided to learn the entire Latin textbook in two weeks, so she did. I could turn to any page and ask her the questions, and she would write down the correct answers.

Anita didn't like the idea that she might be earning high grades just because she was a favorite. She wanted to believe that her hard work and brilliant mind were earning those A-pluses. So, the year before I got to the school, as an experiment, Anita decided to do nothing for a class. She ignored the homework, talked back to the teacher, and deliberately mangled her exams.

But there it was on her report card: an A-plus. And Anita knew she didn't deserve it. That meant there was no way for Anita to measure herself against the work—no way to find out who and what she really was.

So Anita shut down. In the middle of the busy boarding school, she stopped speaking—to everybody. She stopped eating, too, and just about melted away. By the time I got to know her, a psychiatrist was coming to the school once a week to meet with her, but she still did exactly what she wanted.

I try to explain to the therapist how much willpower this took. Not to speak in a busy, chattery boarding school—it's like keeping your mouth shut in the middle of a sleepover.

Anita was absolutely extraordinary. I adored her.

"When she came to tell you she was going to an eating disorder treatment center," says the therapist, "what was your reaction?"

"*Wow! She's talking to me!* It was that unusual for her to speak. And we promised to write, but I couldn't. They wouldn't give me her address. It upset me so much! I knew she was waiting for my letters."

"Your parents kept you from writing?"

"The housemothers. Leave my parents out of this!"

The therapist gives me her best bland smile, but her face isn't quite as expressionless as she wants it to be. The expression and the lack of expression—both of them make me mad.

"You know what?" I say. "I've had it. I'm done explaining myself. There's nobody to blame for What Went Wrong because there's nothing wrong with me. And that goes for Anita, too. This is who we are. This is what we choose! You just hate it that we have the strength of will to achieve it."

The therapist's face sharpens a little. "To starve yourself?" she says.

"To—no, not to starve ourselves! To not be fat slobs! You go down to the high school, and you go counsel all those porkers who are already hanging over the tops of their jeans. They're the ones who'll die early, not me!"

She regards me with a superior, sphinxlike stare.

"Anorexia nervosa shortens the lives of twenty percent of its victims," she says. "It kills young women at twelve times the rate of all the other causes of death combined."

"Well, that's not what I've got, then. Okay? That's not what I've got! Because I'm not a victim—of *anything!*"

I come out of the office still seething and refuse to eat my supper. The nurses lose their tempers and threaten me.

So what? What are they going to do? Lock me up? Oh, wait—they already did that!

The nurse in charge scolds me, but this time, I don't even blink.

She hates you because she's fat, says the voice in my head. *She hates you because you're in control. She'd break down that control if she could.*

So the nurse calls up the psychologist on call. That's the pretty woman from group therapy this morning, with the flippy black hair and dancer's hands. Her peasant blouse is now a sweatshirt, and her chunky necklace is gone. She must have been called in from home.

The pretty woman talks to me in the cooldown room. I can't help but wonder if Karen is behind the futon cushion.

"I know this is hard," the woman says. "But you need to trust us. We know how to help you get better."

Don't listen! says the voice in my head while she cajoles and appeals. *She wants to make you weak like she is.*

But I'm not so sure the pretty psychologist is weak. She looks like she works out.

We come out of the cooldown room to find the other patients clustered around a patient named Melinda. Melinda's in tears. She's decided to leave Drew Center, and she's over eighteen, so she can do this. She's waited out the maximum amount of time she can be held by law against her will: seventy-two hours. But her parents are supporting the doctors and therapists who say she should stay at Drew Center—which is pretty funny, considering that those doctors and therapists are blaming all her problems on them.

"Mom won't let me come home," she sobs. "Mom and Dad say that if I leave the center, that's it. They're done with me. I thought they loved me!"

"They've been brainwashed!" one of the girls says fiercely, and the rest of us murmur in agreement.

"Is there anywhere else you can go?" Susannah asks.

"There's this guy I know," Melinda says. "We've been texting. I think we have a future, but my parents don't like him."

"Your parents aren't going to make you well," Steph reminds her. "They made you sick. You have to do this on your own."

"I would," Melinda says. "I know where he lives, but it's too far away. I'd need a bus ticket, and I don't have any money."

"I have some money," I say.

And so do several of the others.

We scatter to go get it. When we return and pile all of our collected change and bills together, we have almost fifty dollars. Melinda can buy her bus ticket. She has a place to go.

Melinda is radiant. She packs her bag, and we take turns hugging her. One of us is escaping!

We all win when that happens. We all celebrate her victory.

Melinda waves from the door of the waiting room, and we all cry happily and wave back. This is who we are! They want to break us, but we choose the life we want. This is who we are!

The pretty psychologist walks out with Melinda. When she comes back, she looks distraught. She stops at the nurses' station, and I hear the staff talk to her in low voices.

"Is she going somewhere safe at least?" asks the fat one.

The psychologist shakes her head.

"Some man she met on the Internet. I couldn't get a straight answer. I'm not even sure she knows where he lives."

The pretty psychologist rubs her forehead as if she has a headache, and her frown intensifies. Then she rests her elbow on the counter and shades her eyes with her hand.

The fat nurse pats her on the shoulder.

"I know," she says. "I know. But you can't save them all. You know that. You can only save the ones who want to be saved."

7

I am in another hospital gown—a beige gown with gray diamonds. I am in another hospital bed—a bed with a powder-blue blanket.

A bristling cap of probes has been glued all over my scalp. They itch, but I'm not allowed to scratch them. Many gray wires wind down from the probes to a machine beside the bed. I'm Medusa again, with a scalpful of snakes.

But I don't mind. Medusa was so strong, she didn't need anybody. She could kill a man with just one look.

The eating disorder center kept me for seventy-two hours, and then they had to give me up to my parents. But my parents aren't finished with hospitals yet. Dad has left his stressful office and flown over to America to take on the equally stressful job of driving Mom and me across the country to see the Texan psychiatrist Mom trusts. That psychiatrist has put them in touch with a neurologist, so right now I'm undergoing a forty-eight-hour EEG.

The cold, round eye of a camera lens at the foot of my hospital bed watches my every move. Mostly, it watches me watch television. There's a certain static circularity about all this.

I've been listening to Mom describe my fainting fits for weeks now. She's been wild with worry. But me? They mean nothing to me. They've been a nice break from the nastiness of this last month.

The neurologist is a shrewd-looking, slightly grumpy man with grizzled hair and absolutely no bedside manner. I immediately like him for this.

"Do you think you can have one of your seizures now that you're back in a hospital?" he asks.

I had a number of blackouts at Drew Center, but I haven't had any while Mom and Dad and I have been traveling across the country.

"I guess so," I say.

"What brings them on?" he asks, turning to Mom and Dad.

"She doesn't have them when we're with her," Dad says. "I think she'd have one if she was alone."

"Then we'll have your parents leave," the neurologist tells me. "We'll see if the unfamiliar surroundings can produce one."

So I sit in the hospital bed by myself and flip channels. Television in the hospital always seems especially boring, as if it has its own programs just to keep patients from getting too excited. And the picture on this TV is horrible: grainy and full of white flecks. Would it kill hospital administrators to buy better TVs?

The nurse brings in supper and checks on the camera. Then he takes my vitals and leaves me with the supper tray.

You're not going to eat that, right? prods the voice in my head. *You'd be eating on camera. That's even worse than eating when someone's watching you.*

I debate this for only the briefest flicker of time, more for the pleasure of having a choice than from a need to make up my mind. It's been so nice to be out of the eating disorder treatment center. Every bite of food that I choose not to eat feels like its own personal victory. And it's true that I hate to eat in public. That was one of the worst things about Drew Center.

I glance at the camera. It stares back like an alien spy. So I push away the tray with a feeling of relief.

My head aches. These probes have given me a headache. I flip through the channels, but nothing good is on.

I wonder what the Drew Center patients are doing right now. Do they miss me? Did they like me? What did they think of me?

They were just being polite, says the voice in my head. *They didn't really like you. Remember how Susannah looked at you when you said good-bye?*

I try to distract myself by changing the channel again, but it's all mindless noise. My head is killing me. The round, empty camera eye goggles at me over the end of the bed. I wish it would blink. It's making my eyes water.

Another hospital, says the voice in my head. *Your parents have wasted thousands of dollars on you. Your friends back home know you're a mental patient now. You'll walk into school, and they'll laugh behind your back.*

The television speaker in my remote is getting louder and louder. My temples are throbbing. I try to turn down the volume, but it doesn't seem to be working. The blanket, I think. I'll wrap it with the blanket.

People will whisper about you in the cafeteria, says the voice in my head. *They'll whisper about you in the faculty lounge.*

My head hurts so much that tears form in my eyes as I swaddle the loud remote.

They'll say, "Did you hear what happened to Elena? Did you hear what happened? Did you hear?"

The remote slips from my fingers.

The next thing I know, the nurse is shaking me. He's bending over me from a long way away.

"Sweetie," he says, "what on earth are you doing down there?"

I look around. I'm not in my bed anymore. All I can see are shadowy gurney wheels and the dark undersides of equipment.

"I got burned," I say.

It's true. I've been scalded. The stretch of skin across my collarbones feels like it's on fire.

The nurse lifts me into bed and pulls back my gown. My upper chest directly below my collarbones is one giant, oozing scab. The skin is gone from it in a patch several inches wide.

"What happened?" the nurse asks in amazement. He steps back and examines the floor where I fell. "I don't see what could have scratched up your chest and face like that."

My face? Oh, no! My face! What do I look like?

I feel my cheeks. They sting, and my fingers follow the puffy lines of scratches. Where's my makeup? I need my makeup bag. I must look like a mess!

You look like the kind of person they lock up, says the voice in my head. *With a tube up your nose to feed you.*

My head is pounding like it's going to split open. My chest is one solid blaze of pain, and my face prickles and tingles from the scratches. The nurse sprays the chest wound and bandages it, but nothing can make it stop hurting.

The next morning, the neurologist plays the video for my parents and me. I don't want to risk looking at the mirror girl at first, but the image is so small on the monitor that I realize I can't make out its features anyway. It's just a boring movie about an anonymous girl in a hospital gown who's imprisoned on a little flat screen. For hours, she barely moves. Even fast-forward doesn't make her do much.

Then, with great deliberation, she wraps the remote up in her blanket. A few seconds later, her head falls back on the pillow.

The girl's hands and feet twitch. They start twisting in lazy circles. A minute or two later, her head begins to swing from side to side. And, under the girl's half-closed lids, her eyes are rolling, white, in their sockets.

I feel bored. That girl isn't me. This is a movie I'm watching about someone I don't know. It's not even an interesting movie.

As the minutes pass, the girl's circles become more and more pronounced. Each time her hands pivot on their wrists, her fingernails scratch across her chest. Thin lines of blood start to appear where her fingernails have passed.

Little by little, the girl's movements become more violent. The feet kick, and the arms begin to bend from the elbows. The body thrashes from side to side.

Now the body is folding at the waist like an automaton, like a possessed puppet tossing back and forth. Then it flips over the bars of the hospital bed. The screen shows nothing but a rumpled sheet.

"Forty minutes," the neurologist announces, reviewing the footage. "That's how long you were on the floor."

Mom looks grave. Dad looks shocked. But I don't feel a thing.

"It isn't epilepsy," the neurologist continues. "I think it's psychological in origin."

"That's good news," Mom says. "Isn't it?"

The neurologist shrugs.

A nurse comes to disconnect the snakes from my head and pry the probes loose from my scalp. I go back to our motel to wash the glue from my hair, and we drive over to talk to my new psychiatrist.

Dr. Harris looks like a long, tall Texan. He has gray hair, a gray mustache, and twinkling gray eyes. He would make a fantastic grandfather—he'd be the one who would give you the whole train set, plus he'd get down on the floor to help you set it up.

This is the psychiatrist who saw Valerie right before she flaked out and ran away from us to live with a bunch of strangers. That was after England. She was supposed to be turning things around, and Mom and Dad paid their good money to let her go to college in the States. But she dropped out and took off halfway through the semester.

Mom is starting to exchange emails with my sister again. I've forbidden her to tell Valerie anything about me.

Mom and Dad leave Dr. Harris and me alone, and he begins to talk about Valerie. He's slightly apologetic, and I realize that in a way, Valerie betrayed us both. She abandoned me, but she abandoned him, too. I can tell he feels bad about it.

"I'm not like her," I tell him. "Not a thing like her."

Dr. Harris actually looks like he's listening to me. He isn't trying to control his expression so I can't guess what he's thinking. He's interested to hear what I have to say. So we talk about Valerie. Maybe it helps that he already knows so much about what we went through with her.

"She told me that your father can have a pretty explosive temper," Dr. Harris says. I eye him suspiciously, but he doesn't seem to be holding onto a poker face or giving hints about What Went Wrong. He looks like he's just wondering what I think.

"Dad can get mad, sure," I say. "He's half Italian. But he doesn't stay mad. It's over in an hour or two. When we were little, Dad was a lot more . . ." I pause to find the right word. "Dad was a lot more volatile. He got over it, though. He isn't like that anymore."

"So you don't think it was that big a factor?" he asks. "In Valerie's depression?"

I flash to a memory of a much younger, taller, scarier Dad erupting in our midst. He is shouting at Valerie and me in a kind of frenzy. Valerie is so scared that she pees her pants, and me, I'm afraid of everything.

But that was a long time ago, and Dad got a lot better. He wouldn't do that now. Can't people leave the past alone? Can't they give a person credit for improving?

I think about how tired Dad is now in the evenings. It's nothing for him to put in twelve-hour days. He's a hard worker, just like I am. I got that from my dad.

I say, "I think Valerie just used it as an excuse."

Then Dr. Harris starts asking me lists of questions, but this time they don't seem too intrusive because he has such a mild, thoughtful voice. It isn't like he's trying to get at What Went Wrong. More like he's just getting to know me.

Dr. Harris asks about rituals, and I tell him about even numbers. I tell him that in the German boarding school, I once fell downstairs because I was so busy counting my steps that I didn't notice where I was going.

"In the German boarding school," he echoes. Inwardly, I bristle: here is where he gloms on to What Went Wrong. Instead, he gets a wistful smile on his face. "It sounds like a movie," he says.

"It was so much fun," I tell him. "With that many kids, you never knew what crazy thing would happen next. Like the time Maria Engel dropped a whole stack of plates. Or the time Anna Cecile was carrying a sheet of clear glass, and it was so clear, she didn't even notice she'd dropped it."

"Did you count your steps in German or English?"

"In German. That's because Ramona and I counted our steps together a lot of the time."

"Ramona?"

"My best friend. We were in the same class, and we roomed together for a year and a half. We got in trouble a lot, too. We were like the black sheep of the school. Some of the stuff we did really would make a great movie."

Dr. Harris consults his notes.

"Not the anorexic," he says. "Different name."

"No, Ramona wasn't anorexic. She was a binger."

"Bulimic."

"That's right. Ramona would hoard food. Then, when everyone was asleep, she would binge."

"So she made a ritual out of it," he says. "Like the counting."

"That's right," I say. And then I think about that. It's interesting.

"You could never make Ramona cry," I tell him. "Never, no matter what. We'd get in trouble, and I'd cry—mainly because I was mad—but all that would happen with Ramona was that she'd get these red lines across her cheeks. To her, that was crying. But she didn't ever shed a tear."

I tell Dr. Harris that Mona's parents hated each other—*really* hated each other. They used their children as weapons. Like toddlers, her mother and father snatched at the children: "Mine, mine! This one is my favorite! That one can be yours."

At the school, we joked that Mona got the sweetest deal of any kid because her parents tried to buy her love with gifts and crazy permissions. Her mother even took us out to bars.

No matter what hateful, horrible thing her parents did to each other or to her, Mona never cried. But in the middle of the night, she wouldn't be able to sleep, and then she'd wake me up. And we would go up to the attic together and eat.

Binging after lights-out in a boarding school is as risky as it sounds. The nuns did bed checks. Also, the kitchen was at the far end of the big, rambling building. Mona and I would have to sneak on tiptoe through the cold and the dark and then snatch our food out of icy metal cabinets.

But Mona needed me. She needed her ally. So I always went along.

One night, Mona took more food than I had imagined anyone could carry. Pickles, bread, meat, cheese, chocolate, carrots, even more. We slipped up to the attic and huddled on the stacks of old mattresses there, and underneath a moonlit window, Mona laid out all the things she had stolen.

My stomach churned, but she pleaded with me. "You have to help me eat it!"

We didn't talk. We didn't joke. We just got down to the serious business of eating.

Then, when every last scrap of food was somehow crammed inside us, Mona tiptoed downstairs to the bathroom and threw up in the sink.

Without saying a word, she wiped her mouth and left.

I knew I couldn't leave that mess in the sink. There would be a fuss about it in the morning. And when up to five girls sleep in each room, you never know who has seen what. So I grabbed a handful of paper towels and scooped it into the toilet.

My aching stomach lurched. The smell was unbearable. Tears stinging my eyes, I bent over the toilet and retched.

The nicest of the housemothers heard me and came to check on me. She guided me to her room, made a hot water bottle for my poor sick stomach, and made me a cup of hot tea. Then she tucked me back into bed.

"Sorry," Mona whispered after the housemother left. "Are you okay?"

I didn't answer. I could hear her rubbing her hand against the side of my bed.

"Leni, could you maybe scoot over and let me listen to you breathe?"

I scooted over, and she curled up next to me with her head tucked under my chin. Soon her breathing was slow and even. But I stayed awake, knowing I was disturbed by something, unable to place what it was.

Then it came to me.

When I had thrown up, a housemother had come running. When other girls threw up, the noise of the retching came right through the thin walls. But when Mona had thrown up, she hadn't made a sound.

"So she was practiced at it," Dr. Harris comments. "She must have made a habit of purging. And you purged that time, too, or at least you vomited."

I nod.

"Did you make a habit of purging, too?"

I look into Dr. Harris's gentle eyes. He looks like the White Knight from Alice's looking-glass world. He looks like he could never be mean on purpose. I think about the limp little mustache back in Germany, the doctor who yelled at me right in front of my parents, and I wish Dr. Harris had been my first psychiatrist instead of him.

"What?" I ask.

"I was wondering, did you purge, too?" Dr. Harris says. "When you and Ramona binged?"

"Oh. No, you can tell I don't purge. Just look at my teeth."

I show my teeth in a big flashy grin. Dad used to criticize me because my teeth looked yellow, so I worked hard to make them nice and white. I'm very proud of my teeth now.

Dr. Harris looks, nods, and makes a note in his chart.

I wish he'd been my first psychiatrist. But it's too late. I don't trust any psychiatrist now.

That afternoon, Dr. Harris meets with Mom and Dad and me. He tells them he isn't sure I have anorexia, but I do have an eating disorder. This doesn't sound like much of a problem to me. *Disorder*—it's one of those terms that downplays what it is, like *irregularity* or *discomfort*.

I have an eating disorder. My eating isn't in perfect order. Does that sound so bad?

"The Germans have done excellent work in the area of eating disorders," he tells us. "I would advise you to start work with a local psychologist when you get back to Germany. The brain MRI is normal, and the report from the neurologist is good. My guess is that the blackouts will disappear when Elena's back in her own home again. It was the stress of the forced hospitalization that brought them on."

Dr. Harris adds that I should follow up with an endocrinologist and a cardiologist to make sure my heart is continuing to improve. "I'll be happy to put together a report or to consult with anyone you work with," he adds. "Just let me know what you need."

That's it. After four hospitals and more than a month of my life stolen from me, that's it. We get back into our rental car and drive back across the country to catch our flights home.

We could take an extra day or two in Texas to see old friends, but we don't. We creep out of the state like burglars. We pass within twenty minutes of my uncle's house. We could go see him and the family. But we don't. We don't even call him up.

Your parents are ashamed of you, says the voice in my head. *They don't want their friends and relatives to talk.*

I try to distract myself from thinking about this. A plan. I need a plan. Plans always make me feel better. I pull out my journal to write out a to-do list. My senior year starts a week from now. That's not much time.

And now you're fat, says the voice in my head.

It's true. Thanks to Dr. Harris's office staff, I know my number again, and it's not good. If I don't lose weight before school starts, the other students will think I'm losing my edge.

At the thought of facing all those pairs of eyes, the black hole inside me spins a little faster. Do they know about the hospitals? What do they know? What are they saying about me? Will the scratches on my face heal up before the first day of school?

We're in Tennessee. Signs for the Ripley's Believe It or Not museum flash by, mile after mile. All three of us love museums. Valerie's the only one who doesn't care much for them, and Valerie isn't here.

When Valerie moved away to college, she started working with Dr. Harris. He called up my parents to say that she needed to go back into the hospital. Mom and Dad started looking for places to send her and arranging for a loan, but Valerie ran away. Now I think: *what was it like for Valerie in the hospital? Did she tell me it was fun because she was too proud to tell the truth?*

I would run away, too, before I'd go back into the hospital. How different are Valerie and I, really?

You're both losers, says the voice in my head. *You both disappointed your parents. They thought they could count on you to be the perfect daughter, but you've let them down, too.*

That's not right, though. Valerie was a complete screw-up. She made the whole world see how sick she was. I'm not sick. I didn't start any of this. I'm going to go right back to school and go right on being perfect.

"What do you say?" Dad asks. "You want to stop at Gatlinburg? It's the closest thing to a vacation we'll get this summer."

"I vote yes!" I tell him and put my journal away.

I've been in the Louvre in Paris, the British Museum in London, the Rijksmuseum in Amsterdam, the Picasso Museum in Barcelona, the Uffizi museum in Florence, and the Vatican Museum in Rome.

Now I'm standing in the foyer of the Ripley's Believe It or Not museum in Gatlinburg, Tennessee. They have wild exhibits, including a fake mermaid skeleton. "World's largest tire," muses Mom, reading a sign. Dad's snapping photos. After weeks of boring hospitals, it feels good to be in a museum again.

Afterward, we stop at a pancake house. I order French toast because I used to like their French toast when I was little. But it isn't very good.

People are watching you, says the voice in my head. *Eating French toast is worse than eating a lump of sugar. And there's margarine on it, pure fat, the highest-calorie food you can eat. People are actually watching you get fatter.*

Anxiety pricks me, and I remember the students who'll be watching me in a week. There's no room for fear in a high school, and no room for pity, either. I put down my fork and push the plate away.

"Aren't you going to finish that?" Mom wants to know. I can't stand the way she keeps track of everything I eat now. It's not her business, and it's stressing me out. She should leave me alone.

"I'm fine," I say. "We had that huge breakfast. It's still filling me up."

"I'll take your sausages," offers Dad.

Dad hardly ever argues these days. He's flown over here to spend hour after hour driving me across the country, and he only has two days left before he gets back to twelve-hour workdays again. He hasn't had a real vacation in months.

I think about how Valerie and the Drew Center staff wanted me to blame all my problems on him, and that makes my stomach hurt even more.

"Maybe we could get a box for the toast," Mom says. "You could eat it later in the car."

"Stop it!" I say. "Just chill out!"

But all afternoon, Mom keeps bringing up things I don't want to talk about: food diaries, menus, mealtimes, and appointments we need to set up.

"This is my problem," I tell her. "I'll handle it my way."

Dad says nothing. He's focusing on his driving. We're in Virginia now: hill after hill covered with scrubby pine trees.

The sun is going down, but we can't stop yet. I'm beginning to hate being in a rental car with Mom. We've been crammed into the same room now for weeks. There's nowhere to go to get away from her.

Your parents made you sick, says the voice in my head, and I flash to the memory of me crying and begging not to go back to school. *You think she loves you? What loving mother ships her youngest child off to boarding school?*

I push away the thought and flip open my journal again. It's traveled the whole way with me, but I've hardly written a thing. Just one line about Drew Center:

The whole ward here has more locks than a federal prison.

What else is there to say?

I want to write something cheerful and touristy about the Ripley's Believe It or Not museum. When I get home, I'll paste my ticket to the page, and maybe a photograph or two. Mom and me posing in front of the world's largest tire. Dad sitting in the big chair.

But right now, I find myself reading a page from last November. A page I wrote about Ramona, my roommate in boarding school.

Girl, if you were standing in front of me and were hearing this, I would say: You were always the one to do the crazy stuff first. Let's do this, let's do that.

Come on, Lani, don't be so boring. And now, looking at everything, see how we both turned out?

You, overeating—me, not eating.

You, too quick to love—me, too scared to love.

You, blaming others too much—me, blaming myself too much.

You, not caring about school—me, overcaring about it.

You, moving on.

Me, staying behind.

And I'm sorry, I'm sorry, I'm sorry, I'm sorry.

Got to go exercise away this God-awful me.

Maybe I'll forget the God-awful you.

Miss you, Mona.

I'll love you forever.

The tears on my cheeks surprise me. I close the journal and think about Ramona. What's she doing now? Has her life turned out any better than mine?

Mom starts up again. She just won't let it go. "Every meal, you struggle," she says. "You can't finish anything."

"We're eating fast food," I say. "It's awful."

Saturated fat, says the voice in my head. *Food additives. Dyes. Flavor enhancers. You ate chicken nuggets this morning, forty-eight calories per nugget. That's not going to get you ready for school.*

"We eat anywhere you want to eat," Mom says. "We eat anything you say you'll eat."

Chicken nuggets, continues the voice in my head. *Three grams of fat apiece! You can see the fat ooze out of them. It's disgusting!*

"I don't think you can deal with this problem by yourself," Mom says. "I think they're right. You do need help."

She thinks you're a failure, says the voice in my head. *Your own mother looks at you and sees a failure. This summer has made you lose your edge. You don't look like a girl with a great future anymore.*

"I can't believe you think I'm a failure!" I say. "I make top grades, but you think I'm losing my edge. You criticize me all the time!"

"I don't mean you're a failure," Mom says. "You do a great job in school. But you pick at your food. This is too hard for you to handle."

She shipped you off and made you sick, says the voice in my head. *She kicked you out of the house. You do everything right and one little thing wrong, and the one thing wrong is all she sees.*

"Dad! Mom thinks I can't do anything right. She thinks I'm screwing everything up. You believe in me, don't you, Dad?"

"Of course I believe in you, honey."

"That's NOT what I'm saying!" shouts Mom. Which means, of course, that she's lost the argument.

But the fight gets worse from there. Pretty soon all three of us are shouting. Finally, Dad zooms down an exit lane, turns into an empty parking lot, stops the car, and bursts into tears.

Mom and I are stunned into silence.

We decide to find a hotel and stop for the night. But it isn't five minutes before Mom's talking about dinner. It's like she's doing this on purpose!

Still, I act like I don't mind—for Dad's sake, not hers.

We go to Subway, and I order first. I load my sandwich up with pickles, sit down, and tuck right in. Before long, the whole sandwich is gone. Then I start in on the chips—crispy, salty, and delicious.

I eat the entire bag.

Out of the corner of my eye, I see Dad exchanging meaningful glances with Mom. He thinks I'm doing great.

Mom relaxes, too. Pretty soon she and Dad are joking and having fun.

"I'll be right back," I promise, and I head for the bathroom.

Someone is in the next stall. No problem. It could be Mom, and it wouldn't matter. I guarantee that she wouldn't hear a thing.

I bend over and close my eyes, and it all flows smoothly out— soft bread, edges of chips, and hard knots of pickles. Then I wipe my mouth with toilet paper and flush.

I feel like Wonder Woman. I feel fantastic. Nothing brings on a quicker high than purging. I'm not losing my touch. No fear and no pity. This is going to be a great senior year.

Afterward, I stand in front of the mirror, pop two Tums, and chew them cautiously while I fill my mouth with water. Calcium carbonate to neutralize the stomach acid. Baking soda works, too.

Then I pop an Altoid, reapply lip gloss, and grin to check my teeth.

Smooth. White. Perfect.

You can tell I don't purge.

8

Eight months have gone by since the drive across the States to meet with Dr. Harris. Senior year is almost over. Even though that psychiatrist tried to take it away from me, I'm having my senior year in Germany with all my friends. I'm finishing up advanced-placement classes at the high school on base, and every other day, a school bus takes me to the military hospital, where I volunteer in the emergency room for high school credit.

Right now, it's ten o'clock in the morning, and I am where I love to be: in nursing scrubs in the middle of a busy hospital, with patients and staff all around me.

Every room in the ER is full, and the waiting room is packed. Even the hallway is packed, but not with patients. We've just gotten in a new set of Army trainees, and they're clustered by the big dry-erase board—nervous, miserable, hoping not to be asked to do anything too complicated. By the end of the month, each one of them needs to know how to perform basic medical procedures in the field. Then they'll disappear, and a new batch will show up and cluster by the dry-erase board.

I listen to Sergeant Blake lecture the group on how to start an IV. Then he spots me.

"Ah, Elena!" he says. "Accompany . . . ," he scans the group,

". . . Private Henning into Room Six and monitor as he starts an IV on the patient there. The rest of you, come with me."

Inside Room Six is a middle-aged woman with little baggy eyes and a pinched mouth. She's cradling her abdomen like she's carrying a baby, but if she were pregnant, she'd be upstairs in Labor and Delivery. Appendicitis? Constipation? Since starting here, I've been surprised at the number of patients who need emergency enemas. There's even a special "enema" hand signal in the ER: the first finger curled into the thumb to form a butthole.

I wash up and coach Private Henning on how to wash up as we put on sterile gloves. Private Henning is a gangly African American with the words "Only God Can Judge Me" inked in blue letters into his neck. He can't hide his worry as I tear open the IV kit and lay its components out on a sterile tray.

"Couldn't you just do it for me?" he begs in a low voice.

The middle-aged woman with the constipated appendix has picked up on his nerves, and she too looks toward me in mute appeal. I could, and it would go well—undoubtedly better than it's about to go. I've started IVs on several of the techs for practice. "Hey, Elena, find my vein" is a pretty weird pickup line, but hospital techs have to be creative.

I'm not allowed to start IVs on patients, though. No IVs and no medications. I wonder how this pair would feel if they knew I'm only a high school student, bussed to the hospital on alternate school days to work here for class credit. There are four of us students at the hospital this semester: two in Labor and Delivery and two here in the ER.

No need to tell these fearful people that their "expert" is a schoolgirl, though. They're already having a rough day. So I give them both my most reassuring smile.

"You'll do fine," I tell Private Henning. "I'll talk you through it."

A couple of false starts, and Private Henning accomplishes his task. That actually went pretty well. The cluster of nervous newbies has re-formed by the dry-erase board. Private Henning goes to join them, but I notice that he's already walking a little taller.

A short, dark-haired man stomps to the door of Room Five. His scrubs are patched, and his lab coat is so wrinkled, it looks like he's been sleeping in it. He surveys the herd of newbies with a furious frown, but his face clears when he spots me.

"Elena! Good!" he barks. "Get over here right now! I need assistance!"

"Yes, Dr. T."

Dr. T. is from somewhere in the former Soviet Union. He's a fantastic doctor, but his bedside manner is nonexistent: he takes offense just as readily as he gives it. He's already had a run-in with a patient today, but he handled it surprisingly well. A beefy man with chest pains roared with anger and refused to be treated by him: "I didn't come here to see some damn Polack!"

To my amazement, Dr. T. went away like a lamb and transferred the patient to another doctor. It turned out that he and the beefy man were secretly in agreement. He told me, "I would not let a Polish doctor treat me, either."

Now I join Dr. T. in Room Five, where a big young Marine is sitting on the examining table. He's stripped to the waist, and his pecs and biceps are a thing of much work and preoccupation if not beauty. He has pale blond fuzz on his head, and across the baby-pink skin of his shoulder is a skeleton riding a Harley. With him is another big young Marine—possibly his boss.

Dr. T. is an avid doodler. While he's talking with the Marines, he's scribbling away on his pad of paper.

"Draining an abscess is very painful," he says. "I can perform it here, but I would strongly recommend that you get a surgical consult."

I take a few steps farther into the room and scan the patient. On his back is what appears to be a giant red pimple. We see two or three of these a day. They go deep into the tissue and can even cause gangrene. The skin inflammation is only the tip of the iceberg.

But the Marine looks at his Marine friend, and they both burst out laughing.

"Dude, I've been in the *desert*!" he scoffs. "I think I can handle a little *zit*!"

"Very well," says Dr. T. He's doodling daggers and harpoons on his sketchpad.

I wash again, don new gloves, and lay out the sterile kit. Five minutes later, I'm up to my knuckles in the Marine's back, wiping away blood so Dr. T. can see what he's doing.

"*SHIT!*" roars the Marine, gripping his friend's hand so hard that it's white.

"*SHIT!*" roars the other Marine in agreement, and probably in almost as much pain. Only once did I make the mistake of offering my hand for a patient to hold through a procedure. The poor guy almost broke it.

Behind Dr. T.'s safety glasses, a smile lights up his dark eyes. He begins humming softly as he works.

After the procedure, I stand in the hallway to wait for my fellow student to finish up. The newbies are gone, packed off to the chow hall, and it's almost time for us students to catch the bus back to school. Sergeant Blake is here, chatting with a couple of the techs. Things are slowing down in the ER. Several rooms are vacant.

Behind us in Room Two, I hear Dr. Lawrence. He's a fairly new doctor with kind blue eyes and a propensity for ordering mushroom-and-pepperoni pizzas whenever he's having a bad day. I hear him say, "Can you tell me your name?"

A small voice answers him: "Please help me. . . ."

I turn around. A handsome Army soldier is standing in Room Two. His eyes look lost and frightened.

"I'm an American," he tells Dr. Lawrence in a low voice. "They took my money and locked me up here. Please help me escape. I want to see my family again."

Beside me in the hallway, Sergeant Blake shakes his head.

"Remember the guy they pulled out of the cave-in?" he asks a nurse who walks up. "Remember how much trouble he had with doorways?"

She nods. "It took twenty minutes to coax him through the door."

The conversation covers other interesting cases of combat-induced PTSD, but I continue to watch Dr. Lawrence. He's the least frightening medical person I know, and he's using his gentlest voice, but all this is wasted on the soldier, who is still trapped in his memories of trauma.

"Please help me," he begs. "I'm an American. I just want to go home."

The conversation beside me has turned from PTSD to craziness in general. The nurse is detailing a suicide attempt gone awry.

"I have a hard time with it," she admits. "The things they can do with razors . . ."

"The craziest patient I had," says one of the techs, "stabbed himself in the arm with a scalpel from a medical kit while I was out of the room getting his blood transfusion ordered."

"The craziest patient *I* had," says Sergeant Blake, "burned a *smiley face* into her arm!"

"Yeah," I say. "That was my sister."

They break off talking to stare at me. Then they laugh in disbelief.

Why did I say that? Why would I want them to know about Valerie? But I can't help myself. I'm like that soldier—trapped in my memories of trauma. Because I see it all. I remember it all.

It had been a beautiful summer day. Mom and Dad and I were at a party. Valerie had stayed home to lie in bed and listen to her music. Naturally, we were worried, but what could we do? We couldn't just stop living our lives.

At first, Mom and I met in corners from time to time to call home. But by the time dusk had fallen and we were toasting marshmallows around a fire pit, we were actually feeling happy.

That's when Valerie called to tell us:

"I've swallowed a bottle of pills."

As long as Valerie was conscious, she cried and told us she was sorry. She wasn't trying to kill herself, she said, because the psychiatrist had told her the pills wouldn't do that. She was sure it was perfectly safe.

But Valerie wasn't conscious very long.

She lay like an angel in Room One of the ER—the cardiac room—with her long, glossy brown hair fanned out on the turquoise sheets and her lips stained black with charcoal slurry. The burns and slashes on her bare arms somehow added an exotic touch of beauty. Her skin was so pale as she lay there that she looked like she was already dead. She looked like Ophelia, drowned.

Mom and Dad and I sat by her bedside all night long.

At four o'clock in the morning, they transferred my sister upstairs to the psych ward. A tech in green scrubs bundled her into a wheelchair to take her away. She didn't know we were there, and she couldn't have told us good-bye. Her head hung down almost to the plastic bucket propped on her lap. As the tech wheeled her backward through the swinging double doors, all we could see of my sister was that glossy brown hair and her two white hands, dotted with angry red burns.

My sister. My sister! The calm, rational one. The one who talked me down from my fears. My sister, the one who had always been there to save me from the monsters.

You're making a scene! growls the voice in my head.

I come to with a jolt. The techs are looking away, silent. The nurse is studying my face.

"Elena, oh my God. I'm really sorry," Sergeant Blake begins. But I don't want to listen, so I cut him off.

"That was my sister," I say again.

Then I walk away to catch the bus.

The bus back to school takes the same route to the air base that the blue transport bus took last summer the day they loaded me onto the C-17. I look out the window down at the very same asphalt flowing by next to our wheels.

I shouldn't have told them about Valerie. I should have just let them talk. What Valerie did doesn't matter anymore. My sister is dead to me.

Valerie left us. She left and wouldn't tell us where she was going. I remember Mom screaming into the phone, begging for a name, an address—anything. But Valerie wanted out of our lives.

Well, as far as I'm concerned, she's out.

Maybe Mom has forgotten what Val did to us, and that's how she can write to her now. Me, I don't forget. I remember exactly how Dad's face looked when we got the call. I remember how Mom couldn't get out of bed for days.

Nothing can make up for what Valerie did to us.

My sister is dead to me.

9

The bus brings me back to school in time for lunch break, and my friend Barbara and I meet up at her locker. She's a soccer star and a fantastic student. Both of us are overachievers.

"Do you want to walk to Burger King?" she asks. "I feel like having a burger."

Ten minutes' walk there and ten minutes back, says the voice in my head, *at a burn rate of four calories a minute. That's eighty calories you'll lose.*

"Sure," I say.

As we close our lockers, the wrestling guys come by in a noisy group. "Hey, come watch us weigh in," they call. "You can be the judge."

Barbara laughs, and we follow them to the gym.

One by one, they stand on the scale outside the boys' locker room and argue over ounces. Only one member of the wrestling team will eat today: the one who has lost the most weight since Friday.

Curly-haired Stevie steps on the scale and howls out swear words while the others jeer.

"How come I never get to eat on pizza day?" he mourns.

The winner is Vince. He pumps his fist in the air while the others curse. He jingles a handful of change under their noses. "Do I have enough money for ICE CREAM? I think I DO!"

Barbara steps onto the scale while they shove and punch. Vince says, "Hey, Elena, what about you?"

"I don't need to get on that thing," I say with a smile. "You guys are obsessed."

I know my number, of course. But I would never say it out loud. And I never step on a scale in public. It's one of my rules.

"Guess Elena's weight!" Stevie says. He hoists me into the air. "I could bench-press two of you," he says.

Vince snorts. "I'd like to wrestle in her weight category!"

With dignity, I disengage myself. "You people are morons," I tell them kindly. Then Barbara and I leave to walk to Burger King.

Barbara orders a burger and eats it on the way back. I order a chocolate shake and pretend to drink it on the way back.

She's an athlete, says the voice in my head. *She deserves to eat. You don't.*

In the remaining minutes of break, the two of us sit in a corner of the crowded foyer and talk. Mainly, we worry over grades. Barbara has four younger siblings. She needs to earn scholarships. And me, I want to pay my own way.

Lindsay joins us. She's got a container of French fries. It doesn't take me long to realize that she's chewing the fries and then surreptitiously spitting them into her Coke cup.

That's a wannabe trick! scoffs the voice in my head. *Who does she think she's fooling?*

A shake is the only way to go. With the lid on, no one can tell how much or how little you've been drinking.

Five minutes till the bell. Time to check makeup. Barbara and I head to the girls' restroom. On the way, I carelessly drop the chocolate shake through the hole of a covered trash can—my favorite trash can in the school. Because of the cover, no one can see the melted shake pop open and spill.

As Barbara and I check our mascara, I hear a telltale sound: a toilet flush and a soft flurry of noise. A few seconds later, a cheerleader comes out of the stall. She pushes her hair back from her face and pulls a toothbrush out of her Juicy Couture bag.

What a loser move! chuckles the voice in my head. *She's just going to brush the acid in so it will rot those nice straight teeth. Pretty soon it'll be time for veneers.*

Next class is Mr. Burke, AP English, but I won't be going today. I give Barbara my assignment before heading to my locker.

"Will you turn it in for me?" I ask. "And email me the new assignment? Mom's picking me up for a doctor's appointment." And I think but don't add: *Even though I don't want to go.*

"Sure," Barbara says, and I fight my way through the unruly crowd toward my locker.

Herr Braun, my German teacher, intercepts me outside his door. "Elena, I am glad I see you," he says. He puts the stress on the first syllable of my name, the German way, and I love him for that because it reminds me of my friends at the boarding school.

"I'm glad to see you, too, Herr Braun," I say in German.

Herr Braun's eyes twinkle at this. He's such a softie. I love him for that, too.

"Elena, we want you to give one of the speeches at graduation," he tells me in German. "One of the two German speeches. I'll work with you on a topic later, but for now, I need to know if you are willing."

So I'll speak at the graduation ceremony. Take *that*, you son-of-a-bitch psychiatrist who said I wouldn't have a senior year! But I keep my face in control and don't let the glee I'm feeling show.

"It will be an honor," I say.

"You deserve it," Herr Braun says warmly. "You work so hard."

The bell rings, and I hurry away.

As Mom drives me to the doctor, I tell her about the Marine with the abscess. I tell her about Dr. T. and about the new group of Army trainees. I tell her anything, in short, to keep her from asking questions. My stories are like sandbags I pile up on a bank to keep the river flowing where it belongs.

This year, a gap has formed between Mom and me. We're suspicious of each other. She hasn't stopped watching what I eat (or what I don't eat), and I can't stop thinking about what I learned at Drew Center. She makes me feel guilty and uneasy, and I see guilt and unease in her eyes, too. And right now we're driving to a German doctor to see why—after three more trips to the hospital and another cardiology exam—my supposedly healed-up heart still hurts.

That's because it isn't my heart, the doctor tells us. He thinks it's a condition called costochondritis: the cartilage holding my ribs to my breastbone is riddled with small cracks. To test his theory, he gives me an incredibly painful shot in the chest.

"The shot will help us determine exactly what's going on," he says. "If the pain goes away, it's costochondritis without a doubt. If it continues, then it's probably a bad case of acid reflux—that's acid from the stomach inflaming the membrane of the esophagus. So be sure to let me know the results."

We leave the doctor's office and walk back to the car. The shot has left me shaky, and I feel dizzy.

Dinnertime's coming, warns the voice in my head. *Do something, or you're going to get even fatter!*

"Swing by base and drop me off at the hospital," I say. "I want to put in a couple of hours at the chaplain's wing."

"But I want to start supper," Mom protests. "We're having chicken and rice tonight." I try to keep my face blank, but Mom sees me wince. "I thought you loved chicken and rice."

"Sure, when I was seven," I say. "You can just give me a fiver, and I'll eat at the hospital food court. Look, I need to fit in all the volunteer hours I can. It's important for my college applications."

Mom walks a few steps in silence. In her eyes, I can see the battle taking place inside her mind. Mom should work on her self-control. It's way too easy to guess what she's thinking.

"Do you *promise* you'll eat at the food court?" she asks.

"I promise."

So she fishes a five-dollar bill out of her purse.

Mom drops me off by the hospital, and I slouch my way through the long halls. That injection site really hurts. I wish I could stop breathing for a while.

The place I volunteer in the evenings is a little building just off the chaplain's wing. It's full of new clothes, toiletries, and donated odds and ends that we give to the wounded soldiers when they arrive. They get flown in straight from the battlefield, so all their gear is left behind.

"Elena, honey!" the volunteer coordinator calls out with a big smile on her face. "You're just in time. We got five boxes in today, and I need somebody to sort through them."

So I kneel down in a corner with an open box in front of me. It will be Christmas. And it will be hell.

First comes the Christmas part. I open up an envelope full of homemade cards from a second-grade class somewhere in Maine.

My Dady is a solder, one card reads, with a drawing of a stick figure in Army green. *I love you! Come home safe.*

I read the cards one by one, then put them in a box by the door. Patients who come in love to read them. One chief master sergeant who makes trips downrange to the combat zones grabs a big handful of them every time he leaves.

"I send them to the guys who are at the forward outposts," he told us. "They say those cards keep them sane."

Next comes a set of small pillows with a waving flag and *Bless you for all you do* embroidered across them. A note attached to the pillows tells me they're from a grieving mother whose Marine daughter died last year in our hospital.

A young man in a gown and robe shuffles through the door. He's pale under his desert tan. The volunteer coordinator calls out a greeting and starts putting together a duffel bag for him.

"Have a seat," she says. "I'll take care of it. You're a size large. Do you need a toothbrush and toiletries?"

"Yes, ma'am," he says. Then, shyly, "I don't have my per diem money yet. Can you just take my name and room number for right now?"

"All this stuff is free for you," the volunteer coordinator says.

He looks shocked. "Really? Thanks!"

She gives him one of her big, warmhearted smiles. "No, honey. Thank *you.*"

I reach into my box again. There's an expensive get-well card. That's nice. But inside someone has written, *I'm glad you're suffering, you Goddamn babykiller. I hope to God you got your legs blown off.*

This is the part that's hell.

The young man hasn't sat down. He seems not to know what to do with himself. He shuffles over near me and looks into the box. "Good stuff?" he asks.

"Oh, sure," I say, hiding the card. "It's like Christmas!" Except when it isn't. "Do you want me to grab that chair for you? You really don't have to stand."

"Well . . . I kinda do," he confesses. When I look confused, he blushes. "It's shrapnel," he says, pointing vaguely behind him. "They're operating tomorrow."

"Oh. I'm so sorry!" I blurt out.

He shrugs and gives me a sheepish grin. The volunteer coordinator brings him his loaded bag, and he shuffles away.

I reach into the box again. Fifty decals: *I believe in heroes.* I give them to the volunteer coordinator so she can stick them on the duffel bags.

Two women with buzz haircuts and black Army jogging shorts limp in. One is on crutches and has a thigh-high cast. The other has her foot in a big plastic boot. They've been here before, and they're back now just to look around. A hospital doesn't have many places to wander.

The women find the blue satin prom dress on the rack. Laughing, they hold it up to their battered bodies. Then they fall silent as the rich, shiny fabric slips across their rough hands.

I don't know who decided to donate a brand-new prom dress to help out wounded soldiers, but it was a stroke of genius. None of the female soldiers takes it, although any of them could. But they love to hold it and remember what it was like to wear pretty things.

I reach into my box again. A box of chocolates that's suspiciously light, and the plastic wrapper is suspiciously altered. I slice through it and open the box.

Every paper wrapper is empty, and stained. I'm guessing that somebody spit in them.

A tech in green scrubs leads in a burly African American man who's still wearing his ragged desert fatigues. A white bandage wraps across his eyes and all the way around his head. Dried blood has leaked out and crusted on his cheek.

The burly man bumps into a shelf and stands listening as bottles of shampoo tumble to the floor. Then he listens as we scramble to pick them up.

"I'm sorry about that," he tells us sadly. "It's my first day blind."

Shocked silence falls over the room. I don't know what to say. But silence isn't the right answer, either.

"Well, we're glad to have you here, honey," says the volunteer coordinator, and I see the bandaged face turn toward her warm, sincere voice. "It's just fine. Don't you worry about a thing."

My phone rings. Mom is waiting outside—already! And I forgot to eat.

You're lying, says the voice in my head. *You promised her, but you knew you weren't going to.*

"Did you have supper?" Mom asks as soon as I open the car door. No "Hello." No "How did it go?" They're the very first words out of her mouth!

Lie again, prompts the voice in my head. *Go on! You're good at it.*

"Yep," I say. I climb into the backseat and pull out my headphones.

"How's your chest?" Mom asks next—another question I don't need.

"It hurts," I say as she pulls away from the curb.

"Hurts how?" she wants to know. "Like it did before, or different? Did the shot do anything at all?"

"It just hurts."

But the fact is that the pain's different now, and that's not a good thing. The excruciating pain around my breastbone has eased, but it's left behind more excruciating pain. Jolts of fire shoot up and down in the soft tissue inside my chest.

Costochondritis *and* acid reflux—I have both of them. I know it's purging that has brought on the acid reflux. And that's not going to go away.

"Is it pain like rib pain?" Mom asks. "An ache? A stab? When you see the doctor next week, you need to be able to tell him."

"I don't want to see him again," I say. "I told you these doctors are a waste of time."

"You're hurting," she says. "I don't want to see you hurting."

"It doesn't matter. I'm fine."

You're lying again, says the voice in my head.

I turn up the music and lean my head against the window.

It's twilight outside. The days are getting longer, but the sky is overcast and heavy with storm clouds. My chest hurts. The window under my cheek is cold. I'm tired. Tired, tired, tired. But I have homework.

Mom waves her fingers at me to get my attention. I pull an earbud out of one ear.

"Would you like to say the rosary with me?" she asks.

"I just want to listen to music," I say. "Get Dad to say it with you when we get home."

"Your dad's already asleep. Please?"

I try to think of something to say that won't sound completely mean.

"I'm really tired," I say. "And I have homework. I want to nap for a few minutes, and my chest hurts."

"If your chest hurts, you need to see a doctor," she says.

I don't have an answer for that.

Mom starts saying the rosary by herself while she drives. I put my headphones back on and turn up the music.

Three months ago, my dog got sick. I got down on my knees and prayed, "Please, Lord, don't make Chip die. Valerie's gone, and Ramona's gone. Chip's the only thing left from when I was happy. He sleeps with me at night and makes me feel safe now that I'm by myself. I can't fall asleep without him. I don't see why he needs to die. He's not that old. Please don't make him die."

And the next day, Chip got so bad that Mom had to take him to the vet and put him to sleep.

That pretty much told me where I rate with God.

Home. I disappear into my room. It's huge, my room. It's like a whole house by itself. It's upstairs, right under the roof, so it has a sloping ceiling of tan-colored wooden boards and two big clear windows that look out over the red roof tiles of the neighbors' houses.

I made up my bed before I left for school this morning, and the sight of the maroon satin bedspread dotted with colorful sequins lifts my spirits. My old cloth cow lies in the exact center of its six decorative pillows. Two purple couch cushions rest in identical positions on each side of my burgundy pleather loveseat, and the red Chinese-pattern rug in front of the loveseat is free of fluffs. Two identical night-stands frame the bed, with lamps and bright knickknacks arranged in appealing patterns on top of them. By the door is my desk, with my journals in a line on the shelf below my keyboard. A tall curio cabinet between the windows displays Venetian masks and costumed dolls.

I feel a glow of satisfaction and relief at the sight of these orderly possessions. I saved up and bought this furniture myself with my baby-sitting money. It's clean, bright, and modern. And it's mine.

I set my schoolbooks down on the desk, but I can't persuade myself to study. I ache all over now, my injured chest throbs with pain, and my brain feels empty. My stomach is starting to grind into my backbone and send shivers of nausea up to my teeth and jaw. The good feeling at the sight of my immaculate room ebbs away.

I walk to a window and look out at the gathering storm.

Our neighbor raises racing pigeons. In the twilight outside, I see his birds rush by in the same two loops of a figure eight as always, like there's an invisible racetrack laid out in the sky just for them. This evening, the strong, gusty wind is plucking at them and blowing them off course, but they still whirl by my window in the same wild hurry.

No matter how fast they fly, they never get anywhere.

I go back to my desk, fire up the computer, and go online to my forum. It isn't pro-ana. It's just a place where eating disorder patients can talk. We don't teach newbies any tricks or help them diet, but we support one another as we struggle through our days.

Most of the time, I feel closer to my forum friends than I do to my own family.

As I scan the new threads, I realize that it's been a bad day for most of us.

I just feel so helpless, writes one. *I wish I could bore a hole in my heart and let all the hurt flow out.*

I start to write back. Then I realize I have nothing to say.

Instead, I start up the DVD of the American Ballet Company's *Swan Lake* on my computer, as I do almost every night. Immortal, enchanted women in gossamer white weave an intricate dance to the delicate music. The injured White Swan is ageless and timeless. She's translucent, floating grace. Beauty in pain: she dances the entire story with a shimmer of red blood down the center of her chest.

Her cavalier is faithless. Her lover is a monster. Her face is drawn and pale. But the White Swan triumphs over everything. She doesn't miss a single magnificent step. She's forced to show off in front of a mocking crowd, even though she doesn't want to. But she leaves the crowd stunned with admiration. She outshines them all.

Beauty in pain. As I watch, transfixed, I feel the throb of my own injured chest.

Death saves her in the end, clean and splendid. The credits roll. I stop the DVD, pull up my email and find that Barbara has sent me Mr. Burke's assignment. It's an essay:

> In 300–500 words, describe an object that provokes an emotional response in you.

Emotional response? I can't think of one. I don't feel much of anything anymore. I'll write the essay later. I add it to the neat list of things that still need to be done. The sight of that list holds me together.

I'm wiped out. Time for bed. Without my dog, of course.

You were stupid to get so dependent on him, says the voice in my head. *Bad things happen when you let yourself need others.*

Even though I'm exhausted, I can't turn off the light until I've read two pages each in two different books. Twos protect me. They help me close my eyes and hope for sleep.

But pain comes instead, from the acid eating my esophagus. Pain comes from the cartilage cracking around my ribs, from each and every vertebra of my improperly curved spine, from my hip bones, from my neck. Pain throbs behind my eyes. Pain churns in my furious stomach. Each aching part of my body settles into the mattress independently from every other aching part.

With my eyes closed, I mound a pillow into the size and shape of my dead dog, Chip. I snuggle into it, clutch my old cloth cow, and drop into a doze.

Bolt upright!

I sit bolt upright, with a shriek in my throat. My heart is pounding! I can feel it galloping inside my chest.

I reach out blindly. No Chip. No Valerie. No one to save me from the monster in my dreams.

There was a hand over my mouth. Pain. Pain! And a voice yelling in my ear . . .

I've heard that voice yell at me in so many nightmares.

Shivering, teeth chattering in my head, I slip out of bed and make my way to the window. My steps are unsteady. I hold on to the furniture I pass to keep from falling to the floor.

Behind the ghostly curtain, darkness smothers the world. I lean my head against the cold window frame. The pulse pounding in my head lights up a strobe-light pattern of orange sparks behind my eyes that flickers on and off against the blackness outside.

You were stupid! Stupid! fumes the voice in my head. *You were a stupid, stupid little bitch!*

I close my eyes and lean my head against the cold window glass until my heart slows down. I'm so tired, I'm on the verge of tears. I wanted that sleep. I wanted it so badly!

But there's no way I'm going back to sleep now.

It's late. No, it's early. It's early, and that's good. I can get a head start on the new day. There's plenty of homework to keep me busy. There's a whole list of things that need to be done.

I fire up the computer and check my email. I've got one message. It's from an unknown address.

> hey, lani, mom said youve been sick. so i just wanted to say sorry, i know youre mad at me but i did what i had to do. anyhoo mom's not mad anymore, so write me back okay? i miss you. love, val

I stare at the message. It doesn't make sense at first. Then it does, but it's too late to matter.

The craziest patient I had burned a smiley face into her arm! Yeah. That was my sister.

I delete the email. Then I pull out my journal and try to write. But instead, I find myself reading old entries from two years ago. I could have written them yesterday.

> I got to start eating again. I got to start sleep
> ing again. This is not my problem, not my life, not my

burned wrists, not my freaking mental outbursts.
I am me, and I need to let this go.

Elena, she is messed up. Read what you are writing.
She is having problems and you can't change that ever.
Ever. Ever. Ever. No matter how hard you want to.
No matter how bad your heart hurts.

It's almost two years later. But my heart still hurts.

So, at 3:17 in the morning, I write Mr. Burke's essay about an object that evokes an emotional response.

Good-bye to the door downstairs. The door that is
always locked now. The door that we pass by hurriedly,
eyes focused straight ahead. The door that hides
away the room and memories of the other daughter,
the sister, the inky black sheep who lost her way. So
many memories of that door but not so many of her.
Sometimes I think my mind blocked them all, but
then a crystal-clear image of her hits, fractures my
thoughts, paralyzes me with hate—anger—fear—pain—
loss—love. And sometimes—which is even worse—I feel
nothing at all.

Images of her hang in my mind, framed by the strong
wooden doorposts like pictures in an art gallery. A
fleeting glimpse, and she would be gone. On the other
side of the door was her space, her womb, her world.
We were not a part of that and could never hope to be.

Her emotions were released on the door. It was a
shield, blocking the waves of pain and accusations
from crashing into us and knocking us over. At night,

I would wake up to the sound of the door slamming, the grating of the metal key turning in the lock. Sometimes the door was not thick enough, and I could hear her cry.

Scuffed by heavy boots, covered in cigarette burns, graced with tiny drops of rust-colored blood, the door held it all, from the beginning to her end. Like a sponge, it soaked up our memories and feelings. It buffered her rage, it filtered our pain. It sheltered her from her fears of the world, it protected us from seeing too much. In months of confusion and grief, it remained constant.

So, for one last time, I turn the key in the lock. The door makes a soft sound of recognition as I push it open. The room is cool, the colors, subdued, the carpet faded and stained. Shadows flit over the empty bed, the empty chair, empty dresser, empty me. Memories are pungent here, like rotting oranges.

I have an urge to take the door and shred it, gut it open, decipher every sliver of wood. Spread out all the splinters like a giant puzzle, until it tells me why.

Why she left me.

Why she left us.

Why she left.

Why.

10

College, first semester. I'm back in the States in a big auditorium-style classroom in a big featureless university in a state big enough to swallow up the whole country of Germany—twice.

We've been in Texas for three months now. Mom and Dad moved into their old house across town from the university, the house where Valerie and I played when we were kids. I moved into the dorms here, with enough AP credit to polish off almost one full year of college before I even opened a textbook.

Halfway to finals, fall semester. It's the last class of the day.

The professor's teaching assistant trots up and down the risers of the semicircular room and hands back essays. She lays mine on my desk facedown, and I peel up a corner as if I'm in a poker game. A, reads the corner, so I flip the paper over. *Excellent analysis—nice examples!*

Good. Good! After the first two quizzes, the first test, and the first essay, I have an A.

That's because this class is too easy, says the voice in my head.

Fifty minutes grind by. Finally, class ends. With a sudden buzz and bustle, two hundred students turn and stretch and rise to their feet. Now, off to the Social Sciences building, where the Intro to Psych test grades should be out.

I stand up and reach for my backpack.

A wave of blackness rushes in and turns the bright, busy class-room into a hushed world of underwater gray.

No! Not today. Not ever!

While students file past, I grip the back of my chair and fight. I've been here before. Breathe. Just breathe. Find the knot of pain in your chest.

Count: one, two. One, two. One, two, three, four.

The darkness retreats. Like a volume knob turning, the noise and chatter of the big classroom returns. I locate the pen I've dropped, check for my cell phone, and pick up my backpack.

Now I'm just another student, heading down the hall.

Out into sunlight and whipping wind. It isn't white-hot any-more like it was a month ago, but it isn't comfortable, either. After seven years in Germany's cool, rainy climate, it'll take more than a few months in Texas to make me feel at home.

Is this home? says the voice in my head. *Do you have a home?*

As if in answer, a witch in a tall black hat and green face paint whirs by me on a bicycle.

It's Halloween.

I hurry over to the Social Sciences building, climb an open stair-case with limestone banisters, and head down to the end of a long, straight hallway.

Yes! The grades are up. I scan the list. Pretty bad for the most part: Cs and Ds. A scattering of Fs.

Then there's my student number, and there's my grade: *89.*

An eighty-nine? I studied so hard for that test!

You're not smart enough, says the voice in my head. *You'll never get into nursing school like that.*

I walk back across campus, through asphalt parking lots still shimmering with heat. The trees are changing color right now in Ger-many. I think about the yellow birches and fire-red flames of beech trees and thick layers of rust-colored leaves carpeting the forest floor. Homesickness floods through me. No leaves seem to change around here. I'll be lucky if I get to wear a coat before January.

The sidewalk is blocked by construction fencing. I walk beside orange plastic webbing down the dirt path, between clumps of ragged Bermuda and tall, wispy Johnson grass.

Two zombie frat boys in torn T-shirts and ripped shorts are hogging the path in front of me. I debate passing them, but I'm too tired.

"My girlfriend's really pissing me off," says one.

"Why?" asks the other.

"I don't know."

A little silence.

"That sucks."

"Yeah."

They turn toward the older dorms, and I head into the newest housing area, then up the outdoor cement stairs to my unit.

The sight of the cute, tidy, two-bedroom apartment lifts my mood. Sandra, my new roommate, and I share a comforting streak of OCD. I step into the neat little kitchen and drop my backpack onto our breakfast table next to the fake plant, ceramic pumpkin, and set of matching napkins. Beyond is a living room as elegant as our student incomes will allow: framed Japanese calligraphy and balls woven out of twigs in the living room, Hello Kitty posters and colorful pillows in the bedrooms.

I unlock my bedroom door. My old cow lies on the bed, washed-out purple and dirty brown, her white stuffing peeking through holes and rips. I drop onto the satin bedspread next to her, burrow my face into her side, and fall asleep within seconds.

"Elena? Elena!"

I sit up and blink. My neck is stiff. The light has changed. It's getting dark outside.

I stumble out of my room, and Sandra is waiting for me in the little kitchen. Compact and muscular like a cheerleader, with a pretty, heart-shaped face, Sandra has just come from the gym and looks like an ad for Nike.

Loser! You didn't work out today, says the voice in my head.

"I've got your hot dog right here," Sandra says, rustling around in a white paper bag.

A hot dog! says the voice in my head. *That's fifteen grams of fat. Fifteen grams at least!*

"Oh, no, I don't want it right now," I say. "I just woke up. I'll eat it later."

Sandra gives me a look.

"Elena, you know what tonight is. It's a party night. Party means protein before you go out. You know you shouldn't drink alcohol on an empty stomach."

She takes the steaming dog out of its foil wrapper, squeezes a packet of relish on it, and hands it to me. "You'd better eat it," she says with a pout and a determined gleam in her eye. "I already spent student credit on this. If I have to eat one, you have to eat one. You know the party rules."

Oh, well, this isn't so bad, I think. I haven't had anything today since my green tea and granola bar at eight in the morning. I bite into its greasy goodness. Sandra and I eat together, standing at the kitchen counter.

Think of the fat! shrieks the voice in my head. *Think of the chemicals! Remember* The Jungle!

But I wolf down the hot dog so quickly, I'm ashamed of myself.

"Costume time. I claim shower," Sandra sings out, and before I can stop her, she's barreled into the bathroom and locked the door. I'm left to rub my uncomfortable stomach and slouch off to my bedroom. That's what comes of having an athlete for a roommate.

Sandra's got a scholarship function tonight. She invited me to come along, but my friend Meghan and I are hitting the Halloween parties instead with a couple of friends of hers. Meghan's roommate, Regina, is the mopey kind; she's gone again for the weekend back to her parents' house in Uvalde, so I can have Regina's room for the night. Or at least, I can have Regina's room for as much of the night as I'll be sleeping. Some of Meghan's and my party nights have lasted until the next day.

I change into my costume. I'm wearing a cheap German Oktoberfest outfit: white puff-sleeve blouse, black lace-up vest, and blue miniskirt. It doesn't look much like a real dirndl, but it reminds me of home.

You shouldn't be wearing a skirt like that, says the voice in my head. *Everybody will look at your flabby thighs.*

I distract myself with memories of dirndls. In Germany, dirndls can be as important and expensive as evening gowns. Some of my boarding-school friends had to wear them on holidays—dirndls for the girls and lederhosen for the boys. As I lace the vest, I think about Frau Tannenbaum and the green dirndl she wore to church every Sunday.

Then I pull on a pair of black fishnet stockings and step into five-inch heels.

It's a good thing Frau Tannenbaum can't see me now.

A text comes in on my phone: *im here!* I shout good-bye to Sandra through the bathroom door and remind her that I won't be back tonight. Then I grab my keys, slam the front door, and go down the concrete stairs outside as fast as my heels will let me.

A warm breeze ruffles the short skirt, and I reach back to try to hold it down. After wearing jeans all day, it feels strange to be so well ventilated.

Meghan waves from the parking lot. She's wearing a pirate costume, more or less . . . mostly less. She's got the pirate hat on, and
a curved plastic sword at her side, but her shirt is unbuttoned down
the front, showing a black bra underneath. Her skirt is even tinier
than mine.

"God, Elena, hurry up!" she yells. By the way she's holding on
to the car door and leaning, I can tell she's already had a couple of
drinks. I jump into the backseat, and she slides in after me.

The guy driving the car is Kirk, a friend of hers. The guy sitting
up front is Wayne, a friend of his. Kirk pulls away from the curb with
a squeal of his tires, and I think: *Has he been drinking, too?*

Serves you right if you all die, says the voice in my head.

Kirk drives to where the guy in his algebra class said the party
was going to be. It's obviously where the party is. Bumper-to-bumper
parked cars line both sides of the street, and music blares out of an
open doorway.

The neighborhood is full of student rentals with carports, ripped
screens, and dead lawns. Ryan's house looks like a cheaper version of
my parents' 1970s ranch house—if my parents' house held almost no
furniture, forty or fifty ghouls and mummies, and several kegs of beer
in the kitchen.

The host is standing just inside the door in a bright red devil
costume.

"Trick or treat!" he yells over the pounding dubstep, and he
holds out a plastic pumpkin candy dish.

I look inside and see little tablets in muted shades of pink, blue,
and yellow with quirky symbols stamped into them.

"Fantastic!" says Kirk. He grabs a pink peace sign and pops
it into his mouth. Wayne reaches into the candy dish next. Meghan

puts a blue smiley-face into her mouth, then grabs my arm and heads toward the kitchen.

"I hate the taste," she says. "I need a beer."

We push our way through the crowd of capes, masks, and bright-colored underwear. The crowd is so dense, I can barely maneuver. I think about my short skirt and put up with the unpleasant feeling of bumping against people I don't know.

Perverts! warns the voice in my head. *Fat, sweaty perverts.*

But at least in this crush, no one can see my flabby thighs.

Jell-O shots in Dixie cups line the kitchen counter. Two reasonably sober girls with bunny ears are guarding the good stuff in the fridge. A guy who decided that plaid boxers are a Halloween costume is mixing a Jack and Coke. Somebody hands Meghan a plastic cup full of beer, and she chugs it down.

"Yuck!" she says. "Here, you want to wash the taste out?"

"No, I'm good," I say. I don't like pills, even if I don't have to swallow them.

Meghan's face lights up with the beatific look of a preacher talking about salvation.

"Oh, Elena, you've *got* to try Ecstasy," she says. "You've *got* to try it. It makes you so happy, and all calm, and things feel so good. It's just . . . you've *got* to try it."

She hands her plastic cup back for a refill.

"Maybe next time," I say. "I've got what I need right here." I pick up a red Jell-O shot and a green one and slurp them down, then crumple the Dixie cups and toss them past a goggle-eyed Where's Waldo into the big gray trash can by the kegs. "Vodka and Jell-O," I say. "What's not to love?"

I pick up two more on my way out.

We go into the living room, shoo a Smurf in short-shorts out of the way, and plop down on the couch. I'm next to Wayne. He's holding a Corona with lime and is deep in discussion with the guy next to him about one of the Halo levels. His entire costume, I realize, consists of a rubber knife through the head.

I don't know very many people here. In front of me, an angel is dancing with the devil host. If angels really look like that, they should wear bras and maybe check their white stockings for holes before they leave home.

"I'm out of beer," says Meghan.

"I'm out of Jell-O shots," I say. "Let's go."

Time passes, with more trips from the couch to the kitchen. They begin to seem like massive and difficult journeys. Meghan and I have long, complex discussions about them first, as if we are planning a hiking trip through the Himalayas.

I feel a hand stroking my hair and turn to see why.

"So soft . . . ," murmurs Wayne. "So soft."

Then he kisses me—a long, deep kiss. I pull away, but secretly, I'm flattered.

"Jesus, Elena, what are you doing?" says Meghan. She starts to laugh. "Oh, my *God!*"

I find myself laughing, too.

Several more trips to the Himalayas. The loud music and bright colors of costumes have merged into a fantasy landscape that swirls around me in slow motion. But through the haze, a growing awareness dawns on me.

"I need to pee," I tell Meghan.

She doesn't hear me. She's talking to someone else. Nevertheless, I feel good for having told her. It's the sacred duty of friend to friend.

I wend my way to the front hallway, where the bathroom is. That's also where the largest crush of people is. I stand in line for ten minutes, or maybe one minute, or maybe half an hour—it's hard to tell. Then I push through to the front of the line and smack my hand against the door.

"I need to *pee*!" I yell.

From inside the little bathroom come girlish giggles and snatches of conversation. "We're taking *pictures*!" someone yells back.

Tomorrow, Facebook will display fifty-three new and almost identical pictures of a Teletubby, a cowgirl, and the Progressive Insurance lady holding up their phones and shooting photos in a bathroom mirror. But right now, I still need to pee.

Then I realize: *There's another bathroom upstairs!*

For a second, I am stunned by the force of my own brilliance. Then, congratulating myself on my superior, laserlike mind, I abandon the huddled masses waiting for the photo session to break up. I climb the stairs. The carpet grabs at my high heels and threatens me with a fall at every step.

The landing is lit only by the lights from downstairs. I wander into the hall, trying doors. The first door is a darkened bedroom. Wayne is in there, playing some kind of computer game. Past his silhouette, on the screen, men in flak suits shout to one another.

"What are you doing here?" he asks, getting up.

I feel like I've been caught doing something wrong. It's bad manners to snoop in the bedrooms at a party. Wayne's up here because he's friends with one of the guys who lives here. He probably thinks I'm on a treasure hunt, looking for things to steal.

"Finding the bathroom," I say.

"Next door."

I turn to go, and he follows me out. What a jerk! He's actually going to watch me to make sure I'm not taking stuff.

But he isn't. He grabs me around the waist in the hallway and tries to kiss me again.

I push him away and turn toward the bathroom.

"I need to pee," I say firmly.

He grabs me again—roughly this time. "Come on," he says. "I know you want it."

"Let *go*, Wayne!" I say.

Wayne doesn't let go. He gets a grip on my arm and starts to pull me into the bathroom.

"I know the kind of girl you are," he says. "I know what you want—hey, stop fighting, bitch!"

NO! NO! NO!

Not another bathroom! Not another yelling voice!

I wrap my arm around the doorjamb and hang on tight. A burr of metal on the hinge peels its way down the flesh of my forearm, but I barely feel it. This time, it's not going to go like that. It is NOT going to go like that!

I strike out at Wayne with my free hand and scratch him so badly that I feel bunched-up skin under my fingernails. "You *bitch*!" he howls, and he smacks me across the face.

I see red. I literally see red. I can't even see Wayne's face anymore. I am a kicking, slashing, howling she-devil. I am screaming with rage.

"Forget it, bitch," Wayne says, letting go. He pushes past me into the hall. "You're not worth my time."

He's getting away. He is NOT going to get away!

I'm right behind him. I punch and slash and shriek. We're on the stairway now, and Wayne's at a disadvantage because he can't fend me off and handle the steps at the same time. My high heels are catching in the sculpted carpet. If my punches didn't keep landing and bouncing me back upright, I'd fall down the stairs.

We burst into the living room, and all the Ecstasied-out partiers on the couch and chairs and floor look up at us like flower children in the Summer of Love.

"Dude," says the devil host sleepily. "What happened?"

"Get this bitch away from me!" yells Wayne.

"You *dick*!" I shout. "You asshole piece of *trash*!"

Meghan is next to us now.

"Elena, you messed up my high," she says. "Stop hitting Wayne. He's my friend."

"Goddamn bitch! Look what you did!" Wayne shouts, clutching scratches on his arm and chest. He ducks a punch, and then he hits me hard across the mouth.

"Wayne, *Jesus*!" screams Meghan. "Oh my God, Wayne, you *asshole*!"

But I don't feel it. I am swinging again.

Kirk is beside me, too. He says, "Come on, Elena, we're leaving."

Now we're outside the house, but I'm still swinging. Wayne is farther away, and I see guys around him holding his arms, but I keep closing the distance to connect. Somebody I don't know puts his hands around my waist to pick me up off the ground.

"He's not worth it," he tells me. "He's not worth it."

I use this opportunity to kick Wayne as hard as I can in the crotch.

The guy can't hold me and keep his balance, and I end up on the ground. But Wayne's there, too, writhing and groaning. And I'm the one who gets up first.

Then I'm in the car, in the backseat with Meghan again. I've lost one of my shoes. Meghan and I are arguing, explaining, backtracking, and clarifying in grand, sweeping statements.

"What *happened*," I say, "is that guys are assholes. That's it. That's all. That's it."

Meghan nods like a bobblehead.

"And you and me," she says, "we *have* to stick together."

I feel my head bobbing, too. "That's right."

"I mean—I'm not *saying*—I mean, we *want* to stick together."

"That's right."

"But we *have* to stick together. We *have* to."

"That's right!"

And Meghan and I clasp hands with great emotion.

Somehow we have an entire bottle of Smirnoff in the backseat, and we are passing it back and forth like a peace pipe. I don't wonder how it got there because the backseat of the car seems like a place I have always known. It's a dark little room that I've lived in for a very long time.

Now I become aware that the car has a front seat. It's another room—a little room way up at the front of the car. Kirk is up there. Poor Kirk—he's such a good friend to stay so far away in that little room. He has a bottle of Jack Daniels, but he has no one to share it with. He's having to drink it all alone.

I glance at the speedometer: 110.

That's okay. We're on an autobahn. There's no speed limit on an autobahn. You keep to the left lane, and no one bothers you.

Like magic, Meghan and Kirk and I are walking into another party, even though I don't feel my feet move. This party is upstairs in a tiny apartment, and it's more tightly packed than the first one. White sheets have been hung on the walls and then splashed with fake blood. Meghan and I pose for a self-portrait, pouting prettily—two bright, happy college girls out having a good time.

There is a cowboy at this party. He thinks I'm wearing a Wild West barmaid's costume.

"How about setting off across the prairie with me, pretty lady?" he drawls. "Let's leave this here saloon."

"It's a German costume," I say. "It's a dirndl." An unwelcome memory intrudes into my mind of dirndls in church on Sunday.

"How about pouring me a drink?" persists the cowboy. "We can ride off into the sunset together."

"It's a German costume, you *moron*," I say.

There is a wine cooler in my hand. I don't remember how it got there.

Now I'm in Meghan's apartment. Meghan's apartment? Yes, and there is a crisis. What is it? I look around and try to assess.

There's a pounding noise next to me. I feel the walls. No. I feel the door. Yes. The pounding is coming from the door.

Like a genie, Kirk materializes next to me. I realize that we are both listening to the pounding. I try the door, but it's locked.

"Open the door," I say.

Meghan's voice sounds from the other side. "Elena, open the door!"

I look around. I am in the hall outside the bathroom. The bathroom door is locked.

"Meghan, unlock the door."

The pounding continues. Meghan wails from the other side, "Elena! Open the door!"

"Meghan, you locked the bathroom door. You have to open it."

"*Open it!*"

"I can't open it. You locked it! It's on your side. Unlock the bathroom door!"

Meghan pounds with greater urgency. "Let me out!" she howls. "Let me out!"

I turn to Kirk. "Kick in the door," I say simply. Without hesitation, he does. There is a splintering crack, and the door bursts open. Meghan emerges. We are heroes!

Then I sit up. It's daylight.

Bright, bright daylight.

And I feel like I'm going to die.

I look around. I'm in a bedroom that looks like my bedroom, but there's a Harry Potter movie poster on the wall.

Did I come home with a Harry Potter poster? Would I do that? I'm not sure.

My whole body aches, and the room spins. My head and my gut feel like I've been poisoned. I get up to go to the bathroom and slip on vomit.

There's vomit all over the floor.

That explains the smell. I thought it was my breath.

I walk across the hall and slip on more vomit. There's vomit all over the bathroom.

It's Meghan's bathroom. That's right, I'm in Meghan's dorm. That must be her roommate's bedroom.

One mystery solved: that's someone else's Harry Potter poster on the wall. Another mystery to figure out: the bathroom door won't close.

I discover Kirk passed out on the living room couch. There's vomit on Kirk and vomit on the couch.

Meghan is asleep in her bedroom. There's vomit in here, too.

I follow the trail back into the living room, trying to piece events together. What happened last night?

You ate a hot dog, says the voice in my head. *You let yourself get forced into eating a hot dog, therefore you are a spineless, obese, out-of-control balloon.*

I push past the voice and rummage in my memory. I remember a stupid cowboy. I remember Jell-O shots. I remember looking down and seeing blood drips changing color as they soaked into my blue miniskirt.

Blood. Red blood that dripped down my arm, turning black when it hit the blue skirt. I look at my arm. A long ragged gash wraps around it, and dried blood stains the skin nearby.

The door hinge. The doorjamb I am hanging onto because . . .

You bitch! Stop that, you bitch!

You bitch! says the voice in my head.

Rough hands dragging at me, bruising, striking, *You know you want it, bitch!*

You bitch! shrieks the voice in my head. *You stupid bitch!*

Hands are grabbing me, a hand over my mouth, a voice yelling in my ear.

Stupid bitch! Stupid bitch! Stupid bitch!

"Meghan!" I scream as I turn and bolt for her door. But darkness—welcome darkness—gets there first.

Quiet voices. A woman's voice. That's my mother's. Mom is here?

And then a man's voice:

"I suspect we'll find drug use."

That's a doctor. I know. I don't even need to open my eyes. Oh, shit! My college career. My nursing career!

All you do is screw up your life, you stupid bitch!

I open my eyes. I'm in an ER. And an ER isn't a place to be sick. It's a place to be strong and busy and help others.

My parents are standing next to my bed. They look older than I remember.

"I'm fine," I tell them firmly.

I try to sit up, but I'm in restraints. Restraints? Okay, that's weird. But that's not what's important right now. What's important is that I stop this train wreck.

"Don't worry," I say, sinking back onto the pillow again. "This is just a misunderstanding."

"You dissociated," Dad says. "You haven't dissociated in over a year."

"I stood up too fast," I tell him matter-of-factly. "I couldn't sit down in time."

"You were circling," Mom interjects. "A girl named Meghan Harlow called 9-1-1. She thought you were having a seizure."

"Meghan overreacted," I say. "She panicked. Everything's fine. Hello, doctor," I add politely as a stern face slides into view. "I'm sorry you were bothered. I'm fine."

The doctor looks unconvinced and a little cynical. I'm guessing I'm not the first half-naked college chick to show up at his ER the day after Halloween.

"I'm ordering a drug test," he says, and his eyes challenge me to react to this. "What were you taking last night?"

"Nothing," I say with all the cheerful unconcern of a girl who *didn't* do Ecstasy with her friends the night before.

"I'll be sharing the results with your parents," he continues.

Technically, he doesn't have the right to do this since I'm over eighteen. But I say, "Why not?" and give him such a steady look that he appears to rethink his diagnosis.

The nurse unfastens the restraints and draws my blood. The doctor leaves.

I haven't seen my parents in a couple of weeks, so I pretend this is a reunion and chatter away about everything that's been going on — everything except the things I don't want them to know, of course. I tell them about the eighty-nine on the exam and the A on the essay and start filling up the airspace with funny stories.

Little by little, my parents start to relax.

"What happened to bring this on?" Mom asks after a while. "The dissociation, I mean."

"It wasn't dissociation. I fainted," I say. "It was Halloween, and there were a bunch of parties. I had a lot to drink, but don't worry, I wasn't driving."

A scene flashes into my mind: Kirk, tipping up the bottle of Jack Daniels. The speedometer at 110.

It's all I can do to hang onto my cheerful expression. *A hundred and ten?!* What the *hell* was I thinking?

"Still, I know I got dehydrated," I conclude. "That's probably what made me faint."

Sandra comes in with a set of clean clothes for me. She's awkward and doesn't know what to say. I wonder what Meghan told her. Did Sandra see me? Did Meghan call her? Did Kirk wake up? Did he see me, too?

They're whispering behind your back, says the voice in my head. *They're saying, did you see what happened? Did you see?*

But there's no time to worry about who saw what. I need to stay in charge here. So I reassure Sandra just as I did my parents, and she kisses my cheek and hurries away. She's a teaching assistant, and she has to get to a study group.

The doctor returns to report with a slight tinge of surprise in his voice that there are no drugs in my system. But there's still plenty of alcohol.

If he expects to see horror on my parents' faces, he's disappointed. I've already told them that. Plus, they're used to living in a country where the legal age for beer is fourteen and where my boarding school served the older girls a glass of wine with Sunday dinner.

We sign the forms. I wash up and change into my jeans, and we're ready to leave. "Where shall we go eat?" Dad asks.

My poisoned stomach gives a lurch.

Eat? After that hot dog? says the voice in my head. *You can't let them feed you after all that alcohol! Do you have any idea how many calories you packed on last night?*

"I'm not that hungry," I say. "You know how you feel the morning after partying. . . ."

"It's three o'clock in the afternoon," Mom says.

So I let them take me to Olive Garden, and I introduce them to the soup-and-breadsticks deal. Then the meal becomes a kind of game. For every breadstick they eat, I take one, too, so that I am never without a breadstick in my hand. But I eat only a bite or two and stuff the rest into my napkin. Breadsticks smash down into a wonderfully small space.

We have a great time at Olive Garden. Mom and Dad laugh over my funny stories about life as a freshman. Because I tell them so much, they probably think I tell them everything. But I don't tell them everything—for their sake.

"Your sister just got a promotion," Mom says out of the blue. "She's in charge of the Polo section now."

"My sister's a pothead dropout," I say, "who parties with her pothead friends and barely works at all, and she's stuck in a dead-end job for minimum wage."

Mom gives me a look.

"She isn't," Mom says. "She found a perfectly respectable job, and she's been working since February. Even before this, she wasn't making minimum wage, and the promotion comes with a dollar-an-hour raise."

"It's still dead-end."

"It's a place to start. Your sister's not the loser you want to think she is. She and Clint have been together now for a year and a half, and they seem very happy. I like him. He's smart, and he's a hard worker."

Dad is studying the tabletop menu card like it's written in a code he has to crack. Anger swells inside me. Why is Mom stressing us out like this?

She made you sick, says the voice in my head. *Your mother made you sick!*

"I don't want to hear about Valerie, okay?" I tell her. "I know you get along great with her now—it sounds like you're on the phone every day. Fine, but I don't have to hear about it. New topic. What about dessert?"

As usual, Mom won't let it go, not even if it means I'll be eating. *See how much she cares about your health!*

"I've told you that it's up to you if you don't want to talk to your sister," she says. "But I'll tell you the same thing I told her. I refuse to censor my conversation for anybody. I'm going to go right on talking about the people I love, and that means I'll talk about Valerie to you and you to Valerie."

Valerie doesn't want to hear about me? What reason does she have not to hear about me? What right does *she* have to be angry?

"Anyway, we've invited Valerie and Clint out around Thanksgiving," Mom says. "If you don't want to see them, you'll need to make other plans."

Dad pays, and we leave in silence.

When I get home, I go over to Meghan's dorm, and together we clean the apartment. It takes hours. Then I trudge back to my building, smelling like the inside of a Febreze bottle.

Sandra is back from her study group. We make coffee, and I tell her about my night.

"I can't believe you almost got raped!" she says.

"That's not the crazy thing," I say. "The crazy thing is: why am I not dead? I can't *believe* I'm not dead after last night!"

"You would have been one of those headlines," Sandra says. "Another college statistic."

"Seriously, I'm learning from this," I say. "That will never happen again."

"I'll help," Sandra says. "We'll look after each other. We'll make sure we've got a safe ride, and we'll keep track of each other at parties.

And we'll keep an eye on each other's drinks, too." She pauses for thought. "I can't believe that asshole tried to rape you in the bathroom!"

"Yeah," I say. "And guys wonder why girls always go to the bathroom together."

Sandra digs a brick-sized history textbook out of her backpack to get a head start on next week's reading. Time to start on my own homework. Or maybe lie down for a while.

I change clothes to get away from the strawberry odor of the carpet cleaner, but it seems to be embedded in my skin. The smell gets into my nose and makes me queasy. God, my head hurts! I feel horrible.

There's no room in this life for anybody but winners, says the voice in my head. *You're weak. You aren't a winner.*

I think about how my weakness that morning almost led to disaster. If I hadn't snapped out of it . . . If they'd called in a psychiatrist . . .

You won't have a senior year with your friends!

So I stay strong.

First, I change the sheets on my bed and straighten the bedspread and plump all the pillows. Then I dust and tidy up my desk and bookshelves. I pull out my journal and flip it open to write a new entry. But what will I write? What can I say about last night?

The last entry catches my eye:

I don't know what I am doing, and I keep seeing myself and screaming, Please don't let me have kids so they won't have to go through stuff like this

Please

please

please.

What am I going to become? I honestly don't know. I
am in a very deep dark bad place with no way out.

I stare at it in bafflement. I wrote that? When?

Forget it anyway! I flip back to what I wrote in my journal the
first day I got to college:

No junk food.

Exercise every day.

Study hard.

Work hard.

BE hard.

No tears.

No meat.

No eating after 9 pm.

Get up at 6 every day.

Bed before 1 am.

800 calorie max on weekdays.

Weight day is Friday.

Days will be planned, and that plan will be followed.

Tidied room. No slacking. No laziness.

I will not be a failure!

A smile crosses my face. That's the Elena I recognize.

You didn't exercise today, says the voice in my head. *You stupid bitch.*

Strawberry scent wafts by me and carries with it a faint vomit smell. My stomach flops, and the room whirls.

Stupid bitch!

But I shudder and grit my teeth, and the room steadies again. I pull out my day planner and start to fill it in.

Every hour needs an activity. Every activity keeps me strong. Every hour I am forcing myself to do things that don't come easy is an hour when I am building perfection.

No slacking. No laziness. There is no room in my life for failure.

I work on the planner until the page is a thing of beauty. My tomorrow is full of work and study, full of firm, decisive action. But here, in the morning—here's a gap. Gaps aren't acceptable.

I tip my chair back and call to Sandra through the open door, "Do you want to go to the zoo tomorrow morning? You're supposed to do that primate study, remember?"

"Sounds great!" Sandra yells back.

I write *ZOO* in the gap and draw a heart next to it. Then I close the planner with a satisfied sigh.

Tomorrow, I will be Wonder Woman. Tomorrow, I will be alert and in control. I will accomplish everything I set out to do. I will be perfect.

I will even meet my sister next month when she comes out to visit, because that's how strong I am. Then Valerie will see that I am the successful sister now, the one who is completely in charge of her life.

As I put away the planner, the long slice in the flesh of my forearm twinges and makes me draw in my breath. But the cut's untidy edges are hidden away beneath a neat white gauze wrap, and that's how it's going to stay.

There will be no room for chaos in my life.

11

It's almost ten months later. I'm walking across campus in the steamy
heat of a Texas summer. It's so hot I'm sweating, but the sun feels good
on my back and legs. I'm wearing a tank top with the thinnest straps
possible in the hope that they won't leave tan lines. Tanning is hard
enough for my skin to accomplish without straps to mess things up.

Around me on the short Bermuda-grass lawn are bikini-clad students on towels, letting the full force of the evening sun bronze them
into perfection. But I don't have that kind of time. I'm on my way
from my job at the mall to my job at a gym.

Currently, I'm working three jobs.

Freshman year is over. I came out of it with so many college
credits that I'm officially almost a junior. It was fun, too—or at least
it was fun until spring break, when Sandra fell in love. Then we started
to bicker, and the last night in our dorm, we got into a fight.

She was weak, says the voice in my head. *She let a man into her
life. She let herself depend on somebody else.*

But I won't need a roommate when school starts in a week. I've
been a resident assistant in the dorms all summer now, an RA, and
they've chosen me to be an RA in the fall, too. That means I have a
whole dorm apartment to myself, and it's free. Also, I get a nice sal-
ary. I'm practically paying my way, just like I always wanted to do.

Take *that*, you bastard psychiatrist who tried to convince the world that there was something wrong with me! I'm not just a college student, I'm a super student—the kind they pay to be here. I've learned from my freshman mistakes, and I've made the honor roll twice. I even won a departmental award. I've turned down dozens of dates, and I'm still wearing size 00 jeans.

I've even allowed my sister back into my life. Valerie's still working her retail job, hanging up shirts on racks, but I'm trying to talk her into going back to college. You'd never know it now, but Val was a brilliant student once—she made better grades in the boarding school than I did. It drove me crazy that I worked so hard and she did so little, and she still beat me every time.

But those days are long gone. Valerie's crazy risks and lazy life have buried her opportunities, while my hard work and constant discipline are paying off. I'm the sister who gives the advice now. I'm the one with a future.

The meal-skipping I do these days isn't a disorder because it never lacks order. My control over food is the habit of a winner who refuses to give in to mindless grazing. I no longer skip meals because a black hole nibbles away at my core, making me too upset to eat. I'm over that. I've conquered it. I'm winning.

Sure, I face challenges, but I don't let them slow me down. The pain I feel spreading throughout my body day by day is a disability I've worked hard to overcome. The insomnia I live with is a golden opportunity to get more work done in each twenty-four-hour day. The panic attacks I've started experiencing lately are just another obstacle to test my determination. No pity and no fear. I'm the envy of everyone who knows me.

Life is a combat zone. People who say it isn't have already lost the war.

I pass the last of the slackers working on their tans, run up the concrete steps to my apartment, and unlock the door. The space is still cluttered but cheerful. We received our fall dorm assignments just last week, so I'm not finished moving in. I'm in charge of a floor in one of the freshman dorms, and I can't wait for my students to arrive.

Boxes and piles are everywhere, but Dylan, my betta fish, is already at home in his glass bowl. He unfurls blue fins as he sweeps past a little stone pagoda. My red rug from Germany is on the floor, and my blue sequined cushions decorate the slate-colored couch. This room will be the perfect haven for homesick freshmen when I get through with it.

But right now I'm late for my next job, the night shift at an upscale gym. I grab my uniform and roll it up, then stuff it into a workout bag. I'll change once I clock in.

With a schedule this busy, it's a good thing I'm used to skipping meals.

Fifteen minutes of rush-hour traffic later, I'm walking into the gym. Shining black granite counters face me, and golden cherrywood floors are under my feet. I like working here. I like the fact that this is such an upscale place.

Julian, my boss, is behind the counter. "I'm going to change," I say as I whisk by him. "Oh, and don't let me forget, I need to sign the form about next Saturday being my last night."

"I'll let you forget," Julian says with a laugh. "You know I don't want you to leave."

I hurry down the hall. The gym looks like a Japanese temple owned by Bill Gates. Even our climbing walls are things of beauty. Later tonight, I'll clean the women's locker room with a steam vacuum cleaner, and I'll spend the rest of the time folding hundreds and hundreds of fluffy white towels. It can be hard to stay awake at three in the morning when I'm folding my four hundred and ninety-eighth towel.

There won't be time for more than a quick nap in the morning, though. Tomorrow, RA orientation starts.

"Elena, what a beautiful tattoo!"

I turn. Mr. Morrison is just coming out of the men's locker room in a tweed sport coat, brown wool pants, and Crockett & Jones cordovan shoes. His salt-and-pepper hair is impeccable, and his blue eyes aren't as unhappy as usual.

"Thank you, Mr. Morrison," I say, giving him a smile.

I like Mr. Morrison. He's just as driven as I am. He's at the gym every single evening. Also, I feel bad for him because he's got money and a great career, but his wife isn't just a dumb blond, she's an idiot. She makes his life miserable. At the moment, she's cheating on him with one of the gym staff.

He was a fool to get married, says the voice in my head.

"I didn't know you had a tattoo," Mr. Morrison says. "Most tattoos look like stencils, but that one's real art. What is it? Self portrait?"

"No, it's a mermaid," I say, glancing over my shoulder in its direction. But the tattoo is on my back, so I can't see it.

"Well, good-bye," he says as I pull open the door to the women's locker room, and I give him one last smile.

Poor guy. Poor lonely, driven guy. People who work as hard as he does shouldn't have messed-up lives.

He was weak, says the voice in my head. *He trusted other people too much.*

Black leather couches and a big-screen television grace the outer lounge. It's a joke to call this place a locker room. I hurry past the cherry-wood shelves, now depleted of their stacks of white towels, and drop my uniform next to a tall floral arrangement on the granite counter.

But before I change shirts, I turn my back to the mirror and look at my tattoo.

A beautiful woman looks over her shoulder back at me. Her long, willowy arms cross her bare chest and reach up to arrange her thick black hair. A cloud of red and blue butterflies encircles her.

Self-portrait? Sadly, no.

The beautiful woman could be a mermaid. Her portrait stops at the arms; the rest of her body isn't pictured. And I do love mermaids. I have truly elegant mermaid art all over my room.

Mermaids matter deeply to me. I don't know why, but they do.

Years ago, I made up a story about a girl and a mermaid. The girl lived in the air, of course, and the mermaid lived in the water. They could come face to face, like faces in a mirror, but they could never touch. When they first saw each other, the girl thought the mermaid was her face in the water, until the face swam away.

But the tattooed face staring at me right now isn't a mermaid. It's anorexia nervosa. It's the face that I can never touch.

Only once, I thought I saw her, back when I still went to the boarding school. I was home on break, and I hadn't eaten in days; I was terribly weak and tormented with hunger—I still felt those things then. I woke up and rolled over, and beside my bed stood the most slender, beautiful woman I could imagine. One by one, she put on the rings I had left on my bedside table. Then she held her hands out with the fingers pointing down, and the rings slid right back off.

That was how thin she was: even a little girl's rings slid off her fingers. She was hopelessly, magically thin. And before she vanished, she laughed at me—the most heartless, scornful laugh I have ever heard.

But that's not why anorexia is staring at me in the mirror now. She's here because of an appointment I went to a couple of months ago.

After my trip to the ER the morning after Halloween, the university made me meet with a counselor on staff. That counselor asked me to see an eating disorder specialist—just to make sure I was one hundred percent better. I kept putting it off, but the counselor kept calling, so finally, at the beginning of summer, I gave in and drove to Sandalwood, the eating disorder treatment center across town.

Right away, I didn't care for the place. It was crammed into a series of ragtag offices in a rambling old building. Just finding it was like walking through a maze. I sat in the narrow little waiting room and thought back with something like fondness on Drew Center's solid New England doors.

Drew Center had been horrible and barbaric. But at least they treated an eating disorder with respect.

The secretary led me farther into the maze, to the office of Dr. Leben, Sandalwood's codirector. Dr. Leben had slightly untidy light brown hair, wire-rimmed glasses, a mildly crumpled blouse, and a suit skirt that wouldn't quite behave. In spite of her business attire, there was an indefinable air of hippie Earth Mother about her. But Dr. Leben's voice appealed to me. It was a voice that knew its own mind. It seemed designed by nature to command soldiers or—an even harder feat—a roomful of three-year-olds.

The first thing Dr. Leben did was run me through the same questionnaire Dr. Harris had used on me.

"How often do you think about food?"

"All the time."

"How would you characterize your relationship with food?"

"It's a necessary evil and a waste of time."

Dr. Leben paused to give me a glance over her glasses. She said, "For many people, eating is a joyful experience."

That's when I knew my instinct about the Earth Mother thing was correct.

After the questionnaire, Dr. Leben said, "Well. It's clear that you have anorexia nervosa."

The speed with which she summed this up surprised me. I was

expecting things to be like Drew Center: another round of "Well, we can't be sure. . . . We'll have to see."

"My parents didn't make me sick," I told her. "If I have anorexia, it's not their fault." But in my mind, I could hear my childish voice begging not to go back to boarding school.

"I believe you," Dr. Leben said—again, to my surprise. "We used to think anorexia came from stresses experienced in the family, but now we know that that kind of anorexia shows up early in life. You say yours showed up during your teenage years at the boarding school, so your family life didn't cause it."

But who sent you to that boarding school? said the voice in my head.

I told Dr. Leben everything was fine. I told her I knew how to manage my life.

"I'm sure you do," she said.

I told her about my high grades, my many achievements, and the fact that I was one of a handpicked group of students chosen to be a dorm RA for the summer. "I currently work three jobs," I said.

"I'm sure you do."

"Sometimes I do get a little stressed out," I admitted. In fact, I had recently asked our family doctor for medication to help with my panic attacks, but I didn't see any reason to mention this. "I would be willing to see a therapist," I added, "and maybe come to group sessions once in a while."

"That's not going to help," Dr. Leben said. "I'll need to refer you to a residential treatment center. As severe as your case is, you need twenty-four-hour care for several weeks at least. We're not an inpatient facility."

You'll spend six months in a hospital, said the voice in my head, *with a tube up your nose to feed you!*

I arranged an amused expression on my face and adjusted my voice before I spoke. "I really don't have that kind of time," I said sweetly.

"I know you don't," said Dr. Leben. "Ambition and perfectionism go hand in hand with the anorexic mindset. But you need to put your health first. Anorexia won't go away by itself. Starvation studies have shown that the effects of anorexia lead to its self-perpetuation, and those effects continue for months after you've reached your ideal weight. Until you regain the weight, therapy won't help."

Regain the WEIGHT? said the voice in my head. *What does she mean, regain the WEIGHT?*

And that was where our meeting ended.

I didn't go to therapy, and I didn't drop everything to run off and gain a bunch of weight. But I realized that Dr. Leben and I agreed about one thing: I do share my life with anorexia. So I went out and researched tattoo artists until I found one who produced real art. I saved my money, and I had him create my tattoo.

That beautiful, hostile face isn't where I can see her. I don't need to see her. I know every single minute of every single day that she's there. Anorexia is a part of who I am. She's how I deal with the world around me.

And if you don't get to work, you're going to get fired!

Once I'm in my uniform, I head to the front desk, where the staff who will be running the place for the night are gathering to start our shift. Ray has brought in a meal from the nearby burger place, and Julian is giving him a hard time about it.

"I can't believe you're going to eat that shit," Julian says. "It's got like a thousand calories. I thought you were serious about bulking up. You should be drinking that energy mix I sold you."

"It's not that bad for me," says Ray. "Anyway, I like burgers."

"Elena, you tell him," Julian says. "He'll listen to a beautiful girl. Tell him it's got like a thousand calories and it's going to make his face break out."

Beautiful, I think automatically, and I pair that with my number. Then, against my will, I glance in the direction of Ray's meal.

Double-patty burger: three hundred and fifty-four calories, says the voice in my head. *Add the bacon and cheese for two hundred more. Large fries: six hundred and forty calories. Large soft drink: four hundred.*

It all adds up to sixteen hundred calories. But I don't say that, of course. I never count calories out loud. It's one of my rules.

"I'm staying out of it," I tell them with a smile. "You know I don't do math. All you guys ever do is talk about food."

Julian and I work the front desk until two in the morning. Then I steam clean the palatial locker room. After that, we fold towels until it's time to punch out. It's boring work, but at least it's tidy.

At five in the morning, I drive home. Traffic is no longer bumper to bumper.

The two hours' nap I grab before the beginning of RA orientation is just long enough to make me hate waking up, but I'm excited about the day's training sessions. I loved working as an RA over the summer, and I can't wait to help my new group of freshmen hit their stride and find their potential.

Orientation is mandatory, so all of the RAs are there, not just us new ones who worked during the summer. Our managers are going to go over procedures for handling complaints, for setting up dorm mixers and functions, and for calling the police. I've already had to call the police because of an incident when I was the RA on call, and I handled it so well that my manager singled me out for special praise.

It's one of the reasons I was the managers' first choice when the time came to choose RAs for the fall.

First, we go around the room and introduce ourselves.

"I'm Elena Dunkle," I tell the attentive faces, "and I'm a sophomore. This year, I'll be finishing up my prerequisites for nursing school. I hope to be an RN in the Air Force."

Liar! says the voice in my head. *You know that's not going to happen.*

I haven't been to see the Air Force recruiter in months—not since he told me my weight was too low.

"Gain a few pounds," he said carelessly. "Come see me in six weeks."

"No problem," I told him with a smile.

But I knew as I walked out the door that I wouldn't be coming back.

At lunchtime, two of the veteran RAs walk over to say hi. They're going to be responsible for the floors next to mine.

"Girl, you have *such* a figure," one of them says. "How do you do it? No matter what I try, I can't get rid of this big old butt."

God, I love to hear that! It never gets old.

Right before the last session of the day, the managers introduce their new boss. I can tell they're unsure about her. She's never worked on a college campus, she's never held a position dealing with students, and she seems to be some old friend of the Head of Housing. According to the dorm managers, she was having a hard time, and the Head of Housing decided to give her this job.

The new boss is a plain, doughy woman with ragged bangs, a suit that's way too tight, and a sour expression on her face. Either she hates humanity, or she wants us all to know that she won't put up with any shit. That's not a very good attitude to bring onto a college campus. I'm glad she's not *my* boss.

The last session begins. Two psychologists, a man and a woman, have come over from the Counseling Center to guide us through sensitivity training.

"In spite of the strides we've made in the last ten years," the woman tells us, "prejudice against gay and lesbian students is still common. I'd like you to share your own experiences. Has anyone here had a hostile experience due to your sexual orientation?"

No one speaks up, of course. The two gay RAs I know wisely keep silent.

The psychologists go on to discuss the Americans with Disabilities Act and how we should respond to people with special needs. "We all know about the need to provide ramps for wheelchair students," the man says, "but many disabilities are invisible. We all need to be aware that disabled students won't necessarily show up with a wheelchair or a service dog."

"That's right. Think about learning disabilities," the woman chimes in. "Think about psychiatric conditions. Students who make insensitive remarks or jokes may be offending someone nearby who suffers from one of these invisible disabilities."

"What about you RAs?" the man says. "What experiences have you had with a hidden disability? Anyone here with a learning disability? With a psychiatric condition?"

One of the RAs has confessed to me in strictest confidence that he suffers from schizophrenia. I glance his way, but he has no intention of sharing that with his employers and a roomful of strangers.

"Anybody?" the woman prompts. "Can anybody share their experience? Come on—I know this group is more diverse than you're letting on. We can all benefit from your participation."

Nobody.

Still nobody.

Oh, what the hell.

When it comes to speaking up, I'm not shy. Maybe because I had to learn how to argue in a foreign language, I don't have any problem speaking my mind. Maybe because the voice in my head critiques me so sharply, I don't worry about what regular people will think. There's no room in life for that kind of weakness: no pity and no fear. I hold up my hand.

"I have an eating disorder," I tell the attentive faces. "And when I was in the treatment center, I learned that eating disorders come in all shapes and sizes. Sure, there are the skinny chicks like me, but ED patients can be men or even children, and bulimics are often normal weight or overweight rather than thin. So ED patients may be among your students, and they may not look the way you think. That's important to know because when those patients get into a new environment, they can suffer from isolation and depression."

"That's so true," agrees the woman, beaming.

"Thanks for sharing," says the man.

The sensitivity session comes to an end.

That's it for the first day of RA orientation. I pick up my notebook and head to the door.

Some of the RAs are going out to dinner, but I turn them down so I can work on my apartment. In two days, the freshman class will show up. My room needs to be ready for them.

In the boarding school, my room was a haven for homesick girls. I represented them in meetings with the housemothers and the headmistress, and I counseled them on their problems. I even tucked the little girls in at night. It was one of my favorite things about the school.

Now, as I unpack, I daydream about how pleasant it will be to do that again—to champion timid students and watch them gain confidence. Meanwhile, I sort through boxes to find my favorite knickknacks, the ones that have traveled with me from Germany. My Venetian masks can go here on the living room wall. Not in the bedroom—at night, they look too creepy.

My cell phone rings. It's Valerie. Our relationship will never be what it was before, but we've fallen into the habit of talking at least once a day. She and Clint recently got engaged, and I'm going to be her maid of honor—that is, if she stops procrastinating and gets around to planning. So far, all we've worked out is that she wants to be married in black, barefoot, on the beach.

"What up, ho," I say. "I looked at those bridesmaid dresses you liked on the Internet."

"I'm kinda pregnant," she says.

I feel the blood drain out of my face and then come back in a rush.

Your fault that she's getting to you! says the voice in my head. *You were stupid to let her back into your life.*

"It's not that big a deal," Valerie continues. "It's kinda good in some ways. Now I don't have to worry about a big wedding."

"But you haven't finished college! Clint hasn't gotten into the Air Force yet. You can't raise a kid on minimum wage!"

"Hey, I don't make minimum wage!" she says. "And I don't know what you're so upset about. Clint's almost done with the courses they told him to take. He'll get in. We'll handle it."

But I feel myself shaking my head. This is it. This is absolutely it. My bright sister, who charmed her teachers, who mastered German quicker than I did—who grew up, for God's sake, living in Europe, visiting St. Peter's and the Tower of London—has trapped herself in rural Southern poverty.

She'll be a redneck, says the voice in my head. *She'll be a joke! Your sister is going to end up as a mobile-home redneck welfare mom.*

I can see it all: Valerie in her thirties, in a folding chair in front of a trailer, popping open a can of beer as she takes a drag on her cigarette. I can see her son or daughter dropping out of high school to stock shelves at Walmart.

My own niece or nephew!

This is what happens when you let go of perfection, says the voice in my head. *You shouldn't have let her back into your life.*

I get off the phone and try to continue straightening my apartment, but the work doesn't interest me anymore. My head hurts. A stack of books falls over on the counter, and Dylan swirls around his bowl with extra force.

Fish can't pick up on a bad mood, can they?

The next time my cell phone rings, it's my RA manager. "Elena," he says, "could you meet us at the Counseling Center at seven tomorrow morning?"

"Sure," I say. "Is this about Dean? Is he okay?" Dean is an RA who's been having suicidal thoughts.

"Yeah, that's it," says my manager. "You guessed it. It's about Dean. It'll really help us if you can be there."

"Anything I can do to help, you know that. I'll see you there at seven."

The next morning, Day Two of orientation. I didn't get much sleep last night, so I put on my powder and eye shadow with extra care. Valerie's life may be a mess, but I'm different. I'm a successful student and employee, always ready to do that extra bit that distinguishes great from good. Like now—the other RAs are still asleep, but I come rattling down the concrete steps of my dorm building to meet my manager at the Counseling Center.

But here's a surprise: my manager is downstairs, waiting for me. With him is the angry set of bangs, his new boss. She glares at me like she thinks I might try to steal the coffee mug she's holding. And I'm sleepy enough, I just might.

Together the three of us walk to the Counseling Center. They flank me, one on each side. I try to get a conversation going, but neither of them seems to want to talk.

Once we get there, the managers' boss turns to me. "We've arranged for a counseling session for you," she says.

This is a little strange, but it's probably all for the best—anything to keep Dean from feeling singled out. I'm more than happy to help a student get the care he needs.

When I come out of my session, I'm surprised to find my manager and his boss still there. Surely they have more important things to do on a busy day like today than hang around here waiting for me. And the new boss is eyeing me in a very odd way. She smooths her tight skirt.

"Elena," she says abruptly, "we want you to take the day off."

What happened? What did you screw up? says the voice in my head.

"You've been under a lot of stress," she continues as I pause, stunned. "Take a nap. Go see a movie."

"Is this a joke?" I say, settling my expression and finding my smile. "Seriously, I feel great. And orientation is mandatory."

"This isn't negotiable, Elena," she replies.

What the hell? What did you do? shrieks the voice in my head. *You stupid bitch, what the hell did you screw up?*

I walk back to my dorm apartment in a towering rage.

You've got an empty day planner, fumes the voice in my head.

My hands start to shake with anger and nerves. The shakes turn into shivers that slide up and down my spine. I hate this! My busy day is ruined.

You've got an empty day planner, repeats the voice in my head. *Your life is out of control!*

There is nothing—nothing!—worse than an empty planner.

I try to sleep my way through the empty hours, but my dreams are terrible. By noon, I really do feel sick. My aching body feels like it's coming apart.

At three o'clock, my cell phone rings. I lie there staring at the ceiling and listen to it. I don't bother to pick up.

Five minutes later, there's a knock on my door. It's my manager and the manager of one of the other dorms.

"Hi, Elena," the other manager says, looking embarrassed. But my manager's face is a blank mask.

"You didn't answer your phone," he says.

"I'm off today, you know that," I say. "You were there. You heard your boss tell me to take the day off."

"We were worried," continues my manager, "when you didn't answer the phone."

"You were *worried*? What do you mean, you were *worried*? I was asleep! I'm not on call today. I'm not required to answer my phone."

He doesn't respond to that, but the other manager who's with him looks even more embarrassed. I hate that they're seeing me like this—smudged makeup, old clothes. I'll bet I have blanket lines on my face.

"You know as well as I do," I say, "that your boss *told* me to get some sleep. So, if you don't mind, now that you're not worried anymore, I'm going to go do what I was told."

It takes the last of my self-control not to slam the door in their faces.

Ten minutes later, just as I'm drifting off again, there's pounding on my door.

"Welfare check! Open up, or we unlock it!"

What the *hell*? Welfare checks are only performed when a student's life or health is in danger! They must have the wrong apartment number. But the rest of this building is empty!

When I open the door, the campus police are just as confused as I am. "We were told an Elena Dunkle was in crisis," one of them says.

"I'm Elena Dunkle," I snap. "No crisis here."

The other officer walks past me and checks the whole apartment, as if he thinks there might be another Elena Dunkle hiding back in the bedroom who desperately needs his help.

"Well, okay," he tells me as he leaves. "If you *do* need our help, give us a call."

Now I'm far too angry to go back to sleep. But the anger gives me a sense of purpose again, so I channel that energy into work. I sort through stuff in boxes. I fold T-shirts and put them into drawers. I hang up skirts and tops.

By the time I take a break, the sunset is turning the sky golden outside my apartment windows. I'm feeling weak and sick. I haven't eaten all day—not even my granola bar and cup of green tea.

You can't go to the cafeteria, says the voice in my head. *The other RAs are talking about you behind your back. They'll ask you why you weren't at orientation.*

But the only food I have in the apartment is a bag of pixie straws I bought to give to my new freshmen, who arrive tomorrow.

Pixie straws are pure sugar, says the voice in my head. *You're not going to eat pure sugar, are you?*

The sun goes down. Darkness closes in. Because my body is used to nights at the gym and days at the mall, it isn't sure what time it is. My brain has that gummy, gluey feeling that comes from being at loose ends.

An empty planner does to the mind what a day without a shower does to the body.

In a kind of daze, I walk around, unpacking things. But the chaos in my apartment doesn't seem to get any better.

Finally, after midnight, I lie down on my bed and fall asleep in my clothes.

A rustling noise wakes me. I light up my phone: four o'clock in the morning. Then I slip it under the sheet and hold my breath.

Somebody is in my apartment!

I can hear footsteps trail across the packing clutter: the crackle and crunch of paper. Then the pop of a foot crushing a shoe box lid.

I can't move. I don't dare to move. And I'm lying with my back to the door!

Step by quiet step, the intruder creeps into my bedroom. I silently will it to be a thief and nothing more. Mentally, I offer up my laptop lying open on the desk, but the footsteps come toward the bed.

A form leans over me, pressing its weight into the small of my back. Out of the corner of my eye, I see a woman's face.

She raises her hand. There's the faint flicker of light off a knife blade.

Oh, my God! She's going to *kill* me!

The next instant—nothing.

My back can still feel where she leaned against me, but the woman with the knife is gone. I flee the room, sobbing, and huddle outside on the concrete steps.

What *was* that? Was that a dream? Can dreams be so *real*?

After half an hour on the steps, I gain the nerve to creep back inside. I flick the switch by the door, and fluorescent light stabs on and pins all my possessions into place. I look around the apartment. Nothing seems right. The colors are harshly, artificially bright. On the floor by my bed, the fallen blanket has stiffened into unnatural folds. Even my ragged old cow seems to glare at me.

"Hey, Dylan," I say, kneeling down by the round fishbowl and putting a finger against the glass. But the blue fish lies motionless on the gravel by the stone pagoda. His fins and tail droop sullenly.

It's not late, it's early. I can get a jump-start on my day. As I shower, I push the curtain aside every few seconds to make sure no one is there. I apply my makeup with trembling fingers.

Day Three of orientation. I feel like hell. My day of rest has left me jumpy, chaotic, bedeviled, and miserable. But thanks to my nightmare, I have an hour before sessions start to work again on my apartment, and this time, I'm finally making headway. I stick my motivational posters up on the wall and hang my ballerina Christmas ornaments from the corkboard.

At seven-thirty, my cell phone rings. It's my RA manager.

"Elena, do you have a minute?" he asks.

Of course I have a minute! I put extra warmth into my voice just to show that there are no hard feelings. I check my makeup and hurry down to the RA offices, glad to be busy and useful at last.

That's when my manager leads me into the new boss's office.

And the new boss fires me!

"Why?" I ask. It's the only question I can think of. Even the voice in my head is silent.

The new boss looks as sour and suspicious as if she thinks I'm trying to catch her in some kind of trap.

"We aren't required by law to give a reason," she says.

"I've known RAs who got caught with alcohol in their rooms," I say. "And even they didn't end up getting fired."

She glares at me as if I'm firing her and not the other way around.

"I said I'm not giving you a reason!"

My next stop is the office of the Head of Housing, where I appeal the firing. "At least tell me why," I say.

"Elena, you've been under a lot of stress," he tells me kindly. "We don't think this job is good for you."

You've never spoken to this man, have you? says the voice in my head. *Who's been talking about you? What has he heard?*

I say, "So you want to help my stress level by yanking my funding a week before the new semester?"

The Head of Housing steeples his fingers and puts on his gravest, most fatherly expression.

"An RA is supposed to be a role model to these incoming first-year students," he says. "That's an unwritten contract I have with their parents. And, in good conscience, Elena, I cannot say that you are such a role model."

"I have a completely clean record during my time in student housing," I say. "I have a GPA that put me on the honor roll twice. I earned a departmental award. I was asked to serve on the university's welcoming committee. I've never even gotten a speeding ticket. I've logged almost two hundred hours of volunteer time helping wounded soldiers in a hospital setting. *And you don't think I'm a good role model?*"

He doesn't answer. And that's good. He damn well better not!

But he doesn't need to answer. I already know what this is. It's a setup. The Counseling Center meeting, the made-up call to the police—they were building a mental case against me. Because the last thing I did before all this started was announce in public that I have an eating disorder.

It's a beautiful morning. There isn't a cloud in the sky. But as I walk back out into the sunshine, I can find no consolation. None at all.

Today, the new freshmen are arriving. My RA friends have their hands full. All around me, excited young people and happy parents are calling to one another across stair rails and asking one another for help. They are lugging boxes up to their new rooms and pulling brand-new comforter sets out of bags.

All over campus, new adventures are beginning. And they're going to happen without me.

You've been robbed, says the voice in my head. *You let your guard down. You screwed up. You've been robbed.*

Next to the concrete stairs of my dorm, a girl wearing skinny jeans and a lost expression on her face asks me the way to the student traffic office. I stop, and between us, we mark up her copy of the campus map.

"This place is so big," she says. "I'm never going to learn my way around."

"No, you'll do great," I assure her. "You're already getting it figured out."

She brightens up and walks away with her head a little higher, and I realize: that girl is one of my freshmen.

You've been robbed, says the voice in my head. *They stole her from you.*

I trudge up the steps, unlock my door, and push it open.

Not your door. Not anymore.

My room looks great now: cheerful red carpet on the floor by the coffee table, colorful posters, sequined blue pillows on the couch.

Not your room. Not anymore.

I drop my keys on the kitchen counter. Where to start?

My fish isn't sulking and sleepy anymore. Blue fins unfurled, he floats majestically through his bowl. I dip my finger in the water, and he deigns to nibble it.

"We have to leave, Dylan," I tell him. "We've got till noon tomorrow to be out of here. I think I've got a Starbucks cup for you in the bathroom."

You're a loser, says the voice in my head as I drag clothes back out of the closet.

You're a loser, says the voice in my head as I pack up the car.

Only losers live with their parents, says the voice in my head as I walk through the rooms one last time. *Your hard work didn't mean anything. Everything you ever work for will be lost.*

Dylan doesn't like his Starbucks cup. He thumps at the sides while I empty out his bowl.

"Time to go," I tell him.

But before I go outside, I check my makeup. I brush my hair. And as I walk to the car with my fish in a paper cup, I make sure to hold my head up and smile.

They've robbed me. But they can't make me cry.

12

It's November, just three months since I was at the top of my game.

I'm not at the top of anything anymore.

Slowly, still tangled in shreds of dreams, I become aware of my surroundings. Pain has brought me back: dull, throbbing aches where my vertebrae are and sharp stabs of soreness from the cartilage of my ribs. My skull is a tight helmet, clamping my swollen brain. My eyeballs ache in their tender sockets.

I sit up. An orderly bedroom assembles itself around me. But all the sophistication in the world can't cover up the fact that this is the same room where my sister, the dogs, and I slept in bunk beds when I was ten.

The dogs are dead. Valerie is married—no beach wedding, no maid of honor. And I'm still here: the one who tried to make her way out into the world and failed.

You're a loser, says the voice in my head. *They robbed you. You let them win.*

Aspirin. I need aspirin. I need nonsteroidal anti-inflammatory drugs.

I stumble into the bathroom to hunt for the Excedrin, and Dylan greets me with a swish of his long tail. Like a tiny blue dragon in flight, he floats across a big rectangular aquarium though a forest of silk plants that Mom bought him.

Dylan is more Mom's fish than mine now. She spends her spare time teaching him tricks.

The bathroom is 1970s kitsch: glittery Formica and pitted chrome. Dark wood paneling lines the walls, stained by decades of spills and splashes. Not even Dylan's graceful beauty can improve the place.

I wander back to my bedroom and throw myself onto the bed with a sigh. Come back, dreams. Come hide me away.

My phone dings. Somebody messaged me. I don't care.

My phone dings again. Another new message. They crowd in day and night. Why can't people just leave me alone?

But I grope for the phone out of habit.

lanie can u drive me to work? car wont start, love chris

I yawn. Maybe I can, if I still have enough time before my . . .
NO!

Mom is sitting in the living room, typing her new manuscript into her laptop. I hold the phone out at her accusingly.

"My alarm didn't go off!" I shout.

Mom raises an eyebrow. "It went off."

"You heard it? I can't believe this! Why didn't you wake me up?"

"I tried. First you told me that you didn't have to go to class today. Then you told me to go to hell."

"You shouldn't have listened to me!" I insist. "You should have made me get up! My physiology exam starts in forty-five minutes. You know how important this class is!"

Mom just looks at me—a long, steady look. My skull feels like it's cracking at the temples.

The voice in my head is chanting: *Loser! Loser! Loser!*

"I'll never find a parking place in time!" I say. "She'll shut the door. I'll fail the test! Will you take me to school?"

"Will you eat breakfast?" Mom counters.

Anger flashes through me. It is so like Mom to drag food into this! "You know there's no time for breakfast!" I say.

Without a word, Mom goes back to her manuscript.

Once upon a time, Mom's books meant the world to me, back when I was a homesick little girl in boarding school. Mom's stories would arrive from home a chapter at a time and whisk me away to another land. As I read them, I could hear her voice in my ear, saying the words to me. They weren't books yet, but they were more than books. They were Mom on paper.

Now Mom's books are a barricade she hides behind to keep away from me.

She loves her books more than she loves you, says the voice in my head. *You and Valerie let her down. Her books are her favorite children.*

"Okay, look," I say. "If you'll drive me, we can take five minutes to run by Starbucks. I'll grab a caramel macchiato. Those things have protein and about a thousand calories."

Two hundred and seventy calories if you get the whole milk, says the voice in my head. *You're not actually going to drink whole milk, are you?*

But Mom is setting aside her computer and looking for her shoes. I hurry back to my bedroom (Valerie's and my bedroom) and throw on my jeans and a T-shirt.

No time for makeup. I'll do it in the car.

On the way to campus, I keep up a steady stream of talk to deflect my attention from the rich, buttery toffee aroma escaping from my takeaway cup. Normally, I would sip noisily at it, but today I don't trust myself.

Besides, Mom's driving. She won't notice whether I'm drinking or not. Except that she does. As she pulls to the curb, she reaches over and hefts my cup.

"It's full," she says in annoyance. "Those things aren't cheap, you know."

"I'm taking it to class," I say. "You know I don't like to drink things when they're hot. You might at least wish me luck on my exam. I was up till three studying for it."

"Good luck," she says in a softened tone as I slide out.

"Love you," I say.

"Love you, too."

Mom drives away, and I toss the Starbucks cup into the first trash can I see.

Other students breeze by me as I toil across campus. Has my backpack always weighed this much? Why isn't the Excedrin kicking in? Did I take it? Or did I just look for it?

I drop into my seat only seconds before the teaching assistant starts handing out the exams. I hate that! It messes up my whole pre-exam routine. I turn over the paper and stare at it for a few crazy seconds. What unit is this? Did I study the right notes?

Slowly, answers begin to dislodge themselves from the mud between my ears. Yes, I know this one. Or do I?

You're getting them all wrong! says the voice in my head.

God, I'm so tired! Why do I have to do this? Why can't I just sleep?

Because you're a loser, says the voice in my head.

After we've turned in our exams, the professor pulls out her lecture notes and starts in on the new unit. I didn't get to the reading last night. The chalk figures she draws might just as well be hieroglyphs.

As I stare at the professor, a bright halo creeps up around her. Then she turns into a dark silhouette.

There's a noise like the ocean in my ears.

NO!

This is *not* a fainting spell! I am *not* going to faint! I'm sleepy, that's all. I'm falling asleep. Under my desk, I twist one hand with the other until a sharp current of pain sizzles up my arm. The halo disappears, and for a minute or two, the professor almost makes sense.

The other students stand up. I blink in confusion. Then I realize: you moron, it's the end of class.

You moron, whispers the voice in my head. *You moron-moron-moron!*

I am walking away before I realize that the student next to me is talking. I turn around and look back.

"Sorry," I say. "What?"

He is flustered now. Broad shoulders, nice eyes. Has he always sat next to me?

"I was just asking—I mean, I wondered—"

The haze clears, and I know what he was just asking. He doesn't need to tell me what he wondered.

Maybe he thinks I'm beautiful. What number am I? What number made me beautiful?

You don't know because you didn't check this morning, says the voice in my head. *You've gotten fat since yesterday.*

The student is continuing to talk. I give him a closer look. He has nice hands. I like that.

What about putting him on my list? What about adding him to my collection—the collection of men who think I'm beautiful?

But no. He sits next to me in class. It won't be a simple hook-up. He'll think it's the beginning of something. Next time he sees me, he'll greet me with a smile—that secret smile. And when I freeze him with my blankest, most impersonal stare, he'll follow me like a puppy, asking what's wrong.

This is the kind of guy who will keep calling. He'll want to learn all about me. He'll want to save me. So I turn away from those nice hands, and I say, "Sorry, I'm in a relationship."

With who? the voice in my head wants to know. *You've got nobody, you loser! With who?*

I make the hike to my next class, across dead weeds and packed dirt, up outdoor steps, through a building, down indoor steps. My shoulders ache, my neck stiffens up, and my head pounds until the pain of it makes tears gather in my eyes. It's all I can do not to curl up in the hallway and rest my head on my arms.

I must not have taken that Excedrin after all.

I stop in at the student wellness center. "You again," murmurs the gray-haired secretary, giving me the kind of look Mom does. I ignore her and take a sample pack of ibuprofen from the bins by her desk, then tear it open and wash down the pills at the water fountain by the door.

Above the water fountain is a poster of a smiling college boy: SHE SAID NO—I LISTENED.

The poster makes me feel sad and very, very old, as if nothing that happens to me will ever matter again.

My stomach starts burning as I walk away, so I shake a couple of Tums out of the bottle in my purse. Almost out. Better buy more. I can run out of Excedrin, but no way can I afford to run out of Tums.

Ding! Another message. I glance at it.

elani, where are you? i need help! Meghan

I stick the phone back in my pocket. Meghan always needs help.

Another interminable class. Even on the best of days, my brain wasn't made for statistics. I blink at the chalkboard. My gummy eyes splinter the light and make the formulas unreadable.

"Who's willing to lead our study group tomorrow?" asks the teaching assistant at the end of class. "Oh, good, Elena."

Damn! I knew I shouldn't have held up my hand.

Hauling the heavy backpack, I struggle out to the parking lot. Hazy blue sky and dusty metal. It never rains here anymore. Endless rows of small sedans. Here and there, the occasional hatchback.

I scan the lines of inert metal forms, waiting for a tan Hyundai to pop out.

Nothing.

I hit the panic button on my fob.

No answering siren wail.

Fruitlessly, hopelessly, I wander from row to row, holding up my keys and hitting the panic button.

Where did I park? Where did I leave my car?

I am seconds away from crying with frustration when my phone vibrates. I dig it out of my pocket. It's Mom.

"I thought you would have called by now," she says. "Are you ready for me to pick you up?"

And the voice in my head whispers, *Loser! Loser! Loser!*

Mom's white Hyundai rolls up a few minutes later, and I look out the window while she drives me away from campus. It's nice not to have to do anything, and it's pleasantly familiar to be carted around by Mom.

"Can we stop by the tattoo place so I can pick up my sketch?" I ask.

Mom grimaces. "You know I don't like tattoos."

"But this one is Kate. It's your book!"

Mom shakes her head. "You're not a canvas," she says. "You don't need a person from a book on your body to remind you of who you want to be."

"I don't get tattoos to remind myself of anything," I say. "I get tattoos because of who I already am. They're things that come from the inside, not the outside."

Mom says nothing.

"It's just a sketch," I say. "It's on the way home. If I have to go get it, I'll waste gas."

Mom doesn't answer. She stares out over the steering wheel. Her eyes look cold, and she has serious frown lines now.

Mom's gotten so bitchy this year.

"It's not a tattoo yet," I say again. "It's just a piece of paper. Please?"

Mom still doesn't answer, but she takes the turn to the tattoo place.

Tattoos conjure up images of badass bikers, but Andrew, my tattoo artist, is slight, shy, and clean-shaven. His work is colorful but delicate. And when he shows me the new sketch, it's perfect.

At the house, I pull out the sketch and try to explain it to Mom. "See, here's Kate, from the book cover," I say, "alone in the forest at night, and she knows she's being watched."

Mom is cautious but not warm.

"A forest?" she says. "There are no trees here."

"Maybe later we'll add the trees," I say. "Anyway, you can tell by her face where she is."

"Is that the goblin wedding dress?"

"Yeah, I read Andrew the description. When I used to read the book in boarding school, I always wanted a dress like that."

"Hmm," says Mom. And I suddenly wonder: did she write that dress into the book because she wanted one, too?

"But her hair," I say, "floating out in this cloud, that's from Tori Amos, you know—the singer. I showed Andrew a painting of Tori. It's very famous."

I go get my laptop and pull up the painting of a beautiful woman with red hair. The hair floats out in long strands around her body like a protective charm.

"Tori Amos survived rape," I say. "A lot of artists have painted her. Well, she didn't just survive it. She's very strong. . . ."

Mom looks at the picture. She doesn't ask. But even if she did, I wouldn't tell her.

"It's your book," I say again, struggling to explain, but nothing that comes out of my mouth today makes sense. *We don't have a connection now,* I want to tell her. *What's between us now is broken. But back here, back in the past, we still connect.*

Mom shakes her head.

"It's a beautiful sketch," she says. "Put that on your wall. But not on your body." And she opens her laptop again.

My phone buzzes as I walk off to my room (mine and Valerie's room). It's Valerie. "Hey, slut puppy!" she says briskly. "I can't bend over anymore. It's hell putting on my shoes."

Valerie is in her middle trimester. Everything is going swimmingly. She and Clint are happy, and they're both still working to save up money. In the evenings, she helps him study for the college classes the Air Force told him to take.

As she and I talk, I thumbtack the sketch up over my desk, and I try to explain the new tattoo to her. Valerie loves tattoos, but today, she talks over me. The experience of pregnancy is all she can think about.

"I'm getting huge," she tells me. "It's like I've been taken over. I swear, aliens have invaded my body."

Invaded. Huge. My stomach lurches, and I hear myself say, "I can't talk right now."

"Suit yourself," she replies with an edge to her voice. "I was just calling to say hey. If you're too busy with your university buddies, then you shouldn't answer the phone."

She hangs up.

It's two o'clock in the afternoon. I want so badly to lie down and sleep that I force myself not to do it.

You're losing it, says the voice in my head. *You didn't fill in your planner last night. Where's your perfectly planned day?*

So I pull out my planner and my statistics book and write down the problems that got assigned. I need to get started on them if I'm going to lead that study group tomorrow.

The numbers waver and wander around on the page. I blink at them until they make sense. Control, that's the answer. I can't let them get the better of me. I can't let them make me cry.

My phone buzzes. Then the voice mail icon lights up. Somebody left me a voice mail. I'll check it later.

The phone buzzes again, loudly, right in my ear. I jerk away and almost roll off the bed.

The bed? I've been asleep? How did that happen? When did I lie down?

What's going on? says the voice in my head. *What did you screw up?*

"Hello?" I say into the phone. My voice is rough from sleep.

"Elena!" cries a voice. It's Meghan.

"Jesus, Elena, why didn't you call me back?" she says. "I really need your help! If I don't have this paper finished by tonight's class, it'll be the end. I'll fail, and Dad won't pay for next semester, and I'll be a dropout, and I'll end up eating garbage out of cans. I'm not kidding, Elena. You've got to help me!"

"I'm studying," I mumble into the pillow. The pillow feels so good.

"Elena!" wails Meghan. "I can't do this! I'm not like you!"

So I lever myself out of the pillow and drive to Meghan's apartment, and I sit on the floor of her living room and write her five-paragraph essay while she chatters to me and chatters to her dog and chatters to friends on her phone.

When I finish, she invites me to go grab a burger with her.

"No, I have to get home and study," I say. "I don't eat fast food."

"You're amazing!" Meghan gushes. "I don't know how you do it. I wish I could be like you!"

Amazing. My brain automatically records that and links it to my number.

You're not amazing, says the voice in my head. *She's just stupider than you are. And you don't know your number. That's yesterday's number. You're fat!*

I get back into my car, but I don't drive home. Instead, I find myself cruising the fast-food places near Meghan's apartment. Visions of menu items hang in the air before my eyes. Light, fluffy, crunchy fried chicken skin, golden grease, tender, tear-apart meat. Bean-and-cheese burritos as soft and comforting as the pillow I left at home. Crunchy tacos with warm sour cream and spicy ground beef dripping into their paper wrappers.

I hear myself sigh aloud, and my mouth fills with saliva.

You're like Pavlov's dog! growls the voice in my head.

But I can't help myself. I can see the food so clearly, I don't know how I'm not crashing the car. Crusty pizzas cradling gooey melted cheese. Crisp hot French fries dabbed in ketchup. Frosty chocolate milk shakes so thick they have to be eaten with a spoon.

"Welcome to Burger King. May I take your order?" screeches a voice in my ear.

I snap out of my daydream with a start. What am I doing in the drive-through lane? I need to get out—out—out—

"I'll take a double Whopper with cheese, and chicken tenders with ranch dipping sauce, and a large Coke, no ice—no, make that a double Whopper meal, large fries, and—wait, how many tenders? Two or three? Three. And I need—I need—a large vanilla shake."

Is that my voice—that high, squeaky voice? The drive-through speaker screeches, and I screech back. My hands are trembling on the steering wheel. My breath is hot and quick. Like magic, a big white bag appears in my lap. The shake is cool and soothing in my hand.

I pull over into a nearby parking spot and tear into the food like an animal.

What the hell? screams the voice in my head. *What the hell?!*

But I keep right on shoving the hot, greasy food into my mouth.

Stop it! STOP IT! Stupid bitch! Stupid fat BITCH!

At first, I ignore it. Then, as the contents of the bag fill my mouth and then my belly, I begin to slow down. I hesitate, and the voice has its chance.

Look at you! it screams. *Look at what you've done! Did you have to lose it over burgers and fries? Thousands of calories! Thousands and thousands!*

That's right. I'll stop eating now. I'll throw away the rest. I back out of my parking spot and toss the bag into the drive-through trash can.

But who am I kidding? I can feel that the bag is empty.

Stupid bitch! Stupid fat bitch! You've lost it, you stupid bitch!

It's true! Oh, shit. Oh, shit! I shouldn't have gone for this type of food. I can't believe I ate this stuff. I never eat this stuff! Oh my God, oh my God, I'll be morbidly obese in no time. I'm so sorry I lost control. Please please please stop this from happening!

You will fix this problem, says the voice in my head. *You will fix it NOW.*

I pull out of the Burger King parking lot, tires squealing, heart pounding, hands shaking. Next door is a Walmart. I speed around to the back, and when I get to the dumpsters, I hit the brake so hard that my body shoots forward against my seat belt. Frantically, I begin digging through the glove box and under the seats, searching for any type of container. All I can find is a single plastic grocery bag.

I spread the bag out on my lap. Then I unfasten my seatbelt, lean forward, and purge my guts out.

Vomit splatters my face. My hands are smelly and slimy. The plastic bag on my lap is a warm, gooshy mess. But I don't stop. I can't stop. I bend over the bag and expel the acidic stew until my throat is on fire.

The fluid runs clear. Then spots of bright blood come up. Only then do I stop.

Breathing in ragged gasps, I stare at the mess in my lap. Tears are trickling down my face and burning my eyes. I wipe them on the back of my hand.

A black streak on my hand. My mascara is running. I must look like a clown. With vomit still on my lips, I roll down my window and toss the squishy bag next to the nearest dumpster.

And that's when I realize I'm not alone.

A young man in a Walmart vest is standing next to the loading dock. A cigarette dangles from his hand. He's been here the whole time. I know he has. He watched the whole thing.

Slowly, painfully, shame burns through me—shame so deep I wish I could die. As I drive away, my hands grip the sticky steering wheel like it's the only thing in the world that can hold me upright.

Back at the house, I turn on the shower and sit curled up under the steaming spray. Surely I'll cry. I want to cry. But the hot water steeps the last little bit of energy out of me, and with it goes my emotion.

What the hell is this? says the voice in my head. *What are you, twelve? Get to work!*

So I change into my workout clothes and go to the gym. I turn up the music and run on the treadmill till everything feels worse and then feels better.

You didn't get rid of it all, says the voice in my head. *You're getting fat right this minute. You can't exercise away those kinds of calories.*

I make myself do another half hour on the treadmill. What happened this afternoon wasn't a breakdown. My willpower is still there.

You're an out-of-control, binge-eating whore.

Panting, I drag myself back into the locker room to change into my street clothes. The women's locker room is empty, so I let myself step onto the scale and read the number.

Is that right? Is that really right?

I read the number again.

That's the best I've ever done!

That's not so great. You could do better, mutters the voice in my head.

For once, I turn to look in the mirror at the white-faced girl on the other side. I don't meet her eyes, but I follow the tracheal rings of each band of cartilage down her long neck to the hollow of her throat. I notice the undulations of ribs above her bra and admire the clean, simple beauty of her collarbones.

They're like wings, those collarbones. They spring out of the flesh like a bird in flight. I run my fingers in wonder over the beautiful, fragile bones.

My body holds a secret—hidden wings.

Dad's asleep by the time I get home. Mom's sitting at the table, typing on her laptop.

"You missed supper," she says.

"I ate fast food," I tell her. Which is true.

I shut the door of my room (mine and Valerie's room) and turn on cartoons to drown out the voice in my head. Then I sit down to do my homework. Study group tomorrow, and I'm the one who offered to lead it. I better get started on those problems.

The numbers waver and wander on the page. My brain wasn't made for statistics.

It isn't until I put the completed assignment into my folder that I find it: the other completed assignment. I pull out the pages and compare them side by side. I can't believe I did the whole thing twice.

And not only that, but I got different answers on five of them.

Loser! whispers the voice in my head.

My phone dings. It's a new message:

Woof! Woof! Booty call! Beer in the fridge, home alone.
Come over!

I blink to clear my blurry vision and study the name below the text. Does he think I'm beautiful? Could he be on my list? Could I add him to my collection?

I close my eyes and concentrate as hard as I have all day. One by one, I tick off the requirements. Cute. Smart. Doesn't know the others. Doesn't go to any of my classes. Won't follow me around, hurt, demanding explanations, when I don't respond to his texts.

And he'll tell me I'm beautiful . . . for an hour. That's all I really want. He'll make me feel powerful because he'll be stupid enough to feel something, and he'll make me feel nothing at all.

Feeling nothing—that will be the best thing I've felt all day.

I close the textbook on my mismatched statistics questions, and I hunt up an outfit to make him drool. The room whirls while I change. The cartoons skip and snicker on the TV screen beside me, and the ghosts of a young, bossy Valerie, a younger me, and two slightly overweight dogs sit together to watch them.

A lump catches my breath. All gone . . . All gone but me.

Where's my purse? I need this now. I'm feeling too much.

I desperately need not to feel.

As I grab my purse and car keys, my bleary eyes register something white and fluttering. I put a hand out to steady it, or to steady me.

That's right, it's my new sketch. It's the girl lost in the forest.

A forest that isn't even there.

13

How did this happen?

How did this happen, and what's going to happen to me?

I sit in the waiting room with Meghan, too shocked and scared to speak. Meghan doesn't speak, either. She holds my hand. The piped-in music is "Rockin' Around the Christmas Tree." Why does Christmas bring out the worst in us?

I turn over details in my mind, trying to piece together what happened. Trying to figure out What Went Wrong.

I met Kevin during my freshman year of college. But he wasn't even a guy I could add to my collection. He wasn't cute or smart. I was so far above him, I was out of his league.

Nobody's out of your league, says the voice in my head.

Meghan pushes around the magazines on the waiting room table, but she doesn't pick any of them up. An article title catches my eye: "When Should I Let My Baby Cry It Out?"

It started four months ago. Kevin was on the other side of the country, and all he wanted was to call me sometimes. He was lonely. I felt sorry for him. I was doing him a favor. We both knew I was out of his league.

There isn't a league for sluts, says the voice in my head.

A tired-looking woman sits across from us in the waiting room. Her pregnant belly is huge.

I knew what it felt like to be homesick, so I told Kevin he could call me if he wanted to. I didn't even have to talk. Kevin did all the talking. All I had to do was hold the phone.

"You're beautiful. You look like a supermodel," he would say.

"You're drunk," I would say. Because he was.

It didn't occur to me that Kevin would come home every now and then—that he would call but this time he wouldn't be that far away. It didn't occur to me that I'd still feel sorry for him and that I'd want to hear him say in person how beautiful I was. I'm not beautiful. I know that. Even without looking in a mirror, I know it. But I know that I'm beautiful to a loser like Kevin. In *his* world—among the hard-drinking, bar-faced women *he* knows—I actually am something special.

You're not special, says the voice in my head. *You just haven't fallen that far—yet.*

"Elena Dunkle!" calls the nurse from the doorway, and we walk in silence down the hall.

She hates you, says the voice in my head. *She'll talk about you behind your back.*

That's okay. I deserve it.

Now I'm flat on my back on the rustling paper of the examining table, thinking about what a mess I've made of my life. The doctor squeezes ice-cold ultrasound jelly onto my concave abdomen. He presses a probe against me and slides it around. After a few seconds, I hear *whump-whump-whump-whump*, very fast and light, like the wings of a hummingbird slowed down.

The doctor points to a hazy little blob of light twitching around the fuzzy monitor screen.

"There it is," he says. "That's your baby."

Such a powerful wave of love pours through me—such an unaccountable, unexpected tsunami of love—that I know right then, well, of course! This is God. This love that I'm feeling is God. All my doubts and fears are swept away in an instant.

My baby! My baby—baby—baby! *(Whump-whump-whump.)* I watch her (I am sure that the shapeless little blip is a her) as she dances her way around the screen. She is almost not there at all, she's so tiny, but she is heroically, astoundingly present, an image of exuberant, boundless life. And me—I am holding that tiny, tiny precious little life safe in the love of both of us, God and me.

But the doctor is frowning at the ultrasound monitor. White *X*s crisscross the screen. And then he says, "We have a problem."

It's the anorexia. The doctor doesn't call it that. He talks about atrophied uterine walls and insufficient hormones. But I've taken the medical classes. I know what he means. I know what he's too kind to say.

"You did this to yourself," his eyes tell me as he talks. So I don't look him in the eye anymore. I stare at the printout he gives me of the shapeless little blip that is my daughter while he tells me she can't possibly survive.

I keep my head down and hear myself answer him in high, clear, expressionless statements. "Yes, I understand. Yes. Thank you."

"Frankly, I'm surprised that it hasn't terminated already," he says.

Terminated. As in, dead.

Kevin comes into town that afternoon. He's so glad to be home and so glad to see me that I don't tell him the bad news yet. Instead, I tell him I'm pregnant.

That's not the bad news. That's the good news. Right?

Maybe it's not Kevin's fault that he looks less than enthusiastic. He didn't get to hear the heartbeat. He didn't see the beautiful dance I saw. I struggle to understand things from his point of view, but that point of view doesn't make sense to me. It isn't like I've asked for his money or his help. He should know me well enough to know that I don't want those things from anybody. I just want to share this knowledge with him—this amazing love.

We sit on the steps of his mom's house, and he frowns at the passing cars as he drinks his beer. He says, "I'm kinda not ready for this right now."

Like it's a thunderstorm or an IRS audit. Like it's something he had nothing to do with. Like it's something I'm doing to him.

I light up a cigarette and poison myself and my little girl with its soothing smoke. After all, it doesn't matter, does it? Because she can't—she isn't going to live.

But Kevin doesn't know that. And he doesn't stop me.

"To tell you the truth—it's a really bad time," he says, and he doesn't look at me.

What's wrong with Kevin today? Doesn't he want to tell me I'm beautiful? Doesn't he know I'm out of his league?

I take his beer from him, tip it up, and drink it down. It doesn't matter. My baby and I are doomed. But Kevin doesn't know that. He watches me drinking my baby to death, and he doesn't do a thing to try to stop me.

"You know," he says, "what I think you should do. What you really need to do—is get an abortion."

Ha, ha, ha! jeers the voice in my head. *You really know how to pick them! You've shared the most amazing event of your life with a selfish, moronic asshole piece of shit!*

And from that second, I hate Kevin almost as much as I hate myself.

I escape Kevin somehow. I don't even know how. I'm too unbalanced to think clearly. The afternoon rolls by like a train I've missed, all noise and crowded impressions and stress. I have a vague idea that

I've been shouting at my parents, but I can't remember why. I just remember how they look: the same shocked, still expression people get on their faces when they see broken bones.

Now I'm by myself, at my computer. The Google search screen feels solid and real—a friend in need. I type in *minimum weeks early birth viable pregnancy* and hold my breath while I wait for the answer.

Twenty-four weeks. Twenty-four weeks—what is that in months? Six months.

It's too long! She'll never make it!

And I huddle in bed, whispering over and over, "Please . . . please . . . please . . ."

But in the middle of the night, the pains begin.

At first, they feel like menstrual cramps. I stumble into the bathroom. But no! I shouldn't be up, should I? I should be lying down as much as possible. Bed rest, right? That stops contractions. That's why hospitals put expectant mothers in bed.

So I lie on my back on the cold vinyl floor, with the sallow fluorescent lights shining into my eyes.

I want you! I want you! Please don't go! Please . . . please . . . please . . .

Images flit through my mind of every baby I've ever held, every gurgle and wail, every scent of powder, every touch of marshmallow-soft skin. Every memory of holding a warm, sleepy, lumpy little bundle in my arms, till my arms ache with longing and I want to scream from desperation:

I want you! I want you! Please don't go!

But minute by minute, the cramps intensify, until they become a grotesque parody of labor. Or maybe birth is always this hideous and cruel—an expulsion, a rejection: *I'm through putting up with you! Now get out into the real world and see how you like it!*

My baby isn't ready for the real world.

Dylan flits about his aquarium in quick, agitated bursts of blue as I gasp and the blood flows bright, bright red. Is she struggling like I am? Is it already over? Has the swift little hummingbird heartbeat stopped?

My guts are emptying out—disgusting, dark, wet, and sloppy. And then, in the middle of the bloody mess, an infinitesimally tiny pale form.

She shines like a pearl, as pure as a bubble of light. I hold her in a cradle of Kleenex: my daughter.

Hands shaking, I lift her to the sink and start the faucet dripping. In danger of death, Father taught us.

"I baptize you in the name of the Father . . ."

My voice sounds like the croak of a frog.

". . . and of the Son . . ."

The tiny form is almost swept away.

". . . and of the Holy Ghost. Amen."

Then tears blind me, and the water and blood and light run together before my eyes.

Miscarriage. I carried her wrong. I carried my baby wrong.

I sit on the bathroom floor and bawl, soundlessly bawl, mouth open, eyes tight shut, rocking myself back and forth. They were right, all of them—those hateful, yelling doctors. They were mean, and they were right.

This isn't a lifestyle. It's suicide. I'm killing myself. And I just killed my baby.

If I could, I'd cry forever, but the tears dry up. I open my eyes, and the sight of the bloody mess in the bathroom fills me with horror, as if I've just walked in on the work of a serial killer.

I can't leave the bathroom like this. But I have to be quiet. Mom has a way of popping out of bed if she hears a noise. I couldn't bear it if she and Dad knew.

So, while my parents sleep, I clean up the bathroom with bleach and paper towels in the kind of silent frenzy that only murderers know. I tiptoe through the quiet house with my plastic bag of waste, thinking about forensics, thinking about clues.

How is what I've done not a crime?

I throw out the trash bag, totter to my room, and crawl, groaning and sore, into bed. Once I'm there, I realize: this is it. This is as far as I go.

I can't imagine a life that will take me out of bed again.

14

I am waking up. No, no, no, don't let me wake up! I curl tightly into myself and try to burrow back under blankets and dreams. Nothing will change now. I will lie here and sleep forever.

I've been lying here for almost three weeks.

The semester started last week, and it started without me. Classes are hurtling by and flinging themselves into yesterday. Homework, pop quizzes, study sessions—I turned off my phone because people kept calling me about them, thinking I would care.

Somewhere in my distant memories, I used to be so busy that I longed for a pause button for my life. To freeze the whole world for an hour, or an afternoon: that was my favorite daydream. To stroll across green grass, admire the butterflies stopped in midair, stroke the soft feathers of birds at the feeder. To maybe lie down and take a nap in the sunshine and know that absolutely nothing needed to get done. No deadlines ticking closer. No obligations crowding in.

But deadlines don't worry me anymore. Neither do aches and pains. Minor problems like that can't begin to touch the agony I'm in. I lie as still as I can to keep the thoughts and memories from finding me, but sick misery clings to me anyway, as close as a second skin.

Mom and Dad keep coming in to check on me. Once, I would have wanted them to fuss over me, and later, I would have wanted them to leave me alone. Now it doesn't matter. They can do whatever they want. They're as powerless to change this as I am.

First, Mom and Dad thought I was hibernating through the rest of my winter vacation, lying in bed and watching cartoons. Now they think I'm sick, so they talk to me about doctors and bring me medicine and chicken noodle soup.

I'm playing along. With what strength I have left, I try to reassure them that the rest I'm getting is healing me. But what I really am is finished, and there's no cure for that. I've collapsed like a pile of bones.

Where does thin become fat? Where does success become failure? Where does a great future become a horrible past full of heartache and regret?

Light flickers faintly against my eyelids, but it can't break in on my isolation. Between the changeable glow of the silent television and the tightly closed shades, day and night look the same in my room. The only way to know day from night would be to look at my phone. And my phone has been off now for a week.

Eyes shut, I lie absolutely motionless. I'll be ready when sleep returns. It's only in sleep now that I can forget and feel nothing.

There's a knock at my door. Mom walks in and hands me her phone, then walks away before I can hand it back to her. Valerie is talking in my ear, crisp, practical, and sardonic, just like she was in the old days. That's the only nice thing about being a failure now: there's a comfort again in listening to my sister's voice. Valerie knew about the pregnancy, so she's the only one who knows about what I lost.

The phone lies next to my head, and Valerie's tiny, tinny voice is filling up the empty airspace with snippets of news. She's learned not to wait for me to talk.

"I'm so ready for these Braxton-Hicks thingies to stop," she says. "I swear, this kid thinks I'm an exercise wheel."

I close my eyes and picture the Facebook photos of her round belly and glowing skin. I think about her happy life now, her gorgeous husband, her ultrasounds of a healthy baby.

Where does success become failure? And where does failure become success? Because there doesn't seem to be anything in between.

I hang up the phone without telling her good-bye.

Sleep comes for a little while, teasing me with fragments of dreams. Then it slinks back out of the room. I long for it immediately. Sleep is the only thing I still want.

I sigh and roll over. Something crunches under my hand. A folded piece of paper.

Dear Elena, I'm so sorry for how you're feeling these days. . . .

It's from Mom.

Food doesn't help us be, she has written. *It helps us do. It enables us to volunteer, to see the world, to accomplish our goals. It gives us the power to change lives. Your future patients need you. Little children who haven't been born yet need you. . . .*

Not anymore, sneers the voice in my head.

Loss overwhelms me, and I burst into tears.

Mom is standing at my door. I prop myself up on one elbow and start to talk. Words pour out of me—not about the pregnancy, but about the not eating and about how it's too late to fight it. I cry and cry, and I talk and talk about what anorexia has done to me and how I'll never be able to change it.

"I wish I'd done what Dr. Leben told me to," I sob. "I wish I'd gone into treatment last year."

"How about now?" says Mom.

Now is too late. The rest of my life will be too late. But Mom starts putting together plans. The semester's just started. I can withdraw. We can get a refund. I'm not working three jobs anymore.

Mom goes into high gear. From my bed, I hear her talking to insurance people and doctors—one call after another. Then she's handing the phone to me, and I'm talking to an intake specialist at Clove House, a residential eating disorder treatment center.

I've never been to Clove House. It's several states away. But I know all the answers to all the questions the person is going to ask.

"How often do you think about food?"

"All the time."

"How often do you let yourself enjoy food?"

"Never."

Now I'm up and dressed, in the car with Mom. She's driving me to get medical tests. Now she's got me by the arm, and she's towing me across campus, and I'm signing myself out of school. She tows me back to the car, and as we drive, she makes lists out loud of things I'll need to take. Now we're in the drugstore, and she's helping me think through makeup and toiletry choices.

Nothing has changed. It's still too late. If it were up to me, I'd still be in bed. But I can tell this is important to Mom, and her determination overwhelms my apathy. Going into treatment is a penance I accept to make up for the damage I've done. It's a way to say "I was wrong and you were right."

I still can't imagine that it will help. I can't picture any kind of life ahead of me, much less a life without anorexia.

I'm part of you, whispers the voice in my head. *I know what you've done. You'll never get rid of me now.*

Mom and I are out all afternoon in the sunlight. We bring home Greek food for dinner, and Dad and Mom talk while I actually nibble a little of the gyro meat. Then I'm pulling outfits off the floor of my closet, and Mom's running loads of wash. I find myself packing and scribbling things onto lists.

Gradually, it starts to come over me again: that old feeling of racing to meet a deadline. My flight's in a day and a half. A lot of things need to get done. My lists keep getting longer—books to order, worn-out clothes to replace. I'll have to take everything I need with me. Who knows how long they'll keep me there?

You'll spend six months in an institution, says the voice in my head, *with a tube up your nose to feed you.*

Well, maybe I do need to spend six months in an institution. Maybe I really do need a tube up my nose.

Dad goes to bed. Then Mom goes to bed. Amazingly enough, I'm the one who's still awake. In the middle of the night, I'm sitting at my computer, sorting through photographs that I want to take with me.

I always need photos, if only to look at them and say, "Back then, I was happy."

Valerie calls. "Hey, slut puppy," she says. "Whatcha doing?"

"What up, ho. I'm printing out photos to take with me, for my bulletin board or whatever."

"It's not like boarding school, duh," she says. "They won't let you have pins. You'd probably try to swallow them or poke your eye out or something."

"We don't eat, duh," I answer. "This isn't a psych ward like you went to." And I don't let myself think about the harsh rules at Drew Center.

Maybe Valerie's right about pins and bulletin boards. But the old routine of packing for boarding school, left over from a simpler time, keeps me from asking myself questions about what I'm doing.

Because—am I really going to a treatment center? Really? Am I really going to go through with this?

They'll pump you full of calories, says the voice in my head. *They'll get you just where they want you.*

"It's two in the morning," I say to Valerie. "What are you doing up?"

"The Braxton-Hicks thingies are keeping me awake," she says. "They're kinda starting to hurt."

Instantly, my nursing instincts come to the fore.

"Braxton-Hicks contractions don't usually cause pain," I say. "How often are you having them?"

"I dunno. Every few minutes."

"Maybe you're in labor."

She yawns. "Like I'd get that lucky. I don't think this kid's *ever* getting born."

"Well, tell me the next time a contraction comes."

We chat while she watches reruns and I work on photos. Contractions interrupt, then interrupt again. They're coming five minutes apart.

"You're in labor!" I say in excitement. "You need to wake up Clint. Five minutes apart—you guys should go to the hospital." And I wish she lived closer so I could go, too. I wish I could be there.

"Nah," says Valerie, still the procrastinator, even while giving birth. "If it's labor, Clint'll need his sleep. They say this stuff takes forever. I'm going to go back to bed, too."

In the morning, she wakes me up to say that the contractions are strong and four minutes apart now. Yes, they're going to the hospital, but not right away. First, she wants to take a shower.

"It's what the doc would want me to do," she says. "Trust me."

While she's in the shower, I talk to Clint. He's so nervous, he's not making any sense. I hope he lets Valerie drive.

Mom and I hit the stores, and I hunt for treatment center clothing: comfortable, stretchy pajamas and sweats.

Those sweatpants won't stay stretchy for long, says the voice in my head. *They're going to blimp you out. You'll be fatter than ever, you obese binge-eating whore.*

But I don't listen. I set my teeth and buy the clothes. I'm going to do this.

I was wrong, and they were right. I killed my baby. If they fatten me up, I deserve it.

I deserve to suffer.

The busy hours pass with occasional cheerful update calls from Valerie and occasional semi-incomprehensible update calls from Clint. Then comes the text we've been waiting for:

SHES BEAUTIFUL!

And she is.

Gemma is pink and perfect—a compact little woman, ready to take on the world. Valerie holds her as if brand-new motherhood is the most normal thing in the world, and Clint gazes at them both as if he is eyewitness to a miracle. The bonds of love and trust that tie them together almost show up on film. The hospital room is crowded, but they see no one else.

I look at the photos, and my heart bursts with love and joy and grief, and the future that I've been unable to imagine for weeks suddenly comes into focus. I want this for myself someday. I want a future in which I hold my baby. And I want to be a positive force in my new niece's life.

I don't just want to be the kind of aunt who sends Gemma a birthday card once a year. I want to be a part of her world. I know that nothing is going to hold this amazing little person back. She's going to achieve anything she sets her mind to. But one day, she'll find herself struggling. Valerie and Clint will be there for her, but there are things she won't want her parents to hear.

When that day comes, I want Gemma to know that she can call me, and I know I need to get ready for that. I need to be able to tell my niece that things will be okay—that I know she can defeat her demons.

That means I have to defeat my demons first.

15

I stare at the wall while it's happening. It's better if I stare at the wall.
A week at Clove House hasn't made this any easier.

"Let's talk about what happened at breakfast," Emily says.

"Let's not," I say.

The worst part of being in treatment is getting picked apart in therapy. Except for all the other worst parts.

It isn't that I'm trying to derail my recovery. I want to get better—I really do. But there's getting better, and then there's all the stupid and painful stuff they want you to do because they *think* it will make you better. So, okay, I'm an educated person. Show me a medical study that demonstrates how this will help. But they can't, or they won't. They want me to take it on faith.

A lot of what goes on at this place is bullshit.

"I know what we can talk about," I say. "Let's talk about your wedding photo over there. Let's talk about why it doesn't show your face."

Emily is a young woman with limp blond hair and a discouraged expression. She's fresh out of school, and during our first therapy session, she made a fatal blunder: she confessed that she hated her nose so much, she got a nose job.

I can't believe she was stupid enough to tell you that, says the voice in my head. *She's as big a loser as you are.*

"This isn't about me," Emily protests.

Well, it isn't going to be about me, either.

I fold my arms. That's a sign of hostility. I would wear armor if I could. "I tell you what," I say. "You can give me that speech again about how I should learn to love myself just the way I am."

Out of the corner of my eye, I notice that Emily's face crumples a little more.

She thinks you're a bitch, says the voice in my head. *She wishes they would kick you out. She's only doing this for the money.*

"I'm here to help you," Emily says.

"You're here to get paid."

"I just wish you'd tell me why you're so angry."

"Because I hate it here."

This seems promising. Emily perks up. "Tell me what it is you hate."

"I hate therapy."

"I can tell."

This is the first sign of fight Emily has exhibited. Mentally, I give her props. But I don't uncross my arms or look her direction.

"What else do you hate?" she asks.

"I hate the eating."

But there it is—I might as well not bother. Emily can't know what it means to an anorexic to have to force down food six times a day. It's torture. It's terrifying! It's irresponsible medicine.

And Emily wants me to start eating even more.

The session ends. I drag myself out into the main room. It's a big square with a kitchen in one corner. Long tables line up near the kitchen, and Foofs—giant fluffy beanbags—cluster near a fireplace on the opposite side of the room. Big old-fashioned windows fill the wall by the fireplace and let in gray light from the cloudy sky. Outside, the February day is gloomy, and snow is flickering down.

When I first got here, I would stand at a window to watch the snow fall onto the parking lot. Now I don't. The outside world is losing its meaning.

I automatically head toward the fireplace. It won't help, though. No matter what I do, I can't seem to get warm. I can feel the fire heating my skin now, but the heat can't seem to get inside.

About twenty other patients lie curled up in Foofs or bend over art projects at the tables. Bright, amateurish patient art covers the walls. We even have cutout snowflakes on the windows.

The whole place feels like a kindergarten. Sometimes I find that comforting.

That's because you're pathetic, says the voice in my head.

I collapse into a Foof, worn out by the stress of therapy. Ms. Carter, the nurse on duty, comes over with a Dixie cup in one hand and a glass of apple juice in the other. She says, "Dr. Greene wants you to start this immediately."

"Another one?" I say. "I'm already taking two pills in the morning and two at night. I can barely stay awake."

"This one is different."

I sit up and take the Dixie cup from her. A half of a white pill sits in the bottom of it. I pick it out and take the glass of juice.

I used to hate pills. Now I don't even ask what they're for. Like any invalid, I long perpetually for a miracle drug that will reach into my aching body and erase the anguish inside.

Apple juice, one hundred calories per serving, warns the voice in my head. *You're not going to drink that, are you?*

"Is this coming off my lunchtime calories?" I ask. Ms. Carter stops herself from rolling her eyes, but I see the look. So I take the pill with only the tiniest sip of juice.

Ms. Carter walks back to the kitchen, past two scrawny little girls who are giggling and clowning around at a table. One of them jumps up and executes a cartwheel. Ms. Carter says, "Sam! No exercise!" The little girl collapses into her chair again, shrieking with laughter.

Just like a kindergarten.

And you're pathetic.

I lower my head into the Foof, curl up tighter, and try to fight back the tears. But in another second, they're spilling down my face.

Warm, thin arms curve around me in a supportive hug. A fragile girl my age nestles beside me, smiling kindly when I look up. It's Evey. Evey knows not to ask what's wrong. So I put my head down again and sob into the Foof while Evey pats my shoulder.

The dull drowsiness of the medications pulls me down. After a few minutes, I drift into a doze.

"I like your tattoo," says a high clear voice.

I lift my head. Evey isn't patting my shoulder anymore. She's in a Foof nearby, working on her crochet project. The cartwheel girl is standing beside me. She has long brown hair, big soulful brown eyes, and bright green fuzzy pajamas with googly-eyed creatures on them.

The pajamas are way too big for her. They flop along the floor as she fidgets. And her name is Sam. When I was little, I had a cat named Sam.

"Who was he?" she asks. "He's dead, right? Was he your brother?"

She's pointing at the tattoo on my upper arm, the only one she can see. All my tattoos are beautiful, but I'm really proud of this one. It's a simple grayscale portrait of a young man's face, so delicate that it might have been sketched in pencil. I glance down at that face gazing sadly out at the world: the handsomest man in England.

"Did he die in Iraq?" Sam asks.

"No, he died in World War I," I say. "His name was Rupert Brooke. He wrote poetry."

"So was he your grandfather?" she asks as she fidgets in a nervous little dance.

"Sam! No exercise!" calls Ms. Carter again, and Sam flops into the Foof next to mine.

"No, I love his poetry," I say. "I've loved it for a long time." Sam looks at me, baffled but respectful, so I go on. "He wrote, 'If I should die, think only this of me: That there's some corner of a foreign field that is forever England.' And there is. He died in Greece. He's buried there under some olive trees."

Evey sets down her crochet project and leans back in her Foof. In her brittle hands, even crochet looks like hard work.

"I like that," she says. "I like it that it came true. How does the rest of it go?"

As I say the poem, Sheila wanders over. Sheila has shining honey-colored hair and an imperious expression. She's been a patient forever, and she has a PEG tube through her abdomen straight into her stomach. While the rest of us struggle to chew up and gulp down our meals, Sheila's nourishment flows in without her even noticing.

"Whatcha doing?" she demands as she takes over a free Foof.

"Poetry," Evey says.

Sam bounces up and down in her Foof. "Do you know any more?" she asks me.

Residential treatment, with its long boring days under house arrest, is about the only place outside of my mom's house where anyone would ask to hear more poetry. But I'm prepared. Since boarding school, I've kept Rupert Brooke's poems close by.

As I fetch the book from my basket, I seem to skim over the floor. Was I feeling this lightheaded earlier? I glide rapidly back to my Foof and sink into it, and the book swings open automatically.

"I HAVE been so great a lover," I read out loud, and instantly, I have their attention. So I read on, pulling my favorite parts of the poem together.

"I HAVE been so great a lover, filled my days
So proudly with the splendour of Love's praise,
My night shall be remembered for a star
That outshone all the suns of all men's days."

I glance up. Evey has her eyes closed. Sheila looks a little bored. Sam is staring at me wide-eyed and twitching her whole body slightly like she's swaying to music none of us can hear.

"So, for their sakes I loved, ere I go hence,
I'll write those names,
Golden forever, eagles, crying flames,
And set them as a banner, that men may know,
To dare the generations, burn, and blow
Out on the wind of Time, shining and streaming. . . ."

Now all three are staring at me in something like rapture. Wouldn't we all like to think that secretly, somehow, somewhere, someone loved us like that?

"These I have loved:
White plates and cups, clean-gleaming,
Ringed with blue lines; and feathery, faery dust;
Wet roofs, beneath the lamp-light; the strong crust
Of friendly bread;"

"I hate bread!" mutters Sheila.

"Rainbows; and the blue bitter smoke of wood;
  And radiant raindrops couching in cool flowers;
  And flowers themselves, that sway through sunny hours,
  Dreaming of moths that drink them under the moon;
  Then, the cool kindliness of sheets, that soon
  Smooth away trouble; and the rough male kiss
  Of blankets . . ."

Sheila gives a snort. "What does he know about male kisses?"
I could tell her, but Sam's here, and she's only about thirteen.
  "He didn't love people," Sam says, bouncing. "He loved things.
I thought he would list his favorite people, but he didn't."
  "Well," I say, "people made his life pretty complicated." And
I try to explain how many people were madly in love with Rupert
Brooke—just about everybody except the people *he* loved. But I'm
talking too fast. I stop in confusion.
  "I like it that he loved things," Evey says as she closes her eyes
again. "People just hurt you."
  Which is true.
  "Lunch," calls Ms. Carter.
  Not lunch already!
  You can't eat now! says the voice in my head. *Your stomach's
still full. It's going to split open. It's going to rupture!*
  I sit down at the table across from Evey. Sam takes the seat beside
me. Sheila doesn't have to eat. She parks in a Foof by the fire, brushes
her beautiful hair, and takes our bitter envy as her proper tribute.
  A plate appears in front of me, and I fight down panic. The care
team has upped my quota.
  Five cups of Caesar salad! shrieks the voice in my head. *Five cups
at least! There's no room for it all. You'll pop! Your belly will pop!*

Terror floods me, and I have to close my eyes as I eat so I won't see how much food is still left. I'm like a claustrophobic locked in a cabinet. Every bite brings the walls closer together.

I'm being buried alive—from the inside out!

"You did great," Ms. Carter says warmly as she takes the empty plate away. I fight down a crazy urge to punch her. When I stand up, I'm astonished at how rapidly the table moves away.

I progress carefully to a Foof. I'm so nauseated from the bloated feeling in my stomach that it's all I can do to keep the meal down. I don't dare turn my head for fear I'll upset my balance and bring on vertigo.

The nausea slowly subsides, but my stretched stomach is in torment. Now the room is spinning. Some miracle drug this half-a-white-pill has turned out to be—I'm still miserable, sick, and in pain, and now I feel drunk!

"Group therapy," Ms. Carter calls out.

I glide into the group therapy room and arrange myself on a chair. The room populates with other sick, slender girls and women. The therapist is Susan, a smartly dressed middle-aged woman with large gray eyes and a high opinion of herself. I really dislike her. For some reason, she seems to like that about me.

"Elena's been here a week," she tells the group. "Let's take her history today. Elena, is that okay with you?"

I guess it is. I'm feeling sick to my stomach, angry, relaxed, and reckless.

"Tell us about your mother first," she says. "What's your relationship like?"

"Great," I say. "Mom's a writer, and I love books. She wrote her first books for me and my sister, Valerie. Really good books. They win awards."

The other patients make interested noises at this, but Susan asks, "What was she like when you were little?"

"Mom had cancer. I think that was when I was seven or eight. That was before she wrote books. She spent a lot of time in bed, too tired to play with us or do anything but work. She was always working. Everything was hard for her then. Finally, they found out she had anemia. She'd had it since I was born. When I was born, she couldn't stop—bleeding."

Images flood my mind, and the word catches in my throat. I smooth the expression on my face and force myself past it.

"Mom lost half her blood when I was born." Bright red blood on the bathroom floor. "And then—and then—" Bright red blood on my hands. "And then—"

But I can't go on.

Suddenly, there are tears in my eyes. I swallow hard and force them back. Everyone is looking at me. I stare back at them as if they had been the ones who were doing the talking.

Susan says, "Elena, it's okay. We understand. We know about your loss."

"Screw you," I say.

"It's okay," she repeats. "You can let yourself feel sad. You need to get in touch with that sadness."

From the bottom of my broken heart and aching chest and groaning stomach, I say, "Screw you. You don't know anything about me."

The day keeps right on getting better. As soon as group ends, it's time for massage therapy. The masseuse has set up her table in one of the yoga rooms, and she's dimmed the lights and lit candles. Quiet, plinky spa music plays on her portable stereo as I open the door an inch.

"Come in," she says. "You can lie down on the table or sit on the chair."

I sit on the chair. No damn way is she getting me on that table.

"What are you going to do?" I ask warily.

"Whatever you want me to," she says. "If you lie down, I can give you a back massage, or I can massage your feet. Or I can give you a chair massage and loosen up your neck and shoulders. It's totally up to you."

Up to me. If it were up to me, I'd be a thousand miles from this room. My body stiffens up like cardboard in anticipation of a stranger's touch, and I stare at her without speaking.

"How about I just massage one hand?" she suggests. "You can tell me when you're relaxed enough to try something else."

So I hold out my hand, and she begins to press it gently and rub it in circular motions.

I can't bear the pressure of her skin against mine. I grit my teeth and hold myself rigid. I tell myself: I will *not* feel. My hand shakes with the effort to stay tense.

You'll break, says the voice in my head. *You'll lose control!*

But I don't. She might as well massage a brick.

Then, as the gentle pressure continues, unwanted questions begin to intrude. Why am I doing this? What's wrong with a simple massage?

They're trying to make you lose control!

But how is that possible? No one's talking to me. No one's expecting me to do anything. What control do I need to handle a nice, relaxing massage?

You don't deserve it! says the voice in my head. *You're a fat, stupid bitch. Bitches don't get nice things.*

Is that true? Do I really hate myself this much?

I force the questions back. Instead, I concentrate all my energy and willpower on hating the people who put me here. Emily. Susan. The masseuse who's touching me.

This is wasting my time. This is bullshit! It isn't going to help me recover.

When it's over at last, I walk out without a word. I don't respond to the masseuse's good-bye.

Outside in the hallway is another girl with thin arms and a grim, determined expression. You'd think she was getting ready for electroshock therapy. She told us her story last week. She got gang-raped. She didn't tell a single person, and she kept right on making As.

"That woman is such a pervert!" I whisper to the girl, and she relaxes into a giggle, then rewards me with a quick hug before she heads through the door for her massage.

As I navigate back to my Foof, Emily calls me over. "So, how was the massage?" she asks.

"It was bullshit!" I say. "I'm not doing that again. It's a complete waste of my parents' money."

Emily doesn't look surprised.

"It's not an extra charge," she says. "And it relates to something the care team wants me to discuss with you. Do you have a minute?"

I follow her down the hall, take a seat on the couch in her office, and stare at the photo of the back of her wedding veil again.

They're going to ask you to leave, says the voice in my head. *They're giving up on you. You're too much trouble.*

"We reviewed your case today," Emily tells me. "And the thing we kept coming back to was rage. Anger, suspicion, lashing out in almost every interaction."

Here it comes! says the voice in my head. *The heave-ho. The push out the door!*

And I feel myself tense up again.

"Elena, have you ever experienced a sexual assault?"

"Hasn't everybody?" I snap.

Oh. My. God. There it is. There it is! That's what they wanted to know, and I told them. Now they can all trot off and gossip about me and whisper behind my back. I can't believe it. That massage! That damn new pill!

Ha, ha, ha! screams the voice in my head. *Elena Dunkle, queen of the morons!*

I stare at Emily and hope she'll think I was making a joke. But she doesn't. She's not that stupid.

"Do you want to talk about it?" she asks.

"No."

I wait for her to argue or persuade—to fill up the silence. Emily waits, too.

"Look, it doesn't matter," I say at last. "It happened a long time ago. I was at a party, and I shouldn't have been there. I was drinking, and I should have been more careful. I barely remember it, no kidding. It wasn't that big a deal."

She starts to speak, changes her mind, and thinks for a minute. "Was it date rape?" she asks. "Did you know him?"

"No, my boyfriend was downstairs."

You blamed him, though, says the voice in my head. *He couldn't understand why you changed.*

"When did it happen?" asks Emily.

"A long time ago. I was thirteen. Honestly, I barely remember it."

There it is—the look in her eyes. The thing I hate most. Pity. They tell you pity is such a kind thing, but what pity really does is never ever let you forget.

"Look, I'm not a victim," I say. "I am *not* a victim! I'm smart, and I'm successful, and there are guys who would *kill* to go out with me. I know people who will *never* make my grades! And—and—"

And I'm babbling. I feel myself go red with humiliation.

Poor widdle Elena! You're so pitiful, laughs the voice in my head, and the look in Emily's eyes is still there.

"Are we done?" I say, standing up.

"Sure," Emily says. "If you want to be."

I want to be. I storm out.

Sam bumps into me outside the door. "Mindfulness time, Elena," she says, sliding from side to side on the bottoms of her pajama legs. Most of the older girls ignore her, so I find a smile for her in spite of my bad mood.

Mindfulness time is a relief anyway. We lie on mats with our eyes closed. Half of us fall asleep. No one will ask me to pry into my memories and feelings during mindfulness time.

I take my mat, lie down, and close my eyes. The room seems to be rotating gently.

Seriously, I hate this new pill.

The facilitator begins: first, breathing exercises, in and out. My thoughts and breaths are like an erratic windstorm, but as the minutes pass, they calm down.

"You're on a beach, all by yourself," the facilitator says so gently that I don't seem to hear her voice at all. "You're walking barefoot on the sand. Take a minute to look at the wet sand and think about how firm and cool it feels."

I do. And it does.

The voice goes on, just at the edge of awareness, building the world around me. Gulls soar through the air and cry overhead. A little curving edge of water rushes past my feet and buries my toes in the sand as it hurries away.

"You come to some rocks. The waves are breaking against them. You hear the thunder as the waves break, but the rocks stand fast. You see little pools of water in their hollows. You feel the spray of the ocean waves as they break."

I see it all exactly: the wide, straight, shining line of the ocean horizon and the miles of empty beach. I see the wet, slick rocks sticking out into the ocean. They make the waves roar up and smash into foam.

Now I'm looking at the base of the nearest rock. There are pebbles lying here—thousands of pebbles that have broken from the rock. They've been washed clean and polished smooth by the action of the waves.

"Stop and pick up a pebble."

And I do.

"Look at your pebble. See what's unique about it."

My pebble is wet and deep eggplant-purple, with a pure white mark like the print of a baby's foot.

"Throw the pebble out to sea."

But I can't. I stare down at that beautiful little footprint and yearn for it with all my heart.

"Let it go. Send it back to the ocean it came from."

But I don't. I hold so tight to that precious little pebble that I shake from head to foot. I won't let go. Never, never, never!

The more the soft waves reach for it, the harder I grip it, until I scream out loud at the thundering sea.

When I open my eyes, I am lying on the floor with my head on Dr. Greene's lap. Her skirt is slick with my tears. Other faces are bending down over me: Ms. Carter, Emily, Susan.

"You dissociated," Dr. Greene tells me.

"I was circling?" I ask. "Hands and feet?"

She hesitates and glances up at Susan. Susan answers, "Not circling, no."

You were screaming! exults the voice in my head, and when it tells me, I know it's the truth. *You screamed like a lunatic. You made a complete ass out of yourself!*

I sit up awkwardly and dab at my face with the crumpled tissue I find in my hand. It's no use. I can feel that my face is a mess.

Look at the other girls staring. They're afraid of you now! They'll be talking about this for days. You're a sideshow freak!

The patients are hanging back, their faces solemn. Oh, no! What do I look like? What do they see?

Snot, spit, and chaos. Chaos! You're losing it, you crazy bitch!

Soap and water! I've got to wash my face. I need to put on makeup—now!

I scramble to my feet, pushing through the hands that reach out to steady me.

"No, I don't need help," I hear myself saying. "No! I don't need *help*! Leave me alone! I'm *fine*!"

16

It's the beginning of April. I've been in residential treatment for two months—two months of day-and-night monitoring, endless therapy sessions, calorie quotas, and pills.

I'm on eight pills a day now. They still haven't touched the misery. All they've done is make me feel sleepy and stupid.

That's because you are stupid, whispers the voice in my head.

I'm sitting at one of the long tables in the main room with my journal open in front of me. I've been on the same page now for half an hour, but nothing is coming to mind. I hate myself. I hate my life. I hate my new body. I can feel my flabby thighs flattened out wide against the chair.

Every part of me is flabby now.

Even at my lowest weight, I didn't like my body. I wanted it slimmer, smaller, finer, until it erased itself completely. I wanted my body to melt away like mud sliding off a sheet of glass, until the clarity of my soul could shine through.

But in the treatment center, they're piling that mud on.

I can feel it forming around me. It's thickening my arms and thighs and clinging to my midsection. The beautiful wings of my collarbones have sunk into puffy flesh. All over my body, fat has swaddled and expanded me, until I've lost the feel of who I am, the feel of my knee bones joining my tibias and my tibias hooking onto my pointed hips.

All I feel now is pudding—pudding everywhere, under a jiggly skin.

You're a slack-jawed, vacant-eyed swine, says the voice in my head. *It won't be long till your bloated body pops and floods the room with a layer of jelly.* And in an instant, images pour through my mind: bright red blood flowing across the floor.

Breathe. Don't shiver. Breathe. Come on, now, that's no way to think! Focus on calming the anger.

I didn't even know I was angry till I got to Clove House.

My phone dings, and I glance at it. Here's a welcome distraction: Valerie sent me a new photo of Gemma. Valerie's at home with Mom and Dad now because Clint's getting ready to go into basic training. She has my room (her and my room), and Gemma has the media room.

Clint's staying there for a few weeks, too. We've started texting back and forth. Even though he's more responsible than just about every other guy I know, he has a real streak of fun in him. I love him already. If I'd had a brother to grow up with, I would have wanted him to be like Clint.

Homesickness wells up inside me. Everybody's there having fun with the baby, and I'm stuck a thousand miles away.

Your fault! You're a loser. You lose.

I look at the new photo. Gemma's lying in her car seat, snuggled up in a pastel-colored fuzzy blanket. She has dark bangs already, so she doesn't look like one of those bald alien babies. She pretty much resembles an obese dwarf. Gemma's not smiling yet. She's still too little. Instead she's staring out at the world as seriously as if it's a personal goal of hers to figure out just what the hell is going on.

She looks so funny that for a second, I forget my surroundings and laugh. But then I feel my midsection jiggle up and down, and I'm right back where I started: in a state far from home, in a city I don't know, in a mental illness treatment center, in a pair of shabby gray sweats, in an ever-thickening layer of blubber that is crushing my soul like an egg in the belly of a python.

I glance at my journal and discover that I've written:

I feel so fat. It feels like I am going to explode.

That's enough journaling. Too much truth.

But as I close the journal, a note scribbled across an earlier page catches my eye:

Remember when I told you you were too beautiful to be here? Still true.

No name is next to the message, but I know it's Stella.

The first day I got here, right after I arrived, a whole group of patients burst into the main room, screaming and shouting and carrying on. I thought they were having hysterics, but I found out later that they were just celebrating somebody's birthday.

As they rushed by me, Stella broke off and confronted me.

"You're beautiful," she said. "Why are you here?"

"Screw you," I replied.

It was a rocky start, but Stella broke the ice later in her own unique fashion. She's a day patient—in treatment ten hours a day, seven days a week—and she used to bring her own water bottle from home. One afternoon, as I was moping in a corner, she sat down on the floor next to me.

"Have some water," she said and handed over the bottle.

Ugh!

"I don't need to drink your water," I said stiffly. "I can get my own."

Stella looked amused. "No, you can't." So I decided to humor her and took a gulp.

It was straight vodka.

I gasped and spluttered, and then we both laughed. We've been close ever since. But tomorrow is Stella's last day in treatment. She's leaving me here. Evey is already gone. Evey's insurance wouldn't pay anymore. She didn't want to stop treatment, but she had to.

I take the journal to my basket. When I walk back into the main room, Sam is standing in the middle of it in Tree Pose, with her right foot against her left knee.

"Elena! Elena!" she says, hopping a little on her left leg.

"Sam!" Ms. Carter calls from the kitchen. "No exercise!"

"Elena, come do mod-podge," Sam says. So we take a stack of old magazines from the art room and sit down at one of the tables, and we cut out words and pictures to glue together into a collage.

Feeling HUNGRY?

DISAPPEAR Perfect for you!

Pretty soon I'm having fun. Sam's good mood is erasing my bad mood. But then Emily comes out of the office wing and ruins it.

"Elena, Dr. Greene and I need to talk to you."

Shit! What is it this time? Insurance problems? More pills?

They've had enough of you, says the voice in my head.

Can that really be true? I know they don't like my attitude, but I've done just about everything they've told me to. They made me call Mom and Dad and tell them about the rape and miscarriage even though I hated it. Dad sounded so hurt and baffled, and Mom's voice sounded thin and far away.

"It happened a long time ago," I said to Mom. "Maybe you don't believe me."

Mom said, "Remember that German psychiatrist you went to see back then? The one who tested you for hours?"

"That's right, Anita's psychiatrist. I remember going to see him once."

"You went to see him because we could tell something was wrong. From one weekend home to the next, you changed. We would find you awake at one, two in the morning. You couldn't sleep, and you stopped eating."

"Mom, this isn't a big factor in my eating disorder," I said. "It's really no big deal." Because it wasn't the rape that caused my eating disorder, it was being forced to go to the boarding school. But I didn't tell her that.

"I think it's a big deal," Mom said on the phone. Then there was a pause. "Why didn't he find the trouble then—the German psychiatrist?" she said. "Why did he tell me you were fine?"

"Because I lied my ass off," I told her.

Thinking about those phone calls now makes me angry. Look at the pain Emily made me cause! I follow her down the hall, fuming and worrying. What the hell do they want from me now?

Whatever you do, it won't be enough for these people, says the voice in my head. *You're a loser. They want you to lose.*

Dr. Greene is sitting behind her desk. She's both a doctor and a leggy blond, which is an unusual combination, and she's smiling slightly, as always. For some reason, Dr. Greene thinks I'm interesting. I seem to entertain her.

Emily pulls up a chair to sit by Dr. Greene. I don't want to sit, but I do. My instinct tells me to prepare to run. What will it be? Drugs? Medical tests? Dismissal?

"Elena," says Dr. Greene, "the care team needs to move your quota up to five thousand calories a day."

Five THOUSAND? screams the voice in my head. *Five THOUSAND!*

Panic swamps me. It's a good thing I'm sitting down, or I really would run out of the room!

Emily sees the look on my face.

"You've been doing well," she hastens to assure me. "You're gaining weight, but it's not going fast enough. We know this is very hard on you; we understand. . . ."

"You don't!" I say. "You don't understand!"

They look a little startled, and I realize I'm yelling. Okay, dial down the rage. Emily and I have been working on that.

"Here's the thing," I say. "Here's what you don't understand. Here's exactly how I feel. Let's say you have claustrophobia. It's so bad, you don't like to hang up your jacket in the closet, even though the door's open. And now let's say you go into treatment. And your treatment is getting locked inside a tiny box—*six times a day!*"

"It's not like that," Emily says. "You know we wouldn't ask you to do something dangerous."

"Oh, it's not dangerous," I say. "It's not like the staff won't let you out. In fact, they're really sweet. They even let you paint your box your favorite color. And then, when they let you out, they ask, 'How was that for everybody?'"

Dr. Greene's smile is broader now.

"But six times a day," I say, "you have to fold up like a pretzel, with your feet tucked up to your butt. And when you're wedged in as well as you can be, they close the lid and turn the lock. And every few weeks, they call you in and say . . ."

"'We need to move you to a tighter box.'"

That's Dr. Greene. She's really enjoying the box idea.

"It's a very good analogy," Emily says with caution. "It's great that you're expressing your feelings so well. But this is something your insurance company is pushing, and it's a reasonable next step. We need to get you to a two-pound-a-week weight gain."

"Not without a tube," I say. "I need a tube."

"You know we've tried," Dr. Greene answers.

Most of the patients at Clove House have a little yellow tube snaking out of their noses, taped with fabric tape to their cheeks. All day it stays put and does nothing, but at night it's hooked to a pump. When their calorie quota needs to be upped, they get a little backpack to carry around, and then the tube works day and night. The meals they eat stay small, but they still gain weight.

But nose tubes don't work for me. I can't keep them down. I've purged so much that my gag reflex is hypersensitive. I purge as quickly and easily as I cough, whether I want to or not. They've tried repeatedly to place a nose tube, but it comes up every time.

"Then I want a PEG tube," I say.

I covet Sheila's PEG tube. She acts like she's the queen of all of us, and in a way she is because she has the one thing we all want. The PEG tube is my Holy Grail. If I get one, I won't have to eat. The central worry of my life—gone.

Emily shakes her head. "That's a solution of last resort. It's temporary at best, and it's not without risks. It's a significant surgery, and it could affect your eating for days."

No food or drink after eight the night before surgery, gloats the voice in my head.

"The thing is, we've tried," Dr. Greene chimes in. "We've discussed it with your insurance company. They won't go for a PEG tube."

There it is: the insurance company gets in the way again. And I'm one of the lucky ones. At least my company is letting me stay in treatment as long as I need to. Most of the patients here got forced out of treatment after just a few days.

Like Evey. She cried when they made her leave. She knew she wasn't ready.

Evey deserved recovery. You don't, says the voice in my head. *They'll force you out, too. You're trouble.*

I'm afraid of getting in trouble with the care team, but I can't face the thought of another quota increase. I'm already at thirty-three hundred calories, and I eat so much, I feel like a living bomb.

"I won't eat any more food," I say. "I can't do it without a tube."

"We don't have another option," says Dr. Greene.

So I storm out of the office and collapse into a Foof.

Breathe. Just breathe. Don't panic!

Stella looks up from the blanket project she's knotting together. "What happened?" she asks.

"They're upping my calories! They want me to gain X amount a week!"

I don't say the number, and Stella doesn't ask. We don't say numbers because numbers are all we think about. Numbers are magic words. If we hear another patient's number, it sends us into a rush of competition. We start to worry and obsess. The real problem is that we don't know our own number anymore, so all numbers seem ominous and powerful.

If I knew my number, I wouldn't be such a nervous wreck right now, but the staff keep our numbers secret. It's supposed to help us find new ways to define ourselves, but all it's done is make me feel desperate.

There's nothing I can be sure of without my number.

"They won't let me have a PEG tube!" I continue. "It's the asshole insurance company!"

Stella nods. She knows all about the insurance battle. Her last full day of treatment is tomorrow because her insurance company refuses to keep paying.

It's a good thing for my sanity that we're getting out of this place for a couple of hours. Today is Outing Day, when we patients pile into the van and go someplace fun. We've been to the botanical gardens and the zoo, and today we're getting our nails done.

Sam climbs into the van next to me and sings and dances in place to her own music. Ms. Carter isn't here to tell her not to exercise. Mark is our chaperone today.

"Try not to embarrass me too much," Mark says as the van pulls up to the mall. We giggle because that's exactly what we'll try to do.

We love Mark best of all the staff. He's young and good-looking, but we don't think of him in that way. We think of him as a brother, and that's how he treats us, too. He doesn't fuss over us patients and clap his hands and baby us. He growls at us: "Cut it out!" Or he laughs and jokes.

Mark's sister died of an eating disorder. That's why he chose this line of work. His life has been touched by the shadow, and that makes him family.

At the nail salon, I opt for my favorite manicure: French nails. Sam immediately clamors for them, too.

"Your nails are long enough," I tell her. "They'll look great. You'll like it. It's a classy look."

"You know everything there is to know about makeup, don't you?" says Sam.

"I'll help you with your makeup one day if they'll let me," I promise. Then I laugh as she tries to sit still enough to get her manicure.

I hate Sam's parents. I truly do. They're the reason she has her eating disorder. They're evil incarnate, but not the kind of evil that's going to drink blood or take over the world. Sam's parents are worse than that. They're whiny, grasping, greedy, infantile, and completely self-absorbed.

Sam's parents aren't the ones who want Sam to get well. They don't want to be bothered with her at all. Sam's parents have fights over which one of them is going to have to keep her.

Demons with pitchforks look like saints compared to Sam's parents.

My manicurist has snapping black eyes and black straight hair, and she speaks very fast in another language to the worker next to her. She buffs my nails at lightning speed and then applies the white polish to their tips.

I admire my hands while she works. They've changed for the better these last two months. Anorexia is hard on the hands.

In school and at university, I could pick out eating disorder people by their hands. Anorexics develop "old-people hands"—thin skin and popping veins. Then I would look for the hand with the ragged, cracked nails, or the hand that had its nails clipped short while the other hand's nails were long. Or I'd look for the beat-up, faded polish. Stomach acid is hell on nail polish.

And then I would stay as far from that person as I could.

It was nothing personal. It's just that hanging out with anorexics on the outside can be risky. We give each other away. It's like an escaped prisoner partying with other escaped prisoners: spend enough time with them and you'll find yourself back in jail.

But now my hands actually look nice for a change.

We leave the nail salon in a laughing, chattering crowd and slowly make our way down the mall. "Can I go to the bear store?" Sam asks. "I want to look at the bears."

"Sure," says Mark.

But when we get to the bear store, the cashier lady comes out front. "I'm very sorry," she says, "but I can't allow you in."

We stop, stunned. We can't go into the bear store?

"It's our insurance," the lady explains to Mark. "We can't be responsible if one of your patients has . . . some kind of event."

I turn around and survey my friends with new eyes. We're pale. We're in baggy sweats and special hospital support hose. Most of us have nose tubes stuck to our cheeks, and some of us are wearing portable pumps.

I guess we do look like patients, don't we?

"Besides," the lady says in a lower tone to Mark, "there are children in the store. I don't want them to be upset."

Children? What the hell? What the *hell*??

Ha, ha, ha! laughs the voice in my head. *You're so ugly, children run from you! You're so ugly, you make babies cry!*

That's too much for Sheila. She pushes her way through our group. "What do you have against CANCER?" she demands loudly.

The lady changes color and swallows hard. "I really am very sorry," she says.

"Let's go," Mark says as he turns away. Reluctantly, we turn to follow him.

Scary ugly! laughs the voice in my head.

But Sheila doesn't follow Mark. She's still glaring at the cashier lady. She pats her shining, gorgeous honey-brown hair and gives the lady a withering look. She says, "I put on my *wig* for this!"

The cashier lady looks like she's going to faint.

"I'm *so* sorry," she whimpers. "*Very* sorry."

"Stop it!" Mark snaps. "Let's go!" And we walk away, giggling. An unpleasant moment has been salvaged. We've managed to embarrass Mark.

But when we get back to Clove House, we sit down with Susan and have a group therapy session about it.

Stella cuts straight to the point, as always. "Do we look that shitty?" she asks.

Susan is not a woman who is easily rattled. She's not rattled now, but she's picking her words with care. "Here's something you need to think about," she says. "I know I've explained this to some of you before. The fact is that you can't see yourselves the way that store manager saw you."

I say, "*Won't* see ourselves that way, you mean."

"No, *can't*," Susan says. "You physically *can't*."

I don't like Susan, but she does have my attention.

"Our brains—*all* our brains, yours and mine both," she says, "have a special way of coping with starvation. When we drop even a few pounds below our ideal body weight, the part of the brain that assesses our appearance stops functioning. Then when we look in the mirror, we don't see the damage that's being done to our bodies. What we see is somehow normal."

Somehow normal! sniggers the voice in my head.

"This helped our ancestors survive," Susan continues. "If a harvest failed, it might mean months of famine before they would get enough to eat again. Not being able to see what the famine was doing to them kept them from losing hope and giving up. But that same trick of the brain works against patients with eating disorders. You can't see a reason to change."

"So we *do* look like hell is what you're saying," Stella concludes.

"You don't look like hell, no," Susan says. "But you look ill. In fact, some of you look very ill. And that's why you're here: to get better."

I think about this as Sam and I go back to our mod-podge. Is that why the mirror girl turned into a stranger? Because my brain couldn't see who I was anymore?

In between jokes and glue-bottle artistry, I sneak furtive looks around the room. It's true that Stella looks a lot better than when I first met her. Her skin is bright and clear, and her dark blond hair is glossy. So does Sam. She used to look like a little beggar out of a Dickens novel. Now she looks like a happy little girl.

They deserve to get well, says the voice in my head. *You don't.*

After we put our art supplies away, I go to my basket and fetch my makeup bag. Then I sit down in the art room and look at my face in the compact mirror.

Can I see the person who's really there? Can I see the person other people see?

Well, I've broken out since coming here. Thank you, returning hormones! And my hair might look better if the place that colored it the last time hadn't done such a shitty job. And my nose still looks like a squashed potato, but now it's a fatter squashed potato than before. Is that just my imagination? Do noses put on weight?

I hold the mirror farther away and face the stare head-on.

Who's in there?

Me? Or a stranger?

Not me. The girl in the mirror still looks like a stranger. And she doesn't look like a stranger who's happy to see me.

Remember the lady at the bear store, says the voice in my head. *Whatever you see, the reality looks even worse.*

"Balloons!" shrieks Sam as she and her friend Laurie dash through the door. They're trailing a cluster of red and pink balloons. They close the door to the art room and lock it behind them. It's the only door with a lock.

"What's up?" I ask as I tuck away the mirror and zip up the makeup bag.

"HEEEELIUM!" Laurie says.

The central balloon is Mylar. Sam pulls it from its cluster, flops down on the floor of the art room, and pops off the plastic clip. Then she takes a big breath from the neck of the balloon.

"Say something!" says Laurie.

"Something!" squeaks Sam in a screechy Mickey Mouse soprano. They laugh in octaves, with Sam squeaking away at high C.

Laurie grabs the balloon, inhales deeply, and starts singing a popular song. But she can't squeal out more than two or three words before dissolving into surreal giggles.

The door handle turns.

"Hey!" calls a voice. "Who's in there? What are you doing with the door locked?"

Sam slurps in more helium and squeaks out, *"It's Sam."* Then the pair of them fall into each other as they laugh.

"Who is that?" demands the voice. "Who is that really?"

And I'm laughing so hard, I can't breathe.

Next morning, Stella finishes treatment early. I'll see her again because she lives nearby, so she can come to visit, but this is the last time we'll be together on the inside.

"So this is it," she says. "Don't bother with the whole pump-me-up 'you'll do great' speech."

I nod. "If that's what you want."

"Do you think that's true?" she asks after a minute. "What Susan said yesterday? That we don't even see ourselves right?"

"I don't know."

Stella stares at the ground for a moment, deep in thought. Then a grin lights up her face. She's *so* beautiful. And I would tell her that, but I know she wouldn't believe me. She'd think it was that pump-me-up speech she just nixed.

"Oh, well," she says. "I guess it doesn't matter anyway."

Then she's gone.

I'm somber after Stella leaves. She was right to skip the speech. The fact is that she's not ready. She can't go from ten-hours-a-day nursing care with locked bathrooms and supervised meals to all the temptations and opportunities of home. Stella's compulsions are too strong. She won't have the power to stop herself. They've set her up for failure, and she knows it.

You're all going to fail, says the voice in my head. *This treatment is just a waste of your time.*

Ms. Carter comes up to me.

"Elena," she says, "Dr. Greene wants us to try the tube again."

So they can hurry up and get you moved out of here, too.

She can't get it placed. I'm really trying to cooperate, but no matter what I do, I can't help gagging when it hits the back of my throat. Ms. Carter tries again and again, while the tears run down my face and the tube rubs my nose on the inside until it bleeds.

At last, the tube makes it to my stomach. We look at each other in tense silence, hardly daring to hope and certainly not daring to breathe. Two minutes . . . three minutes . . . I'm still keeping it down. Maybe this time it's going to work!

"Okay," Ms. Carter says, "why don't you walk up and down for a while in the hall, nice and easy, to try to get used to it. I'll go tell Dr. Greene."

So I walk up and down, trying not to turn my head, trying hard not to think about the straw-shaped thing dangling down inside my throat. Settle, stomach. Settle. Nice and easy. I need this thing to stay in.

Sam darts out into the hall, sees me, and comes up, all smiles.

"They finally got it to work!" she says.

"Yes," I say. And that's when all hell breaks loose.

Speaking vibrates the tube against the back of my throat—a sensation that does in my esophagus what a tickle in the nose does to make a sneeze. Right there and then, I gag so violently that everything in my system comes up, and the end of the tube flies out and slaps Sam on the cheek.

Ms. Carter comes running up. "Elena!" she says, aghast. "Elena, you did that on purpose!"

I have vomit all down the front of my sweats, and tears are stinging in my eyes.

"I didn't!" I splutter. "I didn't, I swear!"

"You talked!" says Ms. Carter, beside herself. "You *knew* not to talk! Well, you know what? *You* can clean it up!"

I yank the useless tube out of my mouth and throw it into the vomit. "I didn't do it on purpose!" I yell.

Ms. Carter shoves cleaning supplies at me. "Here's a rag. Get to work!"

"Screw you, you bitch!" I yell back.

At this point, Dr. Greene comes out and tells Ms. Carter to leave me alone. But she doesn't say a word to me.

I stalk off to a Foof. When Ms. Carter calls us for supper, I stay there. To hell with them and their rules! I've done exactly what they've wanted for two whole months, and it's never enough for them.

Each time you meet a goal, they make it harder, says the voice in my head. *They want to humiliate you. They want you to fail.*

Ms. Carter says, "Elena, I'm sorry, but if you don't eat, I'll have to write you up as noncompliant."

She's not sorry, says the voice in my head. *She's happy to see you fail. When you succeed, they push you till you break, and when you fail, they yell.*

I curl up in the Foof and close my eyes. I'm angry and lonely and every bit as miserable as I was on the day I arrived. If Stella were here, she'd sit down next to me and talk to me until she made me talk to her. But Stella's gone.

You don't have a friend, says the voice in my head. *These people don't care about you. They haven't helped you get better, and you're not going to get better. This is who you are. Nothing's going to change.*

"Okay, girls," calls Ms. Carter. "Dorm time! Collect your things and wait by the door."

Screw it! I'm not going anywhere. They can call my parents. They can call an ambulance!

That's right, says the voice in my head. *Coming here was a mistake. It's a waste of your time. Don't wait for them to throw you out. Make them let you out! Stay put, and you'll be on a plane home in no time.*

Behind me, a voice whispers, "Elena!"

It's Sam. But I don't turn around.

The next instant, her hand is in mine. Then she pulls away and hurries off.

I open my hand. Pink Sweet'N Low packets.

Sam's precious stolen store of artificial sweeteners. For me.

I look at the packets and try to sort out my raging emotions. Maybe Emily's right: maybe I am too angry most of the time.

Maybe my recovery is like my face in the mirror—maybe I can't see it, either. Maybe I'm getting better and I just can't tell. Maybe this isn't a waste of my time.

But I do know I have a friend. And I know she's worried about me.

For tonight, that's good enough.

I close my hand around the crumpled squares. I take a deep breath. Then I climb to my feet and head to the van.

17

Two and a half months have passed. It's July, and I'm still at Clove House. They've stepped my treatment down to ten hours a day. I get to go home each night now—or I *would* get to go home if home weren't a thousand miles away.

It's morning, and Mom is shaking my shoulder. Mom has had to come out and stay with me because I'm not allowed to live on my own.

"Time to get up," she says.

I try to open my eyes, but sleep clings to me so tightly that I can't bear the thought of lifting my head from the pillow. I'm always sleepy now. No matter how much I sleep, the sleepiness never goes away.

"You take the first shower," I groan with my eyes closed.

"I've already showered," Mom says.

Of course.

I stagger to the small tiled bathroom and shower while Mom makes our beds. There's not much else for her to do. We're staying in a former orphanage that provides lodging to out-of-town visitors who need medical care. This room at the end of the farthest hall has been our home for almost two months. It has three beds, one desk, and three large windows that let in views of lawn and trees and massive black-and-white Canada geese. I thought geese needed ponds and frogs, but these geese spend all their time pecking in the grass.

When I get out of the bathroom, Mom counts out my pills. I'm up to eleven pills a day.

"Let's go," Mom says, and we make the trek down the long hall, past the cafeteria, through the entrance hall, and out the front door of the orphanage.

An orphanage. Our home away from home.

Mom starts the car for the sixteen-mile commute to Clove House. We make this drive seven days a week. Sometimes Mom and I walk outside into rain and mud puddles. Most days we walk outside into sun. But it doesn't matter. Nothing changes the monotony of our routine.

Back home in my room (mine and Valerie's room), Valerie is playing with her baby. Gemma can sit up now and smile and laugh and grab things out of your hand. Back home at the university, my old friends are in summer school. Some of them are nursing students already. Back home on the bathroom counter, Dylan is swimming in and out of his silk plants. He's going around and around in Texas, and I'm going around and around here.

It's the beginning of a new day, but nothing about it feels like a beginning. Every minute that ticks by seems to add a new load to the weight pressing down my shoulders and eyelids. Dull and sleepy, completely fuzzed out, I blink at the scenery flowing past the car window as the miles of city freeway roll by.

"This isn't working," I say.

Mom keeps her eyes fixed on the road. She has new wrinkles these days. The creases next to her mouth are getting deeper.

"This is bullshit," I say. "I'm not getting better. I want to go home. I want to—"

But I can't bring myself to say it.

You want to hold Valerie's baby, says the voice in my head. *Serves you right that you've got no baby to hold.*

"You were the one who wanted to come here," Mom points out. "No one forced you to do this. But now that we're here, I'm not going to leave. Your recovery is important."

"My recovery is a joke," I say. "What do you know about my recovery?"

Mom doesn't answer.

That's because recovery is a thing neither one of us knows very much about.

Especially not me.

When I started treatment, I thought the scary thoughts and overwhelming compulsions would go away. I thought eating would become natural and pleasant again. But after six months, it's still as hard as ever. I no longer expect it to change.

My journal is in my lap, taking the ride with me. Last night I brought it home because I thought I might write in it again, but all I did was go to our room and sleep. I flip it open and read my entry from yesterday. It's only one line:

I want to be stable and even if I can't be happy, I want to at least be somewhat satisfied with myself.

It's pretty sad that even this modest goal is out of reach.

Now we're off the freeway, winding through elegant neighborhoods. The yards are full of roses. Up the hill, past the school, left turn, and there's the parking lot. Mom stops to let me out.

"Elena, you can do this," she says. "I know you can."

I scramble out and shut the door.

Did you see the doubt in her eyes? says the voice in my head. *She doesn't think you can do this, either.*

Inside Clove House, I settle into a Foof and close my eyes. It's all I do nowadays. Conversations swirl around me: new patients laughing and chattering. They come and go so fast that it's depressing.

Sam rushes over. "Wake up, Elena, pleeeeze? I want to show Harper your poet tattoo."

For dear little Sam, I'll sit up and even smile. She's one of the few veterans left. At the moment, she's preaching Rupert Brooke to the newbies. His poetry really speaks to patients with eating disorders.

At Sam's request, I strip off my hoodie so Harper can see Rupert's face. But while they're looking at the poet, I'm running my hand over a tattoo that rings my other arm. A circle of stars, and the letters *V*, *C*, and *E*.

In April, I got to go home for a visit. I got to hold my new niece and sing to her while she fell asleep, and I got to sit with Valerie and really talk with her for the first time in years.

"I think you'll be okay," she told me then. "Because I'm okay now."

"What changed?" I asked her. "What made the difference?"

"Hell if I know," she said. "It just got better. I could feel it getting better, and then it was okay."

I also got to know my brother-in-law, Clint, better. He felt more like my sibling sometimes than Valerie. He'd kick me under the table. Then I'd elbow him. Then he'd elbow me. Then I'd whack him on the arm.

"Stop it! Just stop it, you two!" Valerie would say. "I swear, it's like I've got three kids!"

"Yeah, Elena, show some maturity!" Clint would say with wide, solemn eyes—meanwhile kicking me under the table again.

I loved it. I loved being home with my family.

But I couldn't stay.

Because I couldn't eat.

A couple of days before Mom and I packed the car to bring me back to treatment, Valerie, Clint, and I went out together and got a tattoo. On each of us, it's the same: three stars and our initials. But on each of us, it looks different.

"We've got your back," Valerie said when I left. "Whatever happens, we're family."

Now I rub the circle of stars and think about that.

Eating disorder runs in families. So does depression. So does OCD. Maybe this is just part of how I'm made. If it is, I don't see how it can get any better.

Lunchtime. Another meal that I choke down bite by reluctant bite. And after that, a therapy session with Brenda.

I'm not seeing Emily anymore.

Emily thinks you're a bitch, says the voice in my head. *She refused to work with you when you came back.*

I'm pretty sure that's true.

"So, Elena," says Brenda. "How are you coming along?"

Brenda is decisive and capable. She's also young and pretty. I actually don't mind her. But it takes a lot these days to bother me. Anger requires too much effort.

"This is all genetic, right?" I ask. She knows I mean the anorexia.

"Not all of it, no," she says. "But yes, genetics plays a role."

"If it's genetic, it's not going to get better," I say. "It's going to stay like this—me thinking one thing and trying to do another. The thinking part isn't going to change."

"That's not true," she says. "I have patients who've made a complete recovery."

I wish I could believe her, but I don't. I feel it in my bones: this is going to be me against myself, fighting for every mouthful every single day for the rest of my life.

You can't do it, says the voice in my head. *You'll fail. You can't change who you are.*

Susan pops her head in the door. "Brenda, can you come here?" The anxiety on her face brings us both to our feet.

Sharp, explosive sobs greet us in the main room, and sober faces turn our way. Ms. Carter and Emily are bending over a patient who is wailing out loud. The other patients are clustered nearby in frightened little knots.

I go over to Sam and her new friend Harper. "What happened?" I ask in a whisper.

"Cynthia's roommate died this morning," says Sam. "She just got the call."

Cynthia has anorexia. So does—did—her best friend. They couldn't be separated in high school, and they have—had—a college apartment together. I met Anna a couple of times. She looked the same as the rest of us. But now Anna's different. Now she's dead.

"Heart attack," Sam murmurs.

Without thinking, I put my hand on my chest—my chest that still aches every day like it's coming apart. My chest that maybe still holds a heart with thin walls.

Anna's heart killed her at the age of twenty-one. Now she's one of the twenty percent, the one out of every five ED patients who gets killed by the disorder. It's horrible, but some days I'm so tired and sleepy, I wish I could be one of them.

"Was she bad? Had she gotten worse?" I whisper to Sam.

"Cyn said she wouldn't go to therapy."

You're going to therapy, says the voice in my head. *But it won't matter. You can't change what you are.*

An ambulance comes for Cynthia, and Ms. Carter goes with her. Susan sits down with the rest of the patients to process what they've been through. But Brenda takes me back to her office to finish our session.

"Are you all right?" Brenda asks me.

"No," I say.

"So you're upset."

"No," I answer.

That's the awful part: how little I'm feeling these days. It's like my soul is muffled up in straw. I'm dead inside. I'm cut off from life. But Brenda doesn't seem to understand that.

"It's a hard thing to face," she says, "but this gets back to what we were talking about. Treatment is so important. Never mind full recovery for the moment—statistics show that treatment is vital in helping anorexics survive."

"I want to stay in treatment," I say. "I do."

You do? says the voice in my head.

"Then you and your mother have a decision to make," Brenda says. "You can't keep going to day therapy. You need to move to outpatient care. The care team thinks it would be best if you find an apartment nearby so you can continue working with us."

"Outpatient?" I can't wrap my foggy brain around the idea. "You mean a couple of hours a week?"

"Four hours three or four times a week," Brenda says. "Maybe even five times a week to start with."

"But I'm not ready," I say. "Nothing's changed. I'm not any different."

Of course you're not different, says the voice in my head.

"That's not true," Brenda says. "You've built up your skills in the last six months. It's time to strengthen them through challenges. In outpatient treatment, you'll go on supervised shopping trips and work together with the other patients to cook meals. You could even take a college course or two in your free time."

Free time. No rules. No routine.

You'll fail, says the voice in my head. *You know you will. They want you to fail.*

"I haven't built up shit for skills," I say. "It's a major achievement for me if I can stay awake for ten minutes straight. How am I supposed to go to college when all I'll do is sleep through the classes?"

"I know you're on a lot of medications, and I know the side effects have been rough," Brenda says. "But you have to look at the improvement over time."

What improvement? says the voice in my head.

But I'm too tired to argue.

As a token of my new status, Brenda releases me from treatment for the rest of the day. My first free afternoon in weeks, and all I want to do is sleep. But I'm not supposed to sleep, so Mom takes me to a movie instead. A Disney movie. The bright colors are hypnotic.

"It's over," Mom says. "Time to go."

I blink and look around the theater. Everybody else is gone.

"What did I miss?" I ask. "Was it good?"

"Oh, yeah," Mom says with a sigh. "Amazing."

There's a pet store next to the theater. Mom drags me in. "Look, kitties," she says. "They have an adoption center."

The adoption center is its own small room behind a glass wall. Stacked-up cages hold shelter cats that need a home. A large woman with gray hair is in the room, tending to the cats. Two by two, she lets them out to run around and play.

"You could volunteer here on your days off," Mom says. "You'd love it."

She's right. At least, I think she's right. I do love animals. But no feeling, happy or sad, rises out of my muffled soul.

We go inside the glass room, and Mom talks to the large woman. I spend my time looking in the different cages.

That's how I feel. I'm in a cage. Even when I'm having a free day.

I peer into a shadowy crate near the bottom of the stack. A bright golden eye peers back. A young black cat lolls in the recesses of the cage. He's missing his other eye.

I put my fingers through the bars, and he comes forward, purring loudly. His injury barely shows. The black fur across the right side of his face is almost perfectly smooth. And on the other side, there's that big bright eye.

Still purring, the black cat flips over and bats at my fingers. His single eye glows like a topaz jewel. He doesn't know anything's wrong with him. He's full of life and confidence. He thinks he's a handsome young creature.

I could rescue this cat. He could move into my new apartment with me. The two of us damaged souls could brave the future together.

But no emotion rises inside me at this idea. No feeling. No feeling at all.

"What a nice woman," Mom says as we leave. "I've got her number written down for you. You could volunteer here on Tuesdays and Thursdays. That would give you something interesting to do."

I take the number from her. But in my heart, I know:

I won't be coming back.

The next day, I have another free afternoon. Mom drives me to see an apartment she's found.

"It's between two of the best nursing schools in the city," she says. "I think you could walk to either one of them. It caters to female students and single women. The parking garage is locked, and the front desk is manned at all times."

The day is sunny and hot, and Mom exclaims over how beautiful the neighborhood is. It's full of stately buildings from the 1920s. Tall trees grow in rows beside the streets. Students are everywhere, pedaling bikes or walking dogs.

"Look at that girl," Mom says as we get out of the car. "Doesn't she look like a nursing student?"

The girl is fit and trim, with a serious expression on her face and a thick backpack full of textbooks. She could very well be what I've wanted to be for so long—on her way to becoming a real nurse.

But for the first time in years, my heart doesn't leap and yearn at the thought of the hospital. I stare at the girl as if she's a mirage. I look at the wide streets and multistory buildings around me, and it's as if I'm watching a movie.

I feel nothing. This isn't me. This is not my life.

The apartment house is charming. It's an avant-garde skyscraper that tops out at ten floors. Mom and the caretaker talk together like old friends, and he cheerfully greets each of the strangers we pass. He seems to know the name of every single one of his tenants.

"This building has been a family-owned business from the start," he tells us. "It's still co-owned by the grandsons of the builder. I've got two apartments to show you, an efficiency on seven and a one-bedroom on level ten."

While we squeeze into the tiny elevator, Mom asks him about parking. As luck would have it, he has a free space for rent at the moment in the covered garage.

We walk down a narrow hall, and he unlocks a door. The efficiency on seven has clean white-painted cabinets in the tiny kitchen and an Internet cable trailing around the baseboard in the main room. I stare out the window and look west into golden haze over city suburbs. Birds fly below me, darting from tree to tree.

"Your furniture would definitely fill this place up," Mom says. "Let's take a look at the one-bedroom on ten."

We squeeze into the tiny elevator again and chug up to the top floor. This apartment has a locking screen door as well as a solid door, a reminder of the days before air conditioning. The caretaker unlocks both doors, and we walk inside.

As soon as I enter, a shadow like a black smear flits past me. It hangs at the very edge of my vision.

Mom and the caretaker walk into the kitchen, but I stay in the living room, blinking and shaking my head. An emotion trembles in my straw-stuffed core for the first time in days—maybe weeks.

It's fear.

There is death in this room.

Like an animal, I freeze and sniff the stale air. Whose death? Whose? The shadow dances just out of sight, and I am coldly, suddenly aware:

This death is my own.

As clearly as a movie, I see my future life. I will move in here. I will enroll in college. I will make the drive three times a week to treatment. But family and friends will be a thousand miles away, and I won't stay in touch.

For a while, everything will hang in the balance. I will stock the kitchen shelves with food. But the winter months will set in with their unfamiliar ice and snow. I won't want to go outside anymore.

And a day will come—a gray day in December or January—when I won't get out of bed at all.

The one-eyed cat won't be able to save me. He won't have enough life in him for us both. He'll cry at the door, and the caretaker will unlock it and find my body, and my soul will stay behind to flit from place to place in the shadows.

I can't do this. I'm not ready. I'm standing at the edge of a cliff.

This room contains my death.

We chug back down the elevator and step out into the sunlight. Mom climbs into the car, bubbly and excited.

"So, for the letters of reference," she says, "I think you could get your old boss at the gym, and maybe your German professor."

"I'm not moving here," I say.

"But why not? It's perfect! It's what you said you wanted."

It is what you said you wanted—*you loser!*

I can't explain to Mom about the shadow or the future or my soul of straw. I'm too sleepy to talk.

"It's not going to work," I say.

Mom smacks the steering wheel in frustration. Then she takes a deep breath. "I'm trying to be supportive here," she says. "Why don't you please tell me what it is we're trying to do."

"I want to go home."

"You said you want to stay in treatment!"

You did *say that*—*you loser!*

"It's not going to work."

"Oh, for heaven's sake, Elena! Why isn't it going to work?"

Tell her it won't work because you're not going to recover, says the voice in my head. *Say it! Say you're not going to recover.*

"I want to go home, that's all," I say. And I doze off on the drive back to the orphanage.

Nighttime. I wake out of nightmares to find that the room is almost black, except for a few rays of moonlight that have crept through the closed blinds. They lie in thin white stripes across the floor. With all the medicine I take, I should be able to count on sleeping through the night, but wouldn't you know, it doesn't work that way.

I stumble to the bathroom and pull down my pajama bottoms.

Blood. Bright red blood!

Images flood my mind: red splashes against beige linoleum.

Your fault! Dead baby. Dead baby!

Nightmares come swimming out of the corners of my mind: chopped-up corpses. Bloody limbs.

Dead baby! Dead baby! DEAD BABY!

"Shut up!" I whisper, pounding my fists on my thighs.

The room whirls. Blood surrounds me. It laps up against me like a sea. Its coppery stink overpowers me and upends my sensitive stomach. I turn and grip the sides of the toilet bowl and purge until all that comes out is long stringy ropes of white spit.

Images flicker high-speed through my brain: dead things. Deformed things. Half-formed things.

Blood! Stink! Death! DEAD BABY! The voice in my head is a scream now. *DEAD BABY! DEAD BABY!*

I dig the palms of my hands into my eyes, but I can't block out the images. All I see is the color of blood.

YOUR fault! YOUR fault! YOUR fault! screams the voice. *Dead BABY! Dead BABY! Dead BABY!*

In a frenzy, I snatch up my razor from the bathtub and peel a deep slice through the flesh of my arm.

Instant calm. The panic stills. The voice dies back to a whisper. The only thing left is the harsh sound of air whistling into my aching lungs. I crouch on the floor and watch blood spill out of the stinging cut as my heartbeat gradually slows down.

My period started, that's all. It's normal. It's perfectly normal.

These damn pills are turning me into a crazy zombie!

Hands shaking, I wrap a hand towel tightly around the cut. Then I wipe up the mess and creep back to bed.

But the next morning, I call to Mom as I'm preparing to take my shower.

"The blood won't stop," I tell her.

I don't remember the cut being that deep, but I've sliced through a large vein. When I came into the bathroom just now and pulled off the hand towel, the dried blood gave the cut a tug and popped it back open. Now a compact rivulet of dark burgundy is slipping down my arm into the sink. It's flowing so fast that the stream of blood is still tube shaped, and a ketchup-colored pool has formed by the drain.

It's lucky for me that Mom is hard to panic. She holds my arm over my head and applies pressure. I don't want to go, but I end up sitting in the waiting room of another ER.

For some reason, my mind is clearer today than it has been in weeks. I think about my panic attack last night and my sister's decorations of cuts and burns.

What drove Valerie to self-harm?

Was she trying to shut out bad memories, too?

The doctor is gray-haired and tired. He's also seen too many patients like me—patients who seem to damage themselves for no good reason.

"It's too late for stitches," he tells us. "All I can do is steri-strip it together." He turns to Mom, his eyes weary and contemptuous. "Is that okay with you?"

I see Mom flinch like she's been slapped. But she covers it up immediately and gives him a rueful smile. Mom is getting better at hiding her feelings these days.

"It's as okay as it's ever going to be," she says lightly, and I'm proud that she didn't let him see how much he hurt her.

We find our car again in the massive parking garage and start the drive back to the orphanage.

"Why didn't you tell me?" Mom demands as we wait at a light. "Why didn't you wake me up?"

"Trust me," I say, "you couldn't have helped."

"Trust you? You don't trust *me*. You haven't trusted me in years. You keep me at arm's length all the time—you hardly say two words to me! I came here to help you. I left my grandbaby behind, and Clint and Valerie. . . . How long do you think they'll be living so close that I can hold my grandbaby every day?"

"Don't blame me," I say, looking out at the passing traffic. "I told you I wanted to go home."

"This is supposed to help you," Mom says. "You're here to get better. All day, I'm stuck in a room by myself, and when I pick you up, you tell me you slept right through it."

That's right, says the voice in my head. *You ungrateful little shit!*

"That's it," I murmur. "Tell me what an evil person I am. That's going to help me get better."

"Oh, for God's sake, stop it!" Mom says. "You're not fifteen! Stop talking like some little emo drama queen."

"Emo drama queen—that's a good one, Mom," I say.

Because she's not going to see that she's hurting me, either.

"You know what?" Mom says. "I cannot WAIT until you finally grow up and I'm just another woman to you. I cannot WAIT until you drop this whole me-against-Mom act and I don't have to be the evil witch anymore."

She wishes she weren't your mother, says the voice in my head. *She wishes you weren't her child.*

"I'm sorry you got stuck with me," I say.

"THAT'S NOT WHAT I'M SAYING!" Mom yells at the top of her lungs.

Which means, of course, that she's lost the argument.

They're all giving up on you, says the voice in my head as I watch the cars go by. *First the care team gave up on you and pushed you into outpatient treatment. Now she's giving up on you, too.*

I don't have an answer for that.

After a couple of minutes, Mom breaks the silence again. "I can't take much more of this," she says. "You're an adult. I'm not here to set rules for you. So think hard before you tell me again that you want to leave treatment. The next time I hear it, I'm packing the car."

She's given up. They've all given up. It's just you and me again. Fine—we'll be able to handle things ourselves, like we always do.

"Fine," I say.

"Fine," Mom says. "Just so you know."

We stop by Walgreens on the way home because it's right next to the orphanage. We've spent a lot of money here in the last two months. Mom buys almond M&M's today, which means she's feeling sorry for herself.

Weak-willed grazer! says the voice in my head.

But I'm trying to be nice to Mom, so I make an effort. We walk the aisles and chat for a bit. I talk her into trying a facial mask. Mom's woefully basic when it comes to skin care.

"Hey, can I buy a couple of little makeup things for Sam?" I say. "She's asked me to show her some makeup tricks."

I know this will appeal to Mom because she knows about Sam's parents. Sure enough, she immediately agrees.

Back in our room. I'm feeling surprisingly wakeful and clear-headed. Then I remember. Because of the cut, we forgot my pills this morning.

Shit! I have no idea if anything I'm doing is making me better or worse!

Mom curls up with her computer and watches an episode of *Lost*. I work on a poem:

And I know, I know
you don't want to read this.

And I know
that I am screaming at a world that is too full
to hold anything else.

So I will cram this paper into a crack,
and I will map out my confusion inside
until someone can make me understand
the dance
I cannot stop following.

Then I take my evening pills and fall headlong into sleep. For tonight, at least, they keep the monsters away.

Next morning, Sam is thrilled to get her makeup. She sits down with me, and I show her in the little compact mirror how to put on the eye shadow and use the blush brush.

"You're my big sister," she gushes, throwing her arms around me.

"No PDA!" calls Ms. Carter from the kitchen.

"I'm proud to be your big sister, beautiful girl," I tell her. "You know I promised to help you pick out your prom dress."

But when Brenda calls me into her office a few minutes later, I can see that she's really angry.

"Elena," she says, "Sam's therapist tells me you gave Sam an inappropriate gift."

What did you do? says the voice in my head. *What did you screw up?*

"What are you talking about?" I ask.

"You know how fragile Sam's self-image is, Elena. What on earth were you thinking, giving her makeup?"

You screwed up! What were you thinking, you little shit?

"I was doing something nice!"

"It crossed the line," Brenda says.

You're out of your box, bitch! Stay in your box! You're just a patient to them. It's not like they care.

"For your information," I say, "Sam isn't just a patient. She's also—in case you hadn't noticed—a teenage girl! She's been begging me to help her with makeup for weeks, and the eye shadow made her day."

Brenda's eyes narrow. "This isn't about making somebody's day."

Yeah, stupid bitch! You're not somebody. You're nobody! All you mean to this woman is a paycheck.

"No, it isn't about making somebody's day, is it?" I say. "No, it sure as hell is *not*. You asshole therapists sit in judgment of us. All we are to you is sick. We're not *people*. All we are is a *case*."

"Now you're overreacting."

Don't react, bitch! You don't deserve to have feelings!

"Am I overreacting? Well, how about this, then? How about I've been complaining for weeks that these drugs are sucking the life out of me, and all you people do is up the dose! How about when I say I'm having a good day, you tell me I'm getting better, and when I say I'm having a bad day, you tell me this just takes time. Well, maybe what's going on is that you're screwing up with me! Did you ever stop to think about *that*?"

But Brenda isn't Mom. She's too well trained to get dragged into an argument. She says, "You'll just have to trust us, Elena."

You can't trust her. She's a quack! They've already screwed you up.

"Trust you? I've been trusting you quacks for six months!" I shout. "And what do I have to show for it? Nothing!"

"This isn't about you right now," Brenda says. "We're talking about Sam. Sam's therapist thinks your close relationship with her is having a negative impact on her therapy. We need you to rethink your contact."

Your contact? What the hell?

"My *what*?"

"No, no, no, I don't mean anything bad," Brenda says. "But you *are* so distrustful of us, and Sam is starting to pick up on it. It's changing how she views us. Her therapist thinks it's slowing down her progress."

It turns out that I can feel after all. I feel the blood heat up my face. I'm staring at Brenda, but all I can hear are the housemothers at the boarding school: *Elena has a negative effect on the other children. She's a bad influence.*

Loser! Loser! Loser! I told you they don't care. They care about every other patient but you!

"I'm done here," I say. And I stand up.

"Sit down!" Brenda says with a smile. "You're overreacting again. Of course we know you're not a bad person, and of course we're glad you're friends with Sam. But her therapy has to come first, you know that, right? Elena! Where are you going? Come back here!"

But I'm walking out the door.

I stop in the main room to put on my shoes. There's a halo of red light around everything I see. People are talking to me, but I can't hear them over the heartbeat in my ears. My hands shake as I dig the cell phone out of my basket.

"That's it, Mom," I say when she answers the phone. "That's it. Pack the car. We're going home."

18

It's the end of September. Two and a half months have gone by since I stormed out of Clove House. I'm sitting in class, and I am trying desperately to stay awake. Listening to the lecture isn't an option. I have no idea what the professor is saying. I just want to avoid the embarrassment of nodding off and cracking my chin on the desk.

I open my notebook and write,

So. I purge every meal.

I purge every drink.

I cut the shit out of my legs.

I cough blood.

My heart is getting worse.

I'm on eleven meds.

And I. Don't. Care.

The numbness of the drugs is producing a kind of frenzy inside me. I don't sleep deeply anymore, but I can't stay awake, either. Physical pain sobers me up, but only for a few minutes. Then I sink back into apathy. It takes energy to fight the voice in my head. I don't have energy, so I don't fight anymore.

I think about yesterday's weigh-in at the nutritionist's office. She congratulated me on how well I was doing.

If she only knew!

So. I have two ankle weights and 2 small dumbbells I tape to my legs. I have a waistband of Cling Wrap with coins superglued on it. I have a push-up bra filled with BB pellets where the gel inserts are supposed to be.

I have fishing weights on the inside of my jeans, inside of my belt, as many as will fit in my shoes.

I frown and blink at the paper in front of me. A worry begins to nibble inside.

What will I do next week to add more weight?

The sports jock at the desk next to mine is waving his fingers to get my attention. I glance over, and he slides his notebook across to me. He's written *DO U KNOW WHERE I CAN SCORE SOME BLOW.*

So that's what I look like to him. I don't look beautiful. I look like a skinny, coked-out drug addict.

You were never beautiful, says the voice in my head. *And you're still too fat.*

I shake my head at the student that no, I can't help him find his cocaine. I reread what I've written. Then I sum it up:

I have lost 30 pounds.

They think I'm fine.

I'm not.

It's only been a couple of months since I left treatment, and I'm worse off than before. I can't bear to eat, and even when I'm willing to try, my abused stomach and digestive tract can't take it. The only thing six months of treatment did for me was show me how strong my anorexia is. Now that I know I'm helpless, it's eating me alive.

The phone sitting on my desk lights up. It's a message from Sam.

elena i got a bus ticket to texas if i show up can i stay with u

I grab the phone and text back:

Call you in 5 minutes.

Class ends. Sam and I talk as I head across campus to my car. In the weeks since she had to leave the treatment center, things have fallen apart for her, too. She's already been bounced back and forth between her parents a couple of times. Now they're starting to talk about foster care. She's terrified. If her parents don't want her, how much worse will strangers be?

"I can sneak away," she tells me, her young voice eager. "They won't look for me because they'll be glad I'm gone."

"It won't work," I say. "It's really dangerous, for a start. You shouldn't be traveling alone. Besides, Mom can't let you stay with us. She could be accused of kidnapping you."

Sam pleads with me, and I've never felt so horrible.

You're a loser. You're failing her. You're failing!

"I wouldn't care if it was me," I tell her, "but I don't have my own place."

Now she's crying. Tough little Sam—nothing makes her cry! More than anything, I wish I could be there for her, but here I am, letting her down.

You always let everybody down, says the voice in my head.

"I'm not going to make it till I'm eighteen," Sam says, and I cringe at the sincerity in her voice. "Elena, I don't want to die. I don't! But I can't make it like this."

After she hangs up, I sit down on the steps of a building and cry. I don't even care that people can see me. It's not like they see perfection these days anyway.

One girl sets down her books and fishes a tissue out of her purse. I wipe my face and smile a thank-you.

"You've got cancer, don't you?" she asks me in a low voice. "Is it the chemo? Is it bad?"

I pick up my backpack and walk away.

There was a time when I calmed myself with dreams of purifying fire. I thought my body would melt away like breath off a mirror. Now I know: there's no beauty in what's happening to my body. But what good does it do me to know that?

My teeth are crumbling. All the baking soda in the world can't save them. My voice is hoarse, and my nose burns all the time now from the acid. My eyes are dull, my skin is rough and patchy, and my hair is falling out.

Nobody envies me anymore. Nobody asks, "How do you do it?"

They see a loser, says the voice in my head. *They see a freak. No matter how bad you think you look, just remember that what they see is even worse.*

When I get home, baby Gemma scrambles across the floor with a happy squeal to greet me. She's crawling now, and my parents' mature, overstuffed living room has all but disappeared under a jumble of bright plastic toys. A big picture of Clint in his blue uniform sits on the piano. He's finished basic training, but he still has to go to tech school before he and Valerie can be together again.

"Hey, Miss Mascara," Valerie says cheerfully.

Shit! My makeup must be all over my face.

I plop Gemma down in front of a red plastic centipede that's supposed to teach her the alphabet and hurry off to our messy bathroom. It's absurd that I care what Valerie thinks. Why would that still matter? But it's just one more habit that's too strong to break.

There's nowhere to step in the bathroom. Discarded jeans and wadded T-shirts lie all over the floor in a welter of baby toys and creams and boxes of wipes. The counter has disappeared under makeup containers and stained cotton balls.

Dylan's fish tank is no longer there. He got fin rot while Mom and I were gone. By the time we got home, he couldn't be saved. That beautiful blue spark of life, gone out.

Life doesn't last, says the voice in my head. *Death is the only thing that lasts. Fires go out, but winter stays for a long time.*

I am brushing my teeth to get the stink out of my mouth when Mom comes to the door. "Supper's at six," she says.

My stomach immediately contracts.

"I'm going to a study group," I say. "We have a big exam." Anything to avoid eating.

You do? says the voice in my head. *You liar!*

"You do?" asks Mom. "So early in the semester?"

"They're piling on the work," I mutter. "Oh, school, how I hate thee."

There's a small silence. I turn to find Mom staring.

"What?" I ask defensively, checking the mirror again. The mascara's fixed. I look better. Right?

Better than what? says the voice in my head.

"Elena, you don't hate school," Mom says slowly. "You've never hated school." And she walks off, shaking her head.

Shame burns my cheeks. Mom is right. From grade one, I was the girl who couldn't wait to do her homework, the girl who loved to learn.

What happened to that girl? Where did she go?

You've screwed up your whole life, you stupid bitch.

Acid kicks up in my stomach, and I lean over, gripping the counter. Forget deep questions—all I can do at this point is lie down. I dig the bottle of Tums out of the drawer and drag myself off to bed.

Sometime later, the light flips on. "Elena, time for supper."

I pull the blanket over my head. "I'll eat later, when I get up."

"What about your study group?"

Study group? Oh, yeah.

"It got canceled."

Liar! says the voice in my head.

The light goes off, and I drift back to sleep.

A buzz in my ear jolts me awake. I've been sleeping on my phone again. Its lighted screen glows in the darkness. It's Stella.

"Elena," she says, "Evey is dead."

My eyes fill with tears for the second time today, and Stella and I cry on the phone together. Sweet, quiet, fragile Evey, who helped me through the early weeks at Clove House. She was so bright and gentle. She didn't want to leave treatment. She wanted to live. Now she's lost the fight forever.

"My hair's falling out," Stella sobs. "I look like a scarecrow. All I do all day is pace the floor and panic over the next meal. I've walked so many hours, I've worn a track in the floor. Elena—is it bad that I'm jealous of Evey?"

I can't speak. It's as if she's read my mind.

"I'm overwhelmed," Stella gulps. "It feels like it's never going to get better. You'd understand if I don't make it, right? Tell me you'd understand."

You're not going to make it, either, says the voice in my head.

Panic grips me. "Stella, I need you!" I say. "I need you to fight this with me. I don't know how to get through it by myself."

Stupid bitch! says the voice in my head. *You don't know how to get through it at all.*

"I can't eat," I say. "Even when I want to, I can't. It won't stay down. If you give up, I'll give up. I need you to keep going."

"I'll try," Stella says. "All right. I'll try."

"I need you to call me," I say. "Call me—every day. Promise you'll call. Promise you'll help me figure this out."

"I promise," Stella says. "I'll try."

I hang up the phone and stare at the little ghost light from the screen shining out into the darkened room. Then the light chokes off, and the darkness rushes in.

Lights go out. But darkness lasts forever.

Evey. Poor Evey! I sob out loud. But my body is too worn down to keep up such hard work for long. Sleep tugs at me until I close my eyes again. My pillow is wet and cold against my cheek.

I am in my room. I am looking at a large fish tank set up in the corner of my room. Brilliantly colored fish dart to and fro. But an intruder rushes in and smashes the front of the fish tank. The water comes pouring out. All around my feet on the wet carpet, fish are flopping and dying.

I race to the kitchen to seize a spoon and a saucepan. Spoon by spoon, I fill the pan with water left behind in the bottom of the ruined tank. As fast as I can, I scurry around the room to scoop up the dying fish.

Only they aren't fish. They're tiny copies of my eating disorder friends, crumpled on the floor of my room. And Sam and Stella swim together in the bottom of my saucepan.

Heart pounding, I open my eyes and sit up in bed. Did I save them? Are they safe? Not Sam. Not Stella. Please not them. Please let it be somebody else!

Nobody's safe, says the voice in my head.

The light flicks on again. Mom is standing in the doorway. "Elena, we need you to come out here."

"I'm sleeping. I'll eat later," I groan, collapsing back against the pillow. "I have an ethics quiz tomorrow. I have to study."

"You slept through your ethics class," Mom says. "You wouldn't get out of bed."

This catches my attention. I slept through ethics? But it's Monday night, isn't it? Ethics isn't till Tuesday morning. I pull my phone out from under the pillow and look at the screen.

It's Wednesday evening. How the hell did that happen?

Sleep lasts, says the voice in my head. *Sleep lasts forever.*

"Elena, you've slept for two days," Mom says. "You can be up for a few minutes. We need you to come out here."

I shuffle into the living room in my pj's and fuzzy blanket. Dad and Valerie are sitting on the couch. Mom hands me a piece of paper and joins them.

"What's this?" I say. "I'm not reading this."

Dad and Valerie exchange glances. Nobody answers me.

I look at the paper. It's a contract between me and my parents. There's a line where I'm supposed to sign. And it ties everything—everything!—to how much I weigh, from whether or not I have texting on my phone all the way to taking away my computer, taking back my car, and forcing me to move out—for good.

This is it, says the voice in my head. *They've given up. They don't love you anymore. You were stupid to count on love.*

"What the hell is this?" I cry. "What do you think you're doing?"

"We're trying to help you get better," Mom says.

They're not helping you. They're blaming you. It's your fault you killed their love.

"You're blaming me for being ill. You're blaming me!"

"We're not blaming you," Dad says. "That's not the idea here."

You killed their love, and now they're going to make you pay.

"Well, it sure as hell looks like I'm the one who's going to pay!"

"Elena," Mom says, "we'll do anything—*anything*—to help you get well. But if you're determined to continue destroying yourself, you're not going to use a single thing of ours to help you do it."

You trusted them. You thought they loved you. You were so stupid!

"It's great," I say, "that after everything Valerie did, she turns out to be the one who's the favorite daughter. I like it that I've got almost a four-point grade average, and I'm the one on the street!"

"Hey, I'm not saying I didn't screw up," Valerie says. "But I got my ass in gear."

"This isn't about punishment," Mom interjects. "This is about trying to help you out of a downward spiral."

This is about forcing you out of their lives because they're ashamed of you.

"Well, you know what?" I say. "If you want me out of your life, then I'll be out of your life! You'll know what it's like to lose a daughter!"

"Do you know the reason we're doing this?" Mom says. "Your father started crying the other day. 'She's going to die,' he told me. 'I'm going to walk into her room, and there she'll be, dead. And I don't think I'll survive it.'"

This is so eerily like my own nightmares and premonitions that I stop for a second, stunned.

"Well, he's right," Mom says. "You're killing yourself. But you know what? You won't do it here. You won't have that nice, clean, freshly showered, air-conditioned death you've counted on. If you want to die, you'll have to do it under a bridge."

Dying is quick, says the voice in my head. *But death lasts a long time.*

"I DON'T WANT TO KILL MYSELF!" I scream. Which means I've lost the argument.

I snatch up a pen and sign on the line, and I go back to my room and lock the door. Valerie comes and tries to talk to me. Dad knocks and says he's sorry I'm upset. Mom doesn't come and say anything at all.

Words go away, says the voice in my head. *Silence lasts forever.*

In the morning, I wait until I hear Dad drive off to work, and then I unlock the door. I go to Mom and Dad's room and get a suitcase.

Mom and Valerie are sitting on the living room floor with Gemma. "Where are you going with that?" Mom asks.

"I'm leaving," I announce. "I'm moving out, just like you wanted."

"That's not what I want," Mom says. "And if you're leaving, you're not taking my suitcase. You can use a trash bag if that's what you're determined to do."

See how much she loves you? says the voice in my head. *She's never been anything but a bitch.*

"Fine, bitch!" I say as I drop the suitcase on the carpet. Eyes alight with excitement, Gemma scrambles over and grabs the handle.

Valerie's head comes up as I pass her on the way to the kitchen. "Hey! Don't call Mom a bitch."

They never loved you, says the voice in my head.

"That's choice coming from someone who's got a mouth like a toilet," I say as I fish a trash bag out of the pantry. Gemma lifts her little hands and laughs as the trash bag floats by over her head. Valerie hands her a block and gives a shrug.

"Hell if I care what you think," Valerie says.

Back in my room, I stuff shoes into the trash bag. I start going through the piles of laundry, but I can't find my favorite clothes.

What the hell?

I check the bathroom laundry bin. Not much in there, either.

What the *hell*?

Once more I confront the two women in the living room. Gemma looks up and waves bye-bye.

"Where the HELL are my clothes?" I say.

"We got rid of your extra smalls," Mom says. "We went through them while you were at school. That's not your real size, that was your unhealthy size, and you know you were supposed to get rid of them when you got home. They were sending you the wrong message."

Something like panic grabs my throat. My gray shirt with the three lines of lace . . . my X-pocket jeans . . . my Pink University T-shirt!

"YOU THREW OUT ALL MY CLOTHES?"

I run to the garage. Nothing in the trash can. Nothing in the car. I'm so furious that I'm shaking from head to foot.

"Where are they?" I yell like a maniac as I burst back into the house. "What did you do with my clothes?"

"We donated them to Goodwill," Mom says.

I feel the overwhelming urge to slap her across the face.

That's right, hit her! says the voice in my head. *She doesn't give a damn about you.*

"You don't give a damn about me!" I yell. "You don't give a damn!"

"I *do* give a damn!" Mom says. "All I've done this year is focus on your treatment."

That's not because she cares, says the voice in my head. *She doesn't love you. She just loves to play the martyr.*

"I didn't ask for your help!" I shout. "You chose to be a martyr!"

"It takes two people to make a martyr!" Mom yells back. "Lucky for me I've got you!"

All you do is cause her stress, says the voice in my head. *She hates you, and she wants you gone. That's what this contract is—it's a way to get rid of you.*

"Congratulations on getting rid of me, then!" I yell. "You wanted me gone, so I'm gone. You put me in boarding school to get rid of me, too, even though you *knew* I didn't want to go. You made me sick! You wanted me out of the way so you could write your damn books!"

For one long second, everything in the room freezes. Then Mom jumps up and grabs her purse. The front door slams.

The next thing I hear is the car starting up in the driveway.

"What the *hell*, Elena!" says Valerie. "What the *hell*!"

"Screw you," I say, and I go back to my room.

But I don't keep packing. I sit down on my bed. My head is pounding, and I realize I've forgotten my morning meds again. Hands shaking, I count them out and swallow them with some flat Coke out of an old can sitting on my nightstand.

Seven pills now, plus two at lunch, two at supper, and two more to kiss me good night.

But I didn't take them last night, I realize. Mom always reminds me, but the door was locked. Is that what happened just now? Was that me, or was that the meds?

Valerie comes to the door. She's holding Gemma on her hip. You'd never know to look at this happy young mother now what a hell-raiser she used to be. The scars from her cuts and burns have almost entirely faded away.

"Seriously," Valerie says, "that was not cool. You know Mom puts us first. I've tried her five times, but she won't answer the phone."

The anger that drove me is gone, replaced by bitter unhappiness.

"It was the truth," I say. "The boarding school made me sick."

"Yeah, maybe," Valerie says. "You're sick enough, I'll give you that. Except Mom didn't make you go to boarding school. She let us make the decision."

Leave it to Valerie to take her side, says the voice in my head.

"I remember begging Mom not to go!"

"Sure," Valerie says. "And I remember you saying you loved it so much, you were going to stay at boarding school even if Mom and Dad went home to Texas."

It's crazy, but as soon as she says this, I remember it, too. I shake my head, but that memory won't go away again.

"But I told her I wanted to leave. I remember it!"

"Yeah, well, you weren't what I'd call the most stable little kid in the world," Valerie says. "I remember hearing you say a lot of things."

"I wanted to leave!" I say again. "It was too much stress. I can prove it."

Valerie holds up her hand.

"Hey, look, *I* don't care," she says. "You can pretty much believe whatever you want to believe, and props to you for whatever bullshit story you put together. Fact is, you loved boarding school—except for all the times you hated it."

"I can prove it!" I repeat.

But Valerie walks off.

Valerie goes into the media room to put Gemma down for her nap. I turn to my journals to prove my point. But a journal is missing, a whole year and a half: the journal that I burned.

"Mom still won't answer," Valerie says as she walks by again. "I'm starting to get worried about her."

That's right! Mom has our old letters in her office. That's how I can prove it. I can show Valerie the letters I wrote to Mom, begging to come home.

I go into Mom's study, pull the letters out of a file drawer, and sit down on the floor to read them. A whole sheaf of crackly pages on grid notepaper in the distinctive blue lines of the German school fountain pen—the mere sight of my former self's neat, girlish handwriting makes me feel wistful and sad.

I read through them. But I don't find letters begging to come home.

Guess what! I wrote during my first week at boarding school. *I BROKE THE ICE! Last night, I noticed lots of horse pictures and a halter (used) and a black braid of horsehair on Barbara's billboard. In our room, I pulled out my cowboy book. She asked if I liked horses. Even though my favorite animals are cows, I said I loved them and that they were my favorite animal, casually adding I had gone to riding class. She came over to the bed and it was the first time I had ever seen someone's eyes sparkle!*

The energy and excitement in this old letter makes my heart ache with loss. I was aglow with emotion, on fire to change the world. Where did that bold, ambitious little girl go?

I can't wait till next year! the young me wrote as that first school year came to an end. *I have a feeling I will really miss this place during the summer vacations! It is so orderly and clean and girly!*

I close my eyes and concentrate on the memory I've held on to for so long: my voice begging to leave the boarding school and Mom's voice refusing to let me. The memory opens out. I'm crying over an exam that I've barely passed. And Mom's telling me how proud she is that I passed an exam in German.

I read on into the next school year. The bright, lively, dramatic girl that I used to be lives on these pages, in every silly story and poorly spelled sentence. The months pass. She's still there, riding to the rescue of her less gifted friends.

And then . . .

That girl vanishes.

Overnight, the letters become vague and cynical. They don't say much of anything anymore. They certainly don't tell any more silly stories.

A couple of months after that, the letters stop.

I read the last few pages again. This can't be right! The rape didn't slow me down. I never even thought about it.

But there's no mistaking the pattern.

Before the rape, I'm a child. A ditzy, bouncy, high-strung kid.

And after the rape . . .

I'm gone.

I'm just not there.

A sob surprises me, and I look around the study as if I expect the sound to have come from someone else. Lovingly, carefully, I even out the ragged stack of pages and tuck them all back into the folder. Then I unbend my stiff, aching joints and stagger to my feet.

Soreness radiates from every cracked, malnourished tendon and shrunken muscle in my body. A net of pain surrounds my parched, hungry bones. Thick, toxic blood throbs a drumbeat inside my aching head.

I thought I'd hidden the rape deep inside myself where no one would ever find it. But that's not what happened. The rape hid me. I can't even remember who I was anymore. The person I used to be has been gone for years now—that bright, lively girl who vanished.

I shuffle down the hall and crawl back into bed. Tears seep out of the corners of my eyes. The presence of death clings close to my worn-out body. It flattens me under its weight.

Half awake, half asleep, I lie in a stupor and dredge up old memories—memories that have lain undisturbed in the back of my mind ever since I burned the journal. I see a friend at the boarding school take my hand and hold it as we walk down the hall. I see Mom put her arm around me during church. I see myself put my head on her shoulder.

That's right. I remember now. As hard as it is to imagine, there was a time when I actually liked to be touched.

But in memories after the rape, I see myself jerk away from friends. When Mom puts her arm around me, I flinch and glare. I see myself using sarcasm to build up my defenses. The world begins to divide into enemies and allies. In memory after memory, I watch the walls form around me, until my life stops being about growth and happiness and becomes a matter of cold, stiff pride. The walls around me thicken and harden until it's not me I see anymore. I'm hidden inside a giant, cinder-gray skull.

A skull. A shell of death between me and my life. For years, that skull has stifled my better intentions. The bad people I know—the abusive guys and self-destructive friends—have been right there with me on the inside. But the good ones, the ones who cared for me—the ones I would have had to learn to care for in return—they haven't had a chance to break through.

A skull. A shell of death.

When does life become death?

I've been dying now for seven long years.

Valerie's voice cuts through my daydreams. "I got hold of Mom," she says. "It's crazy! She's on the other side of Austin. But at least she's okay."

I don't open my eyes. I can't find the strength to answer. I can still feel it all around me, blocking out the light—the cold, dead weight of that skull.

Valerie's voice comes closer. "Hey—are *you* okay?"

Tears are sliding out of my closed eyes and down my face. "I feel sick," I whisper.

"You look sick!"

I feel my sister sit down on the bed. I want to take her hand, but the skull is between us.

"So, if I make you chicken noodle soup," she says, "will you just puke it up? Because if you will, I'll save myself the trouble."

"I . . . I don't know. Maybe."

Her weight leaves the bed.

I lie there, ground down to exhaustion beneath the skull. Dear God, is this my life? Is this my future?

This is who we are, says the voice in my head. *I'll never leave. I'm all you've got left.*

The savory aroma of chicken with noodles slides into the room, and Valerie's warm hands help prop me up against the pillow. I open my eyes to see my sister sitting by me in my room (her and my room), giving me that look I remember so well from when we were little.

"Seriously, you look terrible!" she says.

She watches me choke down a few spoonfuls and then takes the bowl back. I'm still crying. I want to say thank you, but I can't.

The rape happened. I can't change that it happened. I can't change what it did to the girl I used to be.

"You know we love you, right?" Valerie says. "You do know that." She turns out the light and leaves the room.

She never loved you! says the voice in my head.

But that's not true. I know she loves me. As crazy as it sounds, I do know that. As unlikely as it seems that anyone could still love what I've become, I don't doubt that love for a second.

I close my eyes and cry myself to sleep.

One by one, the people who love me come into my dream. Gemma, holding up her arms to me. Dad, unable to imagine how he'll survive my death. Valerie, still setting me straight. My new brother, Clint, wearing my initial in his band of stars. Mom, pushed away by my angry words.

I see Valerie and me playing in this room when I was little. I see our old dogs dozing nearby. I see wonderful teachers who cared about my future and wanted to share the excitement of learning with me. I see Mona in the moonlit attic of the boarding school. I see the books I've loved, gifts from extraordinary minds that reached out with their words to touch me. I even see Rupert Brooke sitting barefoot on the green grass that is forever England, and he looks up and smiles at me.

Every single life that has enriched my life has been a separate gift of love. Those lives come pouring into my dream from all sides. Friends and the pets of friends. Aunts and uncles and grandparents. The sweet potato plant that grew on my windowsill, and the big mulberry tree I used to climb. Beautiful blue Dylan, and my cat Sam. My great-grandmother, who gave me the high school ring I wear. The brand-new butterfly I held until it dried its wings and flew away.

One after another, those lives that have touched mine gather until they become an enormous crowd that presses in around me from all sides. The skull can't keep them out anymore. It begins to shrink away. Freed from its shell, I feel the contact of those lives like a living current of love. It flows through the whole vast crowd of us and holds us safe in the cradling hands of God.

Life is love. Life, in all its suffering, is love. And death is powerless to change that.

As I realize this, the skull dwindles down in size until it lies on the ground at my feet. I pick it up, and it's so small now that it fits on the palm of my hand. I hold it for a long moment, debating what to do with it, and I seem to feel the expectant hush of those thousands of other lives jostling close and watching me breathlessly, waiting to see what I decide to do.

I can't throw the skull away. It's too important. It's been part of me for too long. But I won't keep it where I can see it anymore. I won't let it warp my vision again.

So I reach behind me and put it on my back.

I feel it flatten into my spine.

And then I feel strong wings blossoming out.

I wake up. It's dark in my room, and I'm alone. But I can still feel the strong, living current of all those lives joined to mine. I feel the weight of the skull where it rests between my shoulders. And, filling up the darkness around me, I feel the beauty and the power of outstretched wings.

The first thing I do is call Mom's phone. She doesn't answer, but I leave her a message. I tell her how sorry I am. Even though we haven't spoken, I know I already have her forgiveness.

The next day I go to my tattoo artist, and he designs a new tattoo for me.

When Mom sees it, she doesn't say anything because the truce between us is still brittle, but I can tell from her eyes that she's shocked. Dad declines to comment. Even Valerie doesn't care for it, and Valerie likes tattoos.

"Really, Elena?" she says. "Really? A skull with wings?"

But that's all right. My family doesn't need to hear about my tattoo. I know what they need to hear.

"I have an announcement to make," I say. "I'm putting myself back in treatment."

19

It's December. For the last two and a half months, I've been doing eleven-hour days at Sandalwood, the eating disorder treatment center across town. I've gained weight, and I'm on only half the meds I took before. I'm feeling more alert, and I can stay awake for a whole day now. I can go home every night and sleep in my own bed, play with Gemma, and gossip with Valerie.

But the progress I'm making is so ungodly slow that snails would get whiplash by comparison.

It's lunchtime, the end of a long, exhausting morning. Once more, my stomach groans and lurches as I face an enormous meal. Across the table is a twelve-year-old boy with an enormous meal of his own. Trevor has been so brave. For weeks, he hasn't complained. But today, I can see that he's struggling.

The other patients and I sit quietly, spearing pieces of cold chicken and green beans and making the monumental effort to bring the food to our mouths. Finished at last: the staff brings us our after-dinner Ensures, and we sit and sip. The only sound in the room is the clink of Trevor's fork against his plate. We are done, but he still has mounds of food to get through.

"Elena."

Trevor sets down his fork and folds his hands. I can see that his hands are shaking.

"Elena," he says again. "Elena, I just . . . I just . . ."

I reach across the table. My hand flutters against his face, and I struggle for words. What can I say that will help? How can I tell him it will be this hard for a long, long time?

"Sweetie," I say. "It's okay."

The first tear rolls down his cheek and hits my hand with a splash. Then another, and then another. Without asking permission, I jump up and fly around the table and pull him out of his chair and into my arms. The fragile little boy curls up against me, shaking with sobs, and my throat hurts so badly, I can barely stand it.

We anorexics, we cause ourselves pain every day. We toughen ourselves to withstand any hardship. We can deal with the physical torture, the anguish, and the emptiness, but the thing that kills every one of us is having to see what the others suffer.

A staff member looks toward me and hesitates. I shake my head at her: *Please don't make him finish that!* A few seconds later, she slips out of the room.

She's going to fetch Dr. Leben, says the voice in my head. *You're breaking the rules. You're a bad influence. What happened with Sam is going to happen all over again. They want you out of here.*

Anger bubbles up to join the pain I feel. Why does the staff have to be like this?

Poor sweet little Sam, left alone when I walked out of Clove House, passed back and forth between her idiot parents like a bag of trash. Her phone is turned off now, and it's been weeks since I've heard from her. Nobody knows if she's alive or dead.

Cradling Trevor in my arms, I think of the other anorexics who make my heart ache with pain and love. There's the girl whose teacher bullied her incessantly, until she lost hold of who she was. There's the former gymnast, urged to stay small, stay small, control portion size, watch her calories—until one day her malnourished body gave way at the joints, and she took one last tumble off the bars.

So many of us have had to live through pain and trauma. Why can't the staff see how hard this is for us?

There's the girl who begged her mother to take her and her friend out to a movie. Along the way, a car careened into them and took off her friend's face. There's the woman whose parents belonged to a satanic cult and tortured her as part of their rituals. And over and over, there are the rapes: child abuse, gang rape, date rape. The happy, excited almost-a-woman chooses her outfit, checks her makeup, and goes dancing out into the world. What happens there is brutal, demeaning violence.

Like my friend, the beautiful, shy honors student who was brutally raped by classmates on the way home from school. Now her attackers come up and laugh at her in the school hallways, and she can't bear to tell her family what's wrong. She doesn't want to get better anymore. All she wants is to die.

And then there's Evey—dear, dear Evey. She didn't want to die, but she couldn't change.

Dr. Leben appears in the doorway. "Elena, can we see you for a minute?" she says.

I told you! gloats the voice in my head.

Fear and defiance dominate my chaotic feelings as I follow Dr. Leben down a tiny hallway of the sort that might grace a mobile home. Dr. Leben's treatment center has outgrown its shabby office space, and at the end of the week, we're all moving to the new center.

Or at least, *they're* all moving. I'll probably be gone.

Shit!

I'm proud of the hard work I'm doing at Sandalwood. This time, I can honestly say I'm trying. Or at least—I *was* trying. And now this!

It's Sam all over again, says the voice in my head. *It's another treatment center that wants you gone. You're a bad influence—a bad influence on the other patients.*

Interfering in Trevor's mealtime isn't the only strike against me today. This morning I ended up yelling at my therapist, Jen, and I told her I wouldn't work with her anymore. I know I was loud, but each time the psychiatrist takes me off another medication, I go through mood swings, sleepless nights, and bursts of anger.

You'd think Jen would understand that. She's supposed to be a professional. But I never did trust her—not from the start.

You're too much trouble, says the voice in my head. *They can't wait to kick you out.*

Sure enough, when I get to Dr. Leben's messy, colorful office, Jen is already there. She's an older woman with a smart, chic look, and I thought nothing could rattle her. She knows I don't like her, but I thought that at least she liked me.

Nobody likes you here, says the voice in my head.

Connie comes in next: Dr. Leben's co-director. I halfway kind of like Dr. Leben, and I sort of don't like Jen, but I really don't like Connie at all. So they've called in the whole crew. This *is* bad. Shit, shit, shit!

I sink down into Dr. Leben's ultra-soft sofa. Connie sits in the armchair where Dad sits for family therapy. Jen pulls up an office chair, and Dr. Leben sits down by her desk.

"We wanted to talk to you," says Dr. Leben.

Ready? Fight or flight! says the voice in my head. *Here it comes!*

I try to sit up, but the comfy sofa caves in and pitches me back into a slouch. Damn this thing, with its fuzzy afghan and stacks of cheerful little pillows! I want to tell them to go ahead and kick me out if they think I'm such a bad influence on the other patients, but I can't even manage to sit up straight.

Go ahead! says the voice in my head. *Tell them you're done. Tell them they're not getting rid of you; you're leaving* them!

But the fact is, I don't want to leave. This is really scary! I've still got a long way to go.

"Elena," says Dr. Leben, "we've noticed a pattern in your responses to the other people here. You form supportive friendships with the patients, particularly when you can take on a big-sister role. You bond readily with the younger therapists, although you don't tend to recognize their authority. But with the women in charge, you exhibit suspicion and anger."

I stare at her. What does this have to do with kicking me out?

"Let me put it this way," Dr. Leben says. "Can you think of any older woman in a position of authority with whom you *haven't* had a rocky relationship?"

"Um . . . Hold on."

Older women. It's a crazy question, but let's see. Nope, all my favorite teachers were men. Then there was the high school counselor, whom I liked a lot—but not when she tried to tell me what to do. Before that, boarding school. The housemothers really were bitches there, and that wasn't my fault—all except one, and come to think of it, she was the youngest. No, I didn't dislike *every* one of my female teachers. Still, I can see Dr. Leben's point.

"We think it may go all the way back to your birth," Dr. Leben says. "You told us your mother almost died when you were born, and then she was sick for a long time. By the time she could take care of you, you may have already decided, more or less, that you didn't need her."

That's stupid! Of course I need Mom in my life. And yet—and yet—do I trust her?

Or do I view her efforts to help me as meddling?

Connie, the co-director, asks, "What's the first emotion you can remember?"

I stifle my dislike for her and concentrate on the question.

"I was angry," I say. "No—wait. I wasn't angry. A person I didn't know was talking to me, so I wasn't saying anything back."

"You were suspicious and distrustful," confirms Dr. Leben. "Was that an isolated incident?"

Of course it wasn't isolated! When I was little, I was suspicious of everybody. Mom used to tell me that I would point to strangers from my booster seat and announce, "That man in the car next to us is a murderer."

Dr. Leben appears to be reading my mind. "It's a long-standing pattern," she says, nodding.

This makes me angry. She's prying into my business!

And she's an older woman, so of *course* I'm angry.

Damn!

"By the time your mother was ready to participate in your life, it could be that you'd learned to do without her," suggests Jen. "Your critical voice, which is so forceful and perfectionistic, may have filled your mother's place. We all have a critical voice. But your critical voice—your eating disorder voice—is unusually harsh."

That's bullshit! How could my critical voice substitute for a parent when I was only three or four? But then I catch myself thinking of the times when I was little and Mom told me, "There's nothing to be afraid of." And then the voice in my head told me all the things to be afraid of. And which one of them did I believe?

"It's not so simple, of course," says Dr. Leben. "But you do have a pattern of distrust for a certain type of authority figure, and you have a habit of fighting when no one's fighting you back. We'd like you to think about that. I know you told Jen you didn't want to work with her anymore, but we'd like you to revisit your decision. Recognizing that Jen is exactly the type you have trouble with, do you think you can push past your pattern of distrust and give her another try?"

I can't help shaking my head in confusion. "I thought you were going to kick me out!"

Dr. Leben laughs. I'm glad Dr. Leben doesn't try to hide her feelings.

"That's exactly what we *would* do if we were people you couldn't trust," she says. "But Elena, you can trust us. Can you please try to trust us a *little* bit? Remember, we're not the jailors here."

As we take turns sidestepping our way out of the office into the tiny hall, I think about my jailor. A friend of mine at Clove House had a dream once that she was trapped with an ugly old woman inside a stone jail cell. A guard stood outside the door. He would throw a mirror over his shoulder into the cell, and the wrinkled old crone would grab it. She would show my friend her face in the mirror and then smash the mirror on the ground. My friend screamed and tried to protect herself from the flying glass, but she couldn't get away. The guard didn't seem to hear her, and the ugly old crone just laughed.

That's how I see my eating disorder. It's twenty-four-hour confinement with a witch. I'm obsessed with jail shows because their hopeless, restricted, rule-defined lives are the closest approximation to my own.

The very first day I put myself back into treatment, I told Dr. Leben, "I cheat. I'm like those prisoners who can make a knife out of their toothbrush. You'll have to watch me at weigh-in, or I'll hide weights in my bra and socks. You'll have to watch me at mealtimes. I can water down my Boosts with a pinhole prick in the bottom, and you'll never know anything's wrong with them. I've put horseradish into a mayonnaise jar before, and I ate it on my sandwiches for weeks, just to get out of eating the extra calories. If you let me, I can tuck food into boots, pockets, you name it. So don't let me cheat. I'll fail."

It makes me feel good now to remember that even if I don't trust Dr. Leben, at least I made sure she knew not to trust me, either.

Right after snack is spirituality group in the crowded conference room. There's barely space for us patients to squeeze our chairs around the table. I can't wait till we move out of this place. Only four more days.

Connie leads spirituality, and I usually hate it. The whole thing smells of hypocrisy to me. But now I do my best to push my skepticism aside. It's definitely part of that distrust thing they were talking about.

This time, I listen as Connie talks to us about surfing our feelings—observing our emotions and reactions instead of getting swept away by them. She tells us to hold our arms out straight for a few minutes and watch how we respond to the fatigue. I hold my arms out and close my eyes, and she's right: the urge to drop my arms comes and goes. I'll think I can't hold them up any longer, but a few seconds later, I'm fine.

"You can use this to battle your negative behaviors," Connie tells us. "You may feel like you can't hold out any longer, but if you just wait, that feeling will fade."

Then Connie reads us a poem so beautiful that it makes me cry. After spirituality, I stop her to ask if I can copy it down. She doesn't act surprised, although in the last ten weeks, I've never talked to her if I could help it.

"I'm so glad you liked it," she says. "It's beautiful, isn't it? I'll make you a copy right after my session with Trish."

She'll forget, says the voice in my head as she walks away.

But Connie doesn't forget. Before she leaves, she brings me the copy.

At seven in the evening, my fellow patients and I finish dinner, pack our backpacks, and trundle downstairs into the chilly darkness. As always, Mom's waiting in the parking lot. When they started cutting back on my meds, I would get worked up so quickly that I'd bolt out the door and be halfway home before I could think of a better way to handle things. So now Mom drops me off and picks me up every day to keep me from having a getaway vehicle.

I pop open the car door and climb in.

"So, did you have a good day?" Mom asks, as if she's picking me up from grade school. I want to laugh, but considering the fact that I was making flowers out of tissue paper today, grade school sounds about right.

As Mom navigates the dark streets, with their flowing currents of red taillights and white headlights, I think about the hours she's spent with me in doctors' offices over the years. I remember the weeks she spent by my hospital bed during that first horrible summer. I think of the months she spent in our orphanage room so I could stay at Clove House.

Then there were the hours Mom has spent on the phone, patiently unsnarling insurance problems. Mom is the only parent I know who has gotten insurance to pay for all but three days of my months of treatment. She's been at it so long, she actually has friends now at our insurance company.

All that work. All that love. To help me get well.

I flip on the dome light and unfold Connie's photocopy.

"We read a poem today," I say. "It made me think of you."

Mom is the perfect audience for this. She inherited a love of poetry from my grandmother and passed it along to me. We've been known to sit for an hour with our favorite poetry books by us, taking turns reading snippets of verse to each other.

"Who's it by?" Mom asks.

"Daniel Ladinsky," I say. Then I read it out loud:

"There is a Beautiful Creature
Living in a hole you have dug,

So at night
I set fruit and grains
And little pots of wine and milk
Beside your soft earthen mounds,

And I often sing.

But still, my dear,
You do not come out.

I have fallen in love with Someone
Who hides inside you.

We should talk about this problem—

Otherwise,
I will never leave you alone."

By the time I finish it, I'm crying. This poem is Mom's voice to me. The voice of the poem is love and patience and hope and forgiveness, and that's what Mom has always given me. Deep down I've always known that, even when the bitch of a critical voice inside me tried to drown her out.

"I understand," I say. "I understand how you and Dad feel—how hard it's been on you two to try to save me."

And now Mom and I are crying together.

Mom pulls up to our house. We park on the street because a U-Haul trailer is taking up the driveway. After almost a year of living with us, Valerie and Gemma are getting ready to leave. She and Clint will finally get to be together. He's in Mississippi, finishing up tech school. Tomorrow, at four o'clock in the morning, Mom and Valerie will caravan out of Texas to meet him. Valerie's driving her car with Gemma in the baby seat, and Mom is towing the trailer.

Valerie meets me in the driveway with a piece of disassembled baby crib.

"What up, Ho Face!" she says. "Great! You can watch Gemma. She's kinda had enough of her playpen."

White U-Haul boxes form giant baby-block stacks in the entry-way, and Dad bumps into me with another chunk of crib.

Gemma is standing on her tiptoes in the living room in her portable playpen-crib. She shrieks hello and throws a yellow plastic ball at my feet.

"Hey, Itty-Bitty!" I say as I scoop her up, and she rewards me with another happy shriek.

Gemma is almost a year old. I've seen her eat her first solid meal, crawl, and now walk holding someone's hand. But I won't be there to see her take her first steps. She'll do that in Mississippi. I hug her squirming body close and feel her little hands pat me gently on the back.

"I'm going to miss you, Miss Itty," I tell her. But Gemma only laughs. Valerie is such a great mom that Gemma's biggest heartbreak so far has been not getting ice cream for breakfast. She has no understanding of sorrow.

The packing soon winds down. It's funny and sad all at the same time to see how little Valerie and Clint actually own. The majority of the stuff belongs to Gemma. She's a little person, but she has all the biggest boxes.

Dad carries out the last heavy box and goes to bed. Mom walks around the house finding baby socks and teething rings tucked behind bookshelves. Valerie and I go through closets and drawers, packing her clothes. We give each other things we say we don't want but secretly love but hope the other person loves more. We don't say it, but each of us knows we won't sleep tonight. We'll be up till dawn to make this time together last as long as we can.

In the hush of early morning, I carry my warm, limp, sleepy niece out to the car and buckle her into her seat. Mom eases the trailer out of the driveway, and she and Valerie drive off with a rattle and a creak. I watch the red taillights move down to the end of the block and around the corner. Then I go back inside, hug my old cloth cow, and fall asleep.

More boxes greet me when I get to Sandalwood. Only three days left in the old building. I'm tired from my few hours of sleep, but it's crazy: even now, I don't feel as wiped out as I used to after sleeping all night. As the excess meds wash out of my system, I feel like Sleeping Beauty waking up.

Jen calls me into her almost-empty office for therapy. Her knick-knacks nestle in packing paper by the door. She and I go over the meeting the three of them had with me yesterday, and I admit that it makes a lot of sense.

"But my critical voice has gotten meaner," I say. "A lot meaner. It wasn't like this when I was little."

"When did it change?" asks Jen.

"After the rape," I say reluctantly. And I have to fight down a feeling of annoyance when she nods.

I need to work on trust, I remind myself.

"Can you tell me what you remember?" Jen asks. When I'm silent, she adds, "About the rape?"

I want to get mad and tell her that it doesn't matter, that the rape isn't important anymore. Then I think, if it's so unimportant, it shouldn't be a big deal to talk about, right? Then I realize that I'm holding my own hand very tightly in my lap, as if I'm twin girls walking hand in hand through a dark forest. That's silly. I want to let go and smooth my hands on my jeans to show how much this doesn't bother me. But I don't let go. I hold on tighter than ever.

What do I remember? Not much.

"It was a party," I say. "A bunch of the boys' school boys were there. No parents. I think they were gone on vacation. My friend Mona and I were the only girls."

That was the easy part.

"I was drinking beer. The party was in a big room in the basement. I needed to go to the bathroom, so I went upstairs. I . . ."

What do I remember?

"I remember tile," I say. "The tile was cold and hard. My hair was up, and the bobby pins hurt against the tile."

My hands are getting sweaty, clamped together. I am holding the hand of the younger me as she feels the cold, hard tile against her back.

"There was a hand smashing into my face. I tried to bite, but I couldn't. Just palm. Fingers were smashed into my nose. I thought it was broken, it hurt so much." I take a breath. "Finger over my eye. That's what I was afraid of," I say, suddenly discovering. "I was afraid the finger would gouge out my eye."

And I ride the dizzy wave of that sudden fear.

What else do I remember? I don't know. From here on, it all shatters. Time doesn't flow in a smooth line from future to past. It heaves up big blocks with jagged edges. I tiptoe hand in hand with the younger me through the ruined chunks of time.

What do I remember?

Other voices, laughing. Does that mean other boys were watching? What would I say to them if I could? *You were there,* I would say. *Can you tell me what happened? I can't remember. I want to know what you saw.*

I blink. The office is bright. It smells like vanilla even though Jen's candles are already packed. Time is standing still here, too, as Jen waits for more.

But there isn't any more. No more remembering.

"And that's when your critical voice got meaner," Jen says, circling back to the beginning again. And I clutch my hands tightly together in case Jen asks us to go back through that wasteland of not-remembering, the younger me and the older me hand in hand.

But Jen goes in a different direction.

"It's a catch-22," she says. "You don't want to think something as violent and horrible as a rape is out of your control. If it's out of your control, it could happen again, couldn't it? So you tell yourself you were in control. You're the one who caused it. You went down the wrong alley, or you trusted the wrong guy, or you weren't wearing your lucky socks. That's why it happened."

"I went upstairs to the bathroom," I say.

It's the young me who says that. She sounds solemn when she says it, and I realize she's been saying it for years. But as I hear that solemn voice speak out loud, I realize how stupid it sounds. You don't rape a thirteen-year-old kid just because she goes to the bathroom.

"But then," Jen says, "if you make what happened your what can you do with all the disgust and anger you feel? All that negativity turns inward. Because if you *were* in control—if *you're* the one who didn't stop it—then the rape must be your fault."

Your fault, says the voice in my head. *Your fault!*

But the rape wasn't my fault. It certainly wasn't the fault of the dumb little kid who wore her hair in a bun to a kegger.

"I remember how my OCD behaviors flared after it happened," I say. "I counted my steps all day long, everywhere I went. One time, I fell downstairs because I was concentrating so hard on counting. The scrapes and bruises didn't bother me half as much as the fact that I lost count."

"OCD rituals feed that desire for control," Jen says, "that desire to make sure the bad things stay away. Those rituals keep us from coming to grips with the scary idea that sometimes bad things just happen."

"The rape is what it is," I say, echoing one of Jen's mantras. "It wasn't my fault. I didn't cause it to happen."

That doesn't mean you're not a stupid bitch, says the voice in my head.

I don't have an answer for that.

"Now I want you to open your journal," Jen says. "I'm going to say something to you, and I don't want you to answer. Instead, I want you to write down how it makes you feel."

I am instantly defensive and suspicious.

You can't trust her! says the voice in my head.

But I open my journal, take out my pen, and wait.

"The rape is what it is," says Jen. "That's true. Bad things happen, and they're not our fault." She pauses. "And the miscarriage is what it is, too."

Instantly, a flood of horrible thoughts and images pours through me: blood, agony, shame, death.

Your fault! shouts the voice in my head. *Dead baby!*

I am furious. Jen knows not to mention the miscarriage. She knows what I go through when I think about it.

No wonder I don't trust her!

"Don't speak," Jen says, holding up her hand. "Just breathe. Surf the feelings."

And I do.

"Now write down the emotion you're feeling."

I hold my breath like I'm underwater and write *ANGRY* in big block letters. Then I hold the journal up and glare at her.

"Fair enough," she says. "Now, still keeping silent, I want you to look inside that anger. Try not to argue with yourself—we all know how good you are in an argument. Just quietly look at your anger until you can see inside it to find the emotion that it's covering up."

I'm still seething, but I force myself to look inside the bubbling mess that is my current emotional state. Just as I did yesterday, watching my urges to put my arms down, I watch now to see what's coming up.

As calmly as I can, I look at my own anger.

What is it blocking me from? What's it hiding?

Images begin to bubble to the surface. Me, grabbing my razor in the middle of the night. Me, lashing out rather than enjoying a massage. Me, waking up with my head in Dr. Greene's lap after the meditation on the pebble with the baby's foot.

The voice in my head is screaming. *Stop it now, you stupid, stupid bitch! Purge, grab a razor, throw your journal, run out of the room! Stop it, stop it, STOP IT!*

FEAR. I write the word in my journal. I'm afraid of what I'll find if I keep going down. And I just learned something important, something I never knew before:

The voice in my head is the voice of my fear!

"Very good," says Jen as I hold up the notebook. "So your anger was protecting your fear. But what's behind the fear? What is it you're afraid of? Look for that, and write that down."

I stare at the page and trace over the two words until their lines are thick black indents into the paper.

Stop it! Stop it now!

What is it that I'm afraid of? Loss of control? But I've lost control. I've blacked out, and I've woken up cuffed to a gurney in a hospital. It doesn't get much more out of control than that.

Pain? No. I live with pain every day.

The miscarriage? That already happened. It's over and done with, in the past.

But the fear grips me tighter, and the voice of my fear is like a banshee wail:

Stop it! Stop it! STOP IT!

There it is, trembling on the edge of my awareness, like a monster I've spotted out of the corner of my eye. But I don't write it down. I can't write that down. I can barely allow myself to think about it.

Hatred. That's what I'll find if I dig too deep. Hatred—for me.

Because the miscarriage wasn't like the rape. It really was my fault. And I think—I'm almost sure—that I hate myself for it. This isn't like me yelling at Mom, saying, "You hate me! I hate you!" This is the real thing.

The voice of my fears is trying to protect me. It protects me by starving me and abusing me and calling me every loathsome name it can dream up. If that's the protection, what's it like without the protection? How much worse is the monster hiding behind it?

Hatred. There's no way I can possibly survive it.

I close the journal and shake my head. I'm hoping Jen will think I just can't figure this out, but I can feel the hard, expressionless mask settling onto my face.

"You really have done well," Jen says warmly, so I know she knows I'm holding out on her. Does she also know what I'm refusing to write?

She's probably known it all along.

We sit in silence while she studies my face and I fight the urge to throw my journal at her. Stalemate. This isn't going any further. It can't, or I'll end up dead.

"What's her name?" Jen asks.

"Whose name?"

"The name of the baby you lost. Does she have a name?"

"Lilly," I say. "Lilly Arabella." I haven't said those words out loud before.

Pain blazes through me, past defenses that have held for almost a year. A lump swells in my throat, but I swallow it down and blink back tears in a kind of fury. This woman may have hurt me, but she's not going to make me cry.

I've had enough of trust for one day.

Next comes lunch. My twelve-year-old little brother is cracking jokes, and I try to take heart from his good mood, but I pick at my food in dreary misery while waves of nausea attack. It would help if I liked to eat before the anorexia took hold, but honestly, food never had that much appeal for me.

So here I am. I'm stuck with that damn critical voice forever because behind it is something even worse.

At the afternoon group therapy session, Jen asks me to tell the other patients about the miscarriage. I don't want to go back to that place in my mind, but I manage to say a few words. Jen adds a few more and then tells them, "Her name was Lilly Arabella."

Again, hearing the name out loud, I feel tears coming to my eyes.

"Elena, I'm so sorry," says my friend Molly.

She's crying, and she reaches out to hug me. To my surprise, I find myself hugging her back.

During break time, a quiet woman I barely know brings me a small, flat, shiny white stationery box. It says *Arabella* on the lid in lines of glued pearl beads.

"I'm so sorry about your daughter," she says. "I made you a box where you can keep letters to her. That way you can write her whenever you want."

I take the box, feeling awkward and vulnerable, and the woman hurries away. That's good, because I don't know how to respond to this kindness. Even my critical voice can't think of anything to say.

As I put the box into my backpack, I open it. There's already a letter inside.

Dear Lilly Arabella,

I'm sorry I didn't get to meet you. Your mommy misses you so much. She's beautiful, so I know you must be beautiful, too.

You would be so proud of your mommy. She's doing so well.

I'm stunned. The voice in my head is silent. I wrap up the box in my sweater and tuck it into my backpack as carefully as if it's made of glass.

My phone buzzes. It's an unknown number, so I don't pick up. It calls again.

Don't answer! warns the voice in my head. *Stalker—rapist—mugger—creepy serial killer—pervert—*

How did I not notice before that this is just my anxiety feeding me an endless stream of worst-case scenarios?

I answer the phone. A soft, high voice says, "Elena?"

"Oh my God!" I burst out. "Sam! Where are you? Are you okay? I've been so worried! Your phone's been off for weeks!"

"I'm sorry. It kinda got turned off. I kinda ran away. It was really bad, but I'm all right now."

"Are you really all right? Where are you? Are you safe?"

"I'm in foster care," Sam says. "That's how come I have a new number. But, Elena? The foster care family—my new family . . . they're really nice."

I can feel the smile spread across my face.

"Of course they're nice, Sam. They're lucky to have you!"

"It's weird," she says. "I mean, they make me follow all these rules. And you know how I love to break rules! But this time, I actually kind of don't mind about them. Because . . . they're for my own good."

The wonder in her voice as she says this breaks my heart into a million pieces. After so long, to finally live with guardians who want what's best for you . . . I clear my throat to push the lump out of it and cordially wish Sam's parents into the lowest circle of hell.

"I'm so, so glad, baby girl," I say. "That's the best kind of rule you could have. So, hey, where are you now? At school?"

"No, I'm in our backyard. There's other girls here. I got permission to go outside to call you."

"And what are you doing now?" I say. "Because I know you're not sitting down."

"I'm standing in Tree Pose."

"I knew it!"

I'm still laughing when we say good-bye.

As soon as she hangs up, I call Stella.

"Sam's okay!" I blurt out.

"I know," she says. "We both left you messages, but I told her you don't listen to your messages."

The other patients put away their books and file out of the room for mindfulness therapy while Stella fills me in on what happened. Sam ran away, but the police found her. Then she ran away again and got to Clove House. Once they heard what had been happening, they kept her there and arranged for her parents to give her up. So it's thanks to the Clove House staff that Sam's safe now.

Dr. Leben's face appears around the door, with her patented smiling glare, as she gestures for me to get moving.

"Hey, gotta go," I tell Stella as I get to my feet.

"Talk to you tonight," she says.

And she will.

Stella and I have kept the promise we made to each other that horrible afternoon when Evey died. We talk almost every day.

Dad picks me up at seven, and we come home to an empty house. The living room looks forlorn and a bit stuffy with no more rainbow-colored toys to perk it up. But we compensate by ordering pepperoni pizza and watching Asian horror movies till Dad falls asleep.

I'm on an Asian horror movie kick these days. Maybe that's because it isn't Jason or Freddy Krueger who kills people in these films. No, it's the little fourteen-year-old girl in the plaid school uni-form who was so shy while she was alive that she could barely say two words. Now her black hair's coming out of the walls, and her long, slimy fingers are reaching up out of the drain. Grown men crash their sports cars and jump off the balconies of their penthouses to escape the wrath of the dead Asian schoolgirl.

At one in the morning, I wake up to discover that Dad and I have left half the lights in the house on. I shuffle to the bathroom in their unnatural glare and discover: red blood. My period has started again.

Shocking images rush at me—blood and death. My stomach cramps as if the miscarriage is happening again. It happened right in this room.

Your fault! Dead baby! Dead baby!

Surf the feelings. Surf the feelings. Don't get swept away. I start the breathing exercises Connie taught us: long inhale, long exhale. It'll get better, just like the urge to put down my arms. Long inhale, long exhale. I can do this.

Slimy, rotting dead things swarm through my mind. Guilt and shame flood through me, and the room goes gray.

You screwed up! You screwed up! You've screwed up your whole life, you stupid bitch!

Long inhale, long exhale. Get it together. I run cold water on my hands as a distraction. Remember what Jen said. *Don't try to argue. We all know how good you are at that.*

The cold water clears my vision, and I totter on shaking legs back to my room. It's the middle of the night. Mom's gone and Valerie's gone. Dad and the dogs are asleep. But I have a new ally in my fight against the flashbacks. I open the top of his terrarium and lift the hollow rock away.

"Mr. Snaky?" I whisper as I scoop him up.

My red corn snake wakes up and lazily begins to explore my hands. *Mouse?* he thinks hopefully. *Mouse?*

Jen was the one who convinced my parents to buy me a snake. Mom only agreed when she learned that he wouldn't eat live prey.

Since then, the whole family has fallen in love with him. He's very relaxed and friendly. He doesn't let anything ruin his good mood.

Mr. Snaky is also amazingly beautiful: salmon orange with a line of red Navajo-rug diamonds down his back. He's so colorful and pretty that he doesn't look real. He's like a Disney animation of a sweet, happy, peaceful snake.

I concentrate on watching the light glint on his shining scales and focus on the tickly feeling of him winding through my fingers. He flows like taffy from hand to hand to hand as I keep him from reaching the bed. He isn't getting anywhere, but he doesn't seem to mind.

My feelings are like a hurricane. My snake's feelings are so simple that he's more like a computer than a pet. If he's full, he's asleep. If he's awake, he's hunting for food. *Mouse? Bird? Egg?* he thinks as he twines up to my shoulder.

My snake doesn't know a thing about shame or guilt or hatred. I keep up the breathing exercises and do my best to bring my thoughts in line with his.

Warm, he thinks as he explores the pocket of my hoodie. He winds his way back out of it. *Daylight. Mouse? Mouse?*

Your fault, says the voice in my head. *Dead baby!*

"Her name," I say, "was Lilly Arabella."

You've screwed up your whole life. Dead baby!

"Lilly Arabella, Mommy misses you so much."

Now tears are falling onto my snake's bright scales—real, sorrowful tears. Because this isn't about me and my hatred. This is about a little person who danced inside me with the joy of life for a few—too few—short weeks. Even when she was barely there, she was amazing. She lost the chance to be what she might have been.

"Lilly, Mommy's sorry," I say into the still night. "Lilly, I wish I could have watched you grow up. Mommy misses you so much."

The last shreds of my panic dissipate in the warm rain of tears.

Shelter, thinks my wet snake as he hurries into my hoodie pocket. *Storm. Bad weather. Shelter.* And I laugh because he's an outdoor creature who doesn't like rain. I put him back into his terrarium, and he curls up under his heat lamp. *Warm*, he thinks. *Comfy. Sleep.*

I close the terrarium lid and turn out the light, and I go back to sleep, too.

It is a gorgeous spring day. I am standing on a merry-go-round, and all around me, painted horses are frozen in full gallop. Children crowd past me, laughing, and a beautiful little girl with blond hair and a white dress stands beside me, her small hand in mine.

The children are choosing their horses. My little girl tugs me along to join in the search. In her excitement, she breaks away and dances ahead of me, and I lose her in the crowd.

"Lilly!" I call in a panic. "Lilly Arabella!"

The little girl comes running back. Her hair is like sunlight. She hugs me around the legs and looks up at me, laughing.

She says, "Mommy, don't worry."

Now a little pearl box lies at my feet on the merry-go-round platform. It glints in the rays of the sun. I look at the name on the lid: ARABELLA. I open the box and find a dollhouse inside: charming little bed, perfect little toys, postage stamp–sized windows with pink curtains fluttering in the breeze.

Suddenly, my little girl is tiny. Tiny! She fits in the palm of my hand. I put her on the doll bed, and for one last second, I look at her. Then I shut the lid, and my little girl is gone.

How can I face life without that little hand in mine? My heart swells with love and grief. But again, I hear her sweet voice laugh and say, "Mommy, don't worry."

And when I wake up, I swear I can hear it still.

Dad makes me coffee before he goes to work, and I help him find his car keys and his glasses. Then I shower and drive myself to Sandalwood. But on an impulse, I detour by the new building. The clerical staff are already working there.

Nothing is ready yet. Stacks of boxes wait just inside the front door. But Brenda, the gray-haired receptionist, can't contain her excitement when she sees me. "Isn't it fantastic?" she says. "Come on! I'll show you around."

I follow her down the halls, as excited as she is. She's right, the new place is fantastic. I walk past cozy nooks and large, inviting rooms where yoga and movement groups will take place. I can just imagine sitting at a table under that skylight to work on a new art project.

At the heart of the new center lies a wonderful little courtyard, filled with the cool shadows of oak trees. Large windows from the offices open onto its protected space. Plants will bloom here, and a fountain will murmur in the shade.

This is a building that will welcome colorful glass mobiles and shaggy textiles and bright artwork in odd places. Already a pink-and-purple mod-podge sign greets everyone who comes through the door. This is a building that will muffle sobs but magnify laughter. Its wide halls reach out like comforting arms to draw the visitor to the peace of its hidden garden.

It has the right will, this building. It's ready to meet its new people halfway. And its people are ready to move mountains and save lives.

I should know. One of the lives they've saved is mine.

20

Two years have gone by. It's break time at nursing school. Ms. Forbes sees me drinking an Ensure and comes over to chat.

"So, what is it with you and the protein drinks?" she asks. "I always see you eating."

You're always eating, says the voice in my head. *She thinks you're an out-of-control blimp.*

Meaning that I'm nervous about what people think of me when they see me eating in public. But what I'm doing is responsible behavior. It doesn't matter if no one understands it.

"I got permission from the director," I tell her. "It's my thyroid. I have a condition."

"Your thyroid," she says, looking thoughtful.

"I have Hashimoto's thyroiditis," I say. Which is true. "I had to be hospitalized for it a couple of years ago." Which isn't.

Ms. Forbes' face clears, and she gives me a big smile.

"Thyroiditis. Sure," she says. "Well, you keep right on drinking those protein drinks, and I'm glad to see you eating. Those 'thyroid conditions' can result in more than one hospital stay sometimes."

And she winks at me before she walks away.

Ten hours later, I'm helping my friend Daniel keep control of a rowdy party. It's the night before Halloween, and he invited everybody he knows. Daniel knows a lot of people. Half the residents of his apartment complex are here.

Dozens of people in all states of costume and intoxication are crowded into the small two-bedroom apartment. As I squeeze through the tangle of bodies, I keep redrawing fire-exit maps in my head: in case of fire, head toward Pocahontas, turn right at beer keg, and exit through balcony door.

"Bacon!" shouts Pocahontas as I force my way into the kitchen. "Everybody who does a shot has to eat a piece." It's Party Survival 101: you won't get as inebriated if you're eating bacon while you drink.

Eating bacon is barbaric! says the voice in my head, so I remind myself to grab a piece later. It may be barbaric, but it's definitely joyful eating.

Daniel wanders into the kitchen and sticks a piece of bacon on his Wolverine claw. Then he wanders out again, holding the claw over his head so he can make it through the crush. I can see the bacon waving above the crowd of partiers, still stuck to the end of the claw.

A loud knocking sounds at the door—so loud that I actually hear it. I struggle through the crowd (in case of fire, use Elmo as a human shield and continue path to door) and find a policeman there, ringed by a group of staring superheroes.

"What's the matter, Officer?" I ask. He seems relieved that someone here can still say "officer" on the first try.

"It's two in the morning, and we're getting complaints," he says. "Time to wrap up this party."

"We'll shut it right down," I promise.

"Okay," he says. "I'll give you a half hour. Don't make me come back."

He leaves, and I shove my way back into the press again. I tunnel through swaying limbs and cheap nylon capes to Daniel's bedroom (in case of fire, duck behind Frankenstein and follow dining room wall to balcony) and find Daniel and three of his closest friends engaged in a deep philosophical conversation, the sort that alcohol seems to encourage.

"Daniel, you're going to have to tell them to leave," I say. "The cops were here."

He climbs to his feet. "I'll take care of this," he says. And, to show that he means business, he dons his Wolverine claw again.

Daniel forces his way into the living room to take care of the noise problem. Unfortunately, he's feeling relaxed and beatific. As a result, his idea of crowd control is to stand in the middle of the babbling mob, close his eyes, and gently whisper, "Shhhhh!"

Around him, a sea of oblivious, happy people in various colors of theater makeup continues screaming and dancing.

"They can't hear you," I tell him.

"They can," he assures me. He closes his eyes and holds his finger to his lips. "Shhhhhhhhh!"

"*I* can't hear you," I say.

But Daniel is convinced that he has taken care of the problem. Like a second Dalai Lama, he trails clouds of peace and glory back to his room.

Once he's gone, I turn off the stereo. Then I find a chair, drag it through the crowd to the middle of the room, and stand on it.

"People!" I shout. "Cops are here! Let's go!" Then I shove my way to the front door and hold it open.

Icy air curls in. Faces turn my way. Leotards and nylon capes are definitely not weatherproof. Eventually, the group begins hunting down cell phones and shoes. People fan out across the complex to their apartments.

After a few minutes, only about twenty partiers remain, and the noise is down to a reasonable level.

I shut the door and return the chair to the breakfast nook. On the way, I almost trip over Daniel's friend Robin, passed out on his back.

"Hey, that's not going to work," I say as I shake him. "You have to lie on your side."

Robin opens his eyes. He's had a lot to drink. "Elena," he says, squinting in wonder but also great complacency, as though he has personally conjured me up out of another dimension.

"Robin. Roll over on your side," I tell him as I prod him with my foot.

"I will . . . if you come . . . h-here and . . . and cuddle," he says as he attempts to assemble a devastating leer from spare parts lying around his cerebral cortex. Unfortunately, not all the parts arrive at the same time, resulting in facial spasms.

"If you roll on your side," I offer, "I'll tell you a story."

To my surprise, Robin executes a half roll onto his side. I quickly sit down against his back to prop him into place.

"Story," he murmurs contentedly. "What you said."

"All right, this is a story my mom made up for my sister and me when I was little," I say. "It's called 'Baba Yaga and the Glass Cat.'"

"That's *amazing*," Robin breathes. He closes his eyes to better absorb this fact. "It's just . . . It's just . . . *amazing*."

"Baba Yaga lived in the wide, dark forest in a little hut that stood on chicken legs."

"*Chicken* legs!" explodes Robin. "*Chicken* legs? Ha, ha, ha!" It takes quite a bit of effort to settle him back down, and I make a mental note to leave the chicken legs out the next time I tell this story to drunks.

I tell Robin that the king comes to Baba Yaga and asks her to bring a clear glass statue of a cat to life. She agrees, but only on the condition that he return the pieces to her if it breaks. "So the crooked old witch picked up the glass cat," I say, "and she threw it into the thickest, hottest part of the fire. And the flames shot up—red and green and blue."

"Red and green and blue," repeats a female voice dreamily. I glance up. A bee in black thigh-highs has settled down nearby.

"At first, the statue lay there," I say, "with firelight shining on its glossy form. Then it began to glow—first orange—then cherry red. It twisted, and it turned. It gave a sudden shake. And the glowing cat came strolling out of the fire.

"The glass cat lifted its clear glass head, and its eyes were two golden sparks. Its clear glass tail waved back and forth in question marks. It stretched on the hearth, and it had the tiniest clear glass claws. It yawned, and its teeth were the tiniest clear glass needles."

I hear a whispered "Wow!"

I look up. Fifteen or twenty people are sitting in a ragged circle around me. They are staring at me, following my every word. All the remaining partiers have settled down to listen, as eager as preschoolers at library story hour.

So, like a modern Baba Yaga, I weave my spell over the crowd. Why not? My body is inked in symbols and myths, and a dead poet gazes serenely from my shoulder. Lifting my hands, I draw in the air the elegant towers of the king's white castle. I tell them how proud the king is of his unusual pet.

But little by little, the poor glass cat falls out of favor with the king. Stroking the cat leaves fingerprints. It's hard to find because it's clear. And when it tiptoes up and rubs its cold body around the king's bare ankles one morning, it nearly makes him jump out of his skin.

"So the glass cat was banished to the kitchen," I say. "It crouched on the hard stone floor underneath a bench. Along came a little mouse looking for a crumb, and—the glass cat was a cat, after all!

"The little mouse streaked across the floor, and the glass cat did, too. The little mouse raced up onto a table, and the glass cat did, too. The little mouse sprang down onto the stone floor, and the glass cat did, too—and *smashed* into a thousand shining pieces."

"Oh, *shit*!" yells Robin.

"But Baba Yaga knew what to do," I assure him, and I tell them how the king sent her back the pieces of his ruined pet. "She dropped the sparkling fragments into the thickest, hottest part of the fire, and the flames shot up—red and green and blue."

And when the glass cat comes strolling out again and jumps up onto the wily old witch's lap, I see on their faces the same look of wonder that Mom must have seen on mine when I was little.

The next night is Halloween, and I am back home, manning the candy bowl. Mom and Dad have been overseas in Germany since summer, enjoying schnitzel and soccer games. I'm enjoying having the house to myself.

Leela, our new black cat, and I are watching a movie. Mr. Snaky is curled up in my hair. The doorbell rings, and I run to grab the candy bowl, while Leela hops up onto the banister beside the door and stares at the visitors with enough pure evil in her eyes to justify her heritage as a Halloween icon.

Mr. Snaky twines down from my neck to explore the candy bowl. With his bright orange and red body, he blends right in.

Mouse? he thinks as he pokes his nose into the candy wrappers.

"SNAAAKE!" yell the delighted kids.

Mr. Snaky, Leela, and I answer the door for an hour or so, but I've got clinicals early in the morning, so I set the bowl of candy outside and change into pj's.

Time for bed.

I take a minute to fire up my computer and check Facebook.

Valerie has posted photos of three-year-old Gemma out trick-or-treating. Clint is downrange, so she's managing the family single-handedly for the next few months. Facebook is keeping us all together.

The first photo shows Gemma in a gauzy Snow White tutu and a red hair ribbon, ready to go. I scroll to the next photo and laugh out loud. Gemma is sitting in the middle of the street, flat on her bottom. There's a furious scowl on her face. She wouldn't get up and move for a Mac truck, but she's still got a death grip on her candy bag.

Below the photo, Valerie has written, *Aaaaand she was done.*

Clint has been online, too, and he posted a photo of the small plush shark I sent him in my latest care package. The shark is at the business end of Clint's assault rifle. The caption reads *Left him alone for five minutes . . . !*

There's also a message from Sam. The little girl I knew is now a gorgeous young woman in high school who looks sophisticated and aloof in her Facebook pictures. But I know the secret behind why Sam looks so reserved. She has a new set of braces. Yesterday I wrote her and said, *Come on! I want to see them,* so she has emailed a photo just for me. And there she is, wearing a great big braces-filled smile.

She's so beautiful that I almost burst into tears.

Is that talking outside? I hear a murmur of voices.

"*Blah blah* real snake *blah blah* I swear, she has a snake!"

The doorbell rings. Then it rings again.

I go to the door in my pj's and snake to find a dozen little ghosts, zombies, killers, and princesses crowded onto my porch.

"SNAAAKE!" they yell in delight.

Everybody gets a picture with Mr. Snaky, including the parents. A five-year-old pink Whoopee Cushion is inspired into eager speech: "He's a long drippy candy corn candy snake drip!" Her friends and siblings ask tons of questions before snagging some Milk Duds and racing off into the night.

I put Mr. Snaky back into his terrarium and wander into the kitchen for one last Ensure of the day. A poster on my fridge says *WHAT ARE YOU HUNGRY FOR?* I study the food choices it offers as I chug my protein drink.

Sometimes learning to eat is like learning a foreign language.

When I get back to the bedroom, Leela and Mr. Snaky are eye to eye through the terrarium glass.

Mouse? thinks the snake.

Toy? thinks the cat.

Mom's old tan-colored terrier is sacked out on my pillow. She looks like a messy bird nest. Next to her sprawls my black spaniel, Tess, rescued from a Love's truck stop. Tess is resting her head on my old cloth cow, who's wearing a bright, clean, rip-free new hide. Mom found the same cow pattern and sewed her again. She used the old eyes and tail and stashed the ancient ripped-up hide deep inside the new stuffing.

They all look so peaceful that I can't wait to join them. I take my medicine—I'm down to two pills a day now, and they work.

Okay, *now* it's time for bed!

At one in the morning, my phone buzzes. Dad's drinking his morning coffee and worrying about me. He hasn't factored in the time change.

"Are you getting enough to eat?" he wants to know. "I know nursing school is hard. Are you getting enough rest?"

"Really, I'm fine," I mumble. "I've gained two pounds this week."

Leela wakes up, assumes I'm talking to her, and purrs loudly as she crowds under my arm. Tess wakes up and attempts to scooch closer, too, but Leela gives her a smack on the head with her paw. I discover that I'm inhabiting a narrow strip of bed mere millimeters from the edge. When I try to rearrange my fuzzy companions, Leela gives me a smack, too.

"Sorry I woke you up. I just worry," Dad says. "You know I worry about you."

"It's okay," I say as I close my eyes and listen to Leela's loud, rumbling purr. "It's nice to be worried about."

The alarm goes off at six-thirty, and I raise my head. Two old dogs and one young cat gaze at me reproachfully as I struggle out of the warm, cozy blankets.

My day planner is open on the desk. I have an early appointment at Sandalwood, then clinicals. I take out my clothes for the day: a set of scrubs. My heart lifts at the sight of them. I'm in nursing scrubs again!

I wander into the bathroom and attempt to wake myself up with a steamy shower. Singing, I soap my arms. Here's the tattoo for Lilly: *Can a woman forget her own child? And yet will I not forget thee. Behold, I have graven thee in my hands.*

I'll see you one day, dear heart. Your mommy loves you.

There's a scramble by the shower curtain. Leela perches on the edge of the bathtub. She gives me a golden-eyed glare, snatches my razor in her teeth, and races off. I catch up to her in the dining room, where she is in the process of dragging the razor under a chest of drawers to join four tampon wrappers, two pill bottles, one credit card, two pieces of junk mail, two bottles of nail polish, one toy mouse, three ChapSticks, two headbands, and one straw.

My cat has a hoarding problem.

I grab the razor, adjust my sopping towel, and squelch back to the bathroom. It's 6:45, and I've already flashed the neighbors.

I finish my shower and put on the set of scrubs. I put on my makeup. Then I tighten my ponytail, clip on my ID, and meet the gaze of the mirror girl.

Staring out at me from the mirror is a student nurse, crisp and professional in neat navy-blue scrubs. Her tattoos are hidden away beneath a bland white long-sleeved T-shirt. The look in her eyes is friendly and assertive.

You're ugly, says the voice in my head.

That means I still can't see what other people seem to see when they look at me. I still hate my nose. But I accept that I'm loved, and I look neat and pulled together.

Recovery is a path, not a destination.

At Sandalwood, Dr. Leben and I dissect the week that has just ended. I'm having to double down to gain weight after the damage I did to my digestive system, but I'm making slow progress, and I'm even starting to find a few foods I like. That isn't easy. Repeated purging has destroyed about half of my taste buds and most of my sense of smell. But at least I don't have to be on laxatives for life. I have eating disorder friends who do.

"I'm so, so proud of you," Dr. Leben says as we walk to the door after our session. "You're just doing so well. You know, this is a learning process for all of us. The field of eating disorder therapy is evolving very quickly. We've tightened up our protocol here thanks to you, you know. It isn't so easy to cheat here anymore."

I laugh. "I'm sure you've worked on it. But you've still got the vase."

I point to a big red vase by Brenda's desk. Dr. Leben looks puzzled. So I tip the vase over, and a quart or more of pretzels and goldfish pour out.

Dr. Leben bursts out laughing.

"Well, we're getting rid of *that*!" she says. "You get on out of here, Missy. Have a good, healthy week. And behave!"

I make it over to the hospital in time for shift change. Before walking into the post-surgical ward, I wash my hands for the first of many times today. Right thumb, left hand, rotate and rub. Left thumb, right hand, rotate and rub. Left wrist, right wrist, fingers down. Nursing is a great place for people who take comfort in little rituals.

"Student, I need help!" a nurse barks as soon as she sees me. "She's crashing. We have to get her down to ICU."

A very tiny little old lady has just come through surgery, and her body isn't responding well at all. I help the nurse switch out her leads and tubes and put her on a gurney. Her weeping daughter hurries after us.

In the elevator, I stand by the head of the little old lady's gurney. The wrinkles around her eyes and mouth tell me that she laughs more than she frowns. She's conscious and in great pain, but she talks to me as formally and politely as if we are meeting for coffee.

"That's my daughter," she says. "I have two girls and one boy. And I have five grandchildren."

"You must be very proud of them," I tell her with a smile. "Your daughter is beautiful."

We get to the ICU floor, and the nurse goes off with her colleagues to get a bed prepared. The daughter steps away to call her family and tell them what the doctor said: that if they want to say good-bye, they'd better hurry.

The little old lady looks around vaguely. Her eyesight is going fast. I step up close beside her, and she reaches out to seize my hand, and when she touches me I know in every bone of my body that I love what I am doing right this minute more than I love anything else on earth.

"Are you going away?" she asks me anxiously. "I thought everyone was going away."

I give her my other hand to hold. "I'm not going anywhere," I say.

Her fading eyes find my face and see its smile, and she smiles back—just a hint of a smile, but it's enough.

There is a circle of stars hidden under the sleeve of my T-shirt, and stars are hidden in the sky above us, and the little old lady and I have met for the very first time at the crossroads of life and death.

"I don't want to be left alone," she whispers. "Just please . . . just don't leave me alone."

"I'm right here beside you," I say.

There is a skull on my back. But there are also wings.

AFTERWORD

This book is an accurate description of how I have lived with my eating disorder. No part of it is intended to be a guide for how others should live. If you or someone you know has an eating disorder, please do not take any part of this book as a suggestion for how to handle your own journey to recovery.

Many of the things I chose to do were extremely dangerous. Purging, for instance, can kill without warning, and it can kill at any weight. It upsets the balance of electrolytes in the body and can cause cardiac arrest, seizures, or kidney failure. And some of the things the adults around me chose to do were equally dangerous. The contract that my parents made me sign, for instance, that tied my weight to a list of privileges, could have driven me to suicide instead of to treatment. Please do not take it or any of the other actions in this book as a model for how to handle an eating disorder.

If you or someone you love has an eating disorder, the one thing I will advise you to do is seek professional help. Do not try to manage an eating disorder on your own. Do not think that you can quietly share your life with anorexia. Anorexia will take it all.

Educate yourself with up-to-date information. Eating disorders are complicated, and the professionals are trying out new approaches all the time. In the years since my eating disorder began, I have seen treatments and theories change radically. I recommend going to the websites run by the National Eating Disorders Association (NEDA) and the National Association of Anorexia Nervosa and Associated Disorders (ANAD). Their websites will help you find the latest resources available.

You may be wondering why I chose to write this book with my mother. The memoir was my idea. It took me years to talk my mother into helping me.

For years, I wanted this book more than I wanted anything else. The experience I was living through didn't match the experiences in the books I read. The memoirs I read either seemed to glorify eating disorders or seemed to focus only on the rosiest, most hopeful side of recovery. The truth as I lived it was more complicated than either of those two extremes.

Nothing about eating disorders is simple.

But I couldn't write this book on my own. Saying the words, describing details, remembering snippets, answering questions, even writing paragraphs . . . okay. But the thought of sitting in front of the keyboard for the entirety of the book from beginning to end, watching the words march onto the computer screen at a painfully slow, steady pace, immortalizing my indiscretions, failures, vulnerabilities, self-hatred, fears, and destruction in a series of cold, neutral Word documents—it would have been impossible.

It took me six and a half years to say I was raped. Not even to describe it. No, just to say the sentence took me six and a half years. Six and a half years, four schools, two countries, six therapists, three psychiatrists, two treatment centers, four hospitals, two thousand three hundred and seventy-two days, fifty-six thousand nine hundred and forty hours, three million four hundred and sixteen thousand four hundred minutes to say that sentence to my parents over the phone and hang up. It took even longer to let other people discuss it in therapy. Longer still to say the hows and when and whys.

My mother allowed me to tell my story to her sporadically, skipping to different moments when things got too painful. I jumped around in my paragraphs and interviews, avoiding full descriptions, revealing key information in pieces, sometimes weeks or months apart. I could share a memory, and then, as soon as the words had tumbled from my mouth, I could seal it back into my vault. She had to place the pieces together, formulate the order, group the sentences, and make the story understandable and smooth flowing. She had to reread and rewrite the most painful parts of our lives for hours and hours and hours, down to the italics and exclamation points. Everything that influenced my decisions, she had to analyze. I would have given up the moment I saw the computer screen crawling with my pain.

What you have just read are my words, my descriptions, my feelings, my memories, my pain, my fears, my inside look at a world that has lost me many friends and that I have been judged for my entire adult life. This book is the purest, truest definition of those years and myself as I lived them. Without my mother, it would never have seen the light. It would still be racing violently through my head, waking me up every night, whispering softly in my ear, reminding me in spurts and flashes that my past still dictates my life and it will forever. I scooped it up and threw it out, and my mother took the bits and pieces and glued together the perfect picture of who I am.